Origami Gnomes of the Forest Wonderland

Crafting 41 Gnomes, Mushroom, & Forest Creatures

Books by John Montroll
www.johnmontroll.com
Instagram: @montrollorigami

Origami Symphonies

Origami Symphony No. 1: The Elephant's Trumpet Call
Origami Symphony No. 2: Trio of Sharks & Playful Prehistoric Mammals
Origami Symphony No. 3: Duet of Majestic Dragons & Dinosaurs
Origami Symphony No. 4: Capturing Vibrant Coral Reef Fish
Origami Symphony No. 5: Woodwinds, Horns, and a Moose
Origami Symphony No. 6: Striped Snakes Changing Scales
Origami Symphony No. 7: Musical Monkeys
Origami Symphony No. 8: An Octet of Cats
Origami Symphony No. 9: Ode to Australia
Origami Symphony No. 10: Lucky & Dangerous Sides of Origami
Origami Symphony No. 11: Folding on Land, Air and Sea
Origami Symphony No. 12: Where are the Gnomes?

Animal Origami

Jungle Origami
Arctic Animals in Origami
Origami Aquarium
Dogs in Origami
Perfect Pets Origami
Dragons and Other Fantastic Creatures in Origami
Bugs in Origami
Horses in Origami: Second Edition
Origami Birds: Second Edition
Origami Gone Wild
Dinosaur Origami
Origami Dinosaurs for Beginners
Prehistoric Origami: Dinosaurs and other Creatures: Third Edition
Mythological Creatures and the Chinese Zodiac Origami
Origami Sea Life: Third Edition
Bringing Origami to Life: Second Edition
Origami Sculptures: Fourth Edition
African Animals in Origami: Third Edition
North American Animals in Origami: Third Edition
Origami for the Enthusiast: Second Edition
Animal Origami for the Enthusiast: Second Edition

Geometric Origami

The Magic of Origami Polyhedra
Origami Stars: Second Edition
Galaxy of Origami Stars: Second Edition
Origami and Math: Simple to Complex: Second Edition
Origami & Geometry
3D Origami Platonic Solids & More: Second Edition
3D Origami Diamonds
3D Origami Antidiamonds
3D Origami Pyramids
A Plethora of Polyhedra in Origami: Third Edition
Classic Polyhedra Origami
A Constellation of Origami Polyhedra
Origami Polyhedra Design

General Origami

Magical Origami Gnomes: 38 Gnomes. Infinite Fun.
Origami Gnomes of the Forest Wonderland: Crafting 41 Gnomes, Mushrooms, & Forest Creatures
Origami Fold-by-Fold
DC Super Heroes Origami
Origami Worldwide
Teach Yourself Origami: Third Edition
Christmas Origami: Second Edition
Storytime Origami
Origami Inside-Out: Third Edition

Dollar Bill Origami

Dollar Origami Treasures: Second Edition
Dollar Bill Animals in Origami: Second Revised Edition
Dollar Bill Origami
Easy Dollar Bill Origami

Simple Origami

Fun and Simple Origami: 101 Easy-to-Fold Projects: Second Edition
Origami Twelve Days of Christmas: And Santa, Too!
Super Simple Origami
Easy Dollar Bill Origami
Easy Origami
Easy Origami 2
Easy Origami 3
Easy Origami Coloring Book
Easy Origami Animals
Easy Origami Polar Animals
Easy Origami Ocean Animals
Easy Origami Woodland Animals
Easy Origami Jungle Animals
Meditative Origami

Origami Gnomes
of the Forest Wonderland

Crafting 41 Gnomes, Mushrooms, and Forest Creatures

John Montroll

Antroll Publishing Company

To Omri

Origami Gnomes of the Forest Wonderland: *Crafting 41 Gnomes, Mushrooms, & Forest Creatures*

Copyright © 2025 by John Montroll. All rights reserved.
No part of this publication may be copied or reproduced by any means without the express written permission of the author.

ISBN-10: 1-877656-75-5
ISBN-13: 978-1-877656-75-0

Antroll Publishing Company

Introduction

The forest is full of adventures—brimming with playful gnomes, enchanting mushrooms, and small woodland creatures. With a single sheet of paper, you can fold each of them and create your own magical forest scenes where the gnomes spring to life.

All the models are designed by origami master John Montroll, each folded from one square sheet of origami paper. Every gnome, mushroom, and forest creature is paired with a humorous story that adds charm and adventure as you wander deeper into the woodland world.

The journey spans five whimsical chapters:

Greeting at the Edge of the Forest—Gnomes who welcome you and prepare you for the fun ahead.
Friendly Forest Mushrooms—a delightful variety of fungi that fill the forest floor.
Rambling Through the Forest—Gnomes who explain the wonders and secrets of their woodland home.
Small Forest Animals—Creatures who interact with the gnomes and offer their own forest wisdom.
Deep in the Forest—More whimsical gnomes and the inventions, noises, or mischief they create.

All 41 models in this collection are designed to be as simple as possible for their level of detail and complexity. Most can be folded in 20 to 30 steps, A detailed spider with eight legs takes only 27 steps, and the super-detailed grasshopper requires just 26. The squirrel is diagrammed in 20 steps. The final two gnomes—with their splendid curling mustaches—are the most challenging models, each taking over 30 steps. Presenting intricate designs in surprisingly few steps is part of the magic of origami.

The models are easily folded from origami paper that is white on one side and colored on the other. Standard paper sizes from 6 to 10 inches work well.

The diagrams are drawn in the internationally approved Randlett-Yoshizawa style. Origami supplies can be found in arts and craft shops, or at Dover Publications online: www.doverpublications.com. You can also visit OrigamiUSA at www.origamiusa.org for origami supplies and other related information including an extensive list of local, national, and international origami groups.

Please follow me on Instagram @montrollorigami to see posts of my origami.

I want to thank the folders who proof-read the diagrams.

The gnomes are ready to pop out of the pages and share their forest fun with you.

John Montroll
www.johnmontroll.com

Contents

Symbols 9
Basic Folds 10
Appreciating Forest Gnomes 14

Greetings at the Edge of the Forest

15
Flint Oakentoe

18
Dandelion Pipwhistle

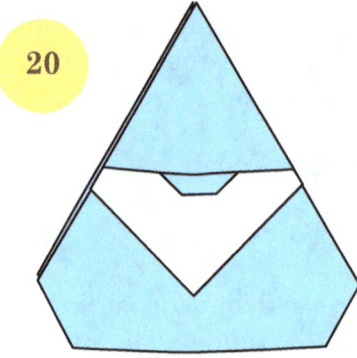
20
Murk Hollowpocket

22
Sprigley Bramblebright

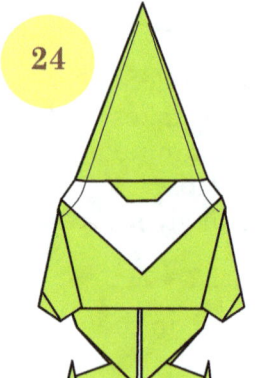
24
Thornwick Bramblebright

26
Mossroot Bramblebright

28
Elmwick Driftstone

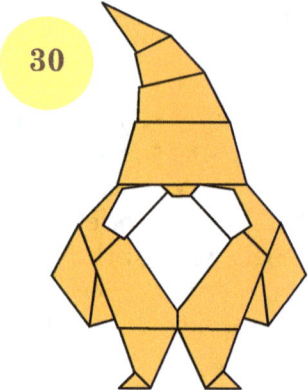
30
Pebblecrest Underbough

Friendly Forest Mushrooms

32
Skyfloat Fungi

34
Sporevine Jellyshrooms

36
Embercaps & Frostbell Caps

39
Sparklecap

6 *Origami Gnomes of the Forest Wonderland*

Rambling Through the Forest

42 Snicket Bramblecoat
45 Pompel Oaktwist
48 Cobble Thrumtwig
51 Wizzlewick Moonwhistle

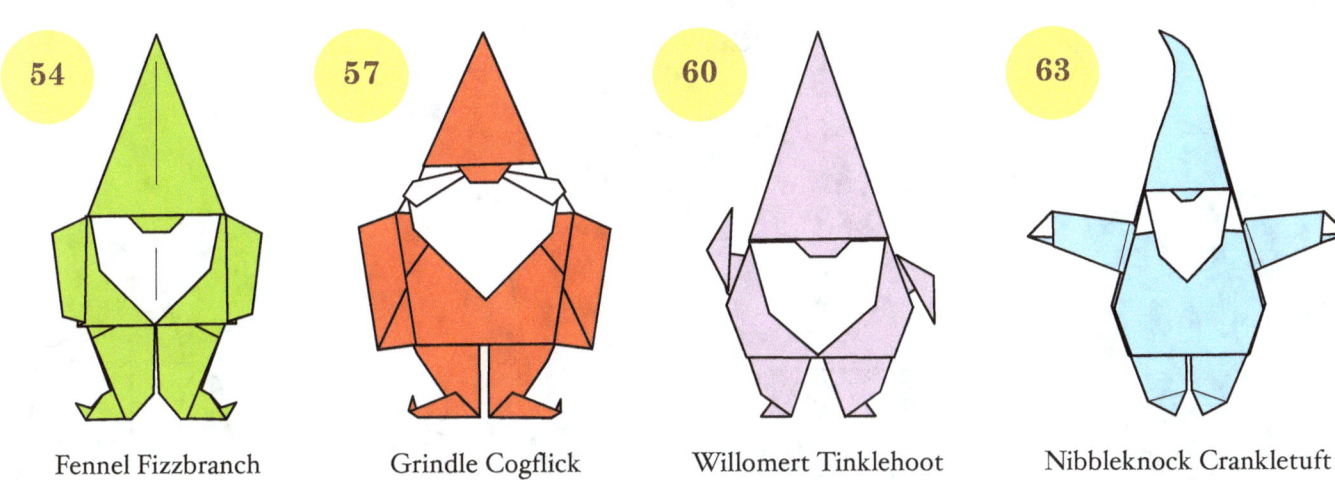

54 Fennel Fizzbranch
57 Grindle Cogflick
60 Willomert Tinklehoot
63 Nibbleknock Crankletuft

Small Forest Animals

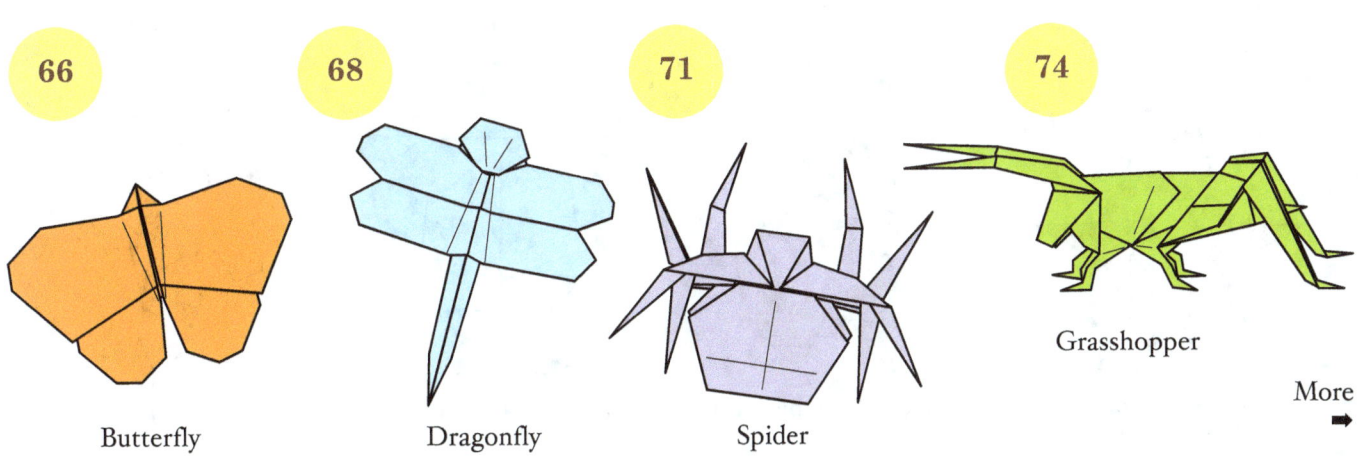

66 Butterfly
68 Dragonfly
71 Spider
74 Grasshopper

More ➡

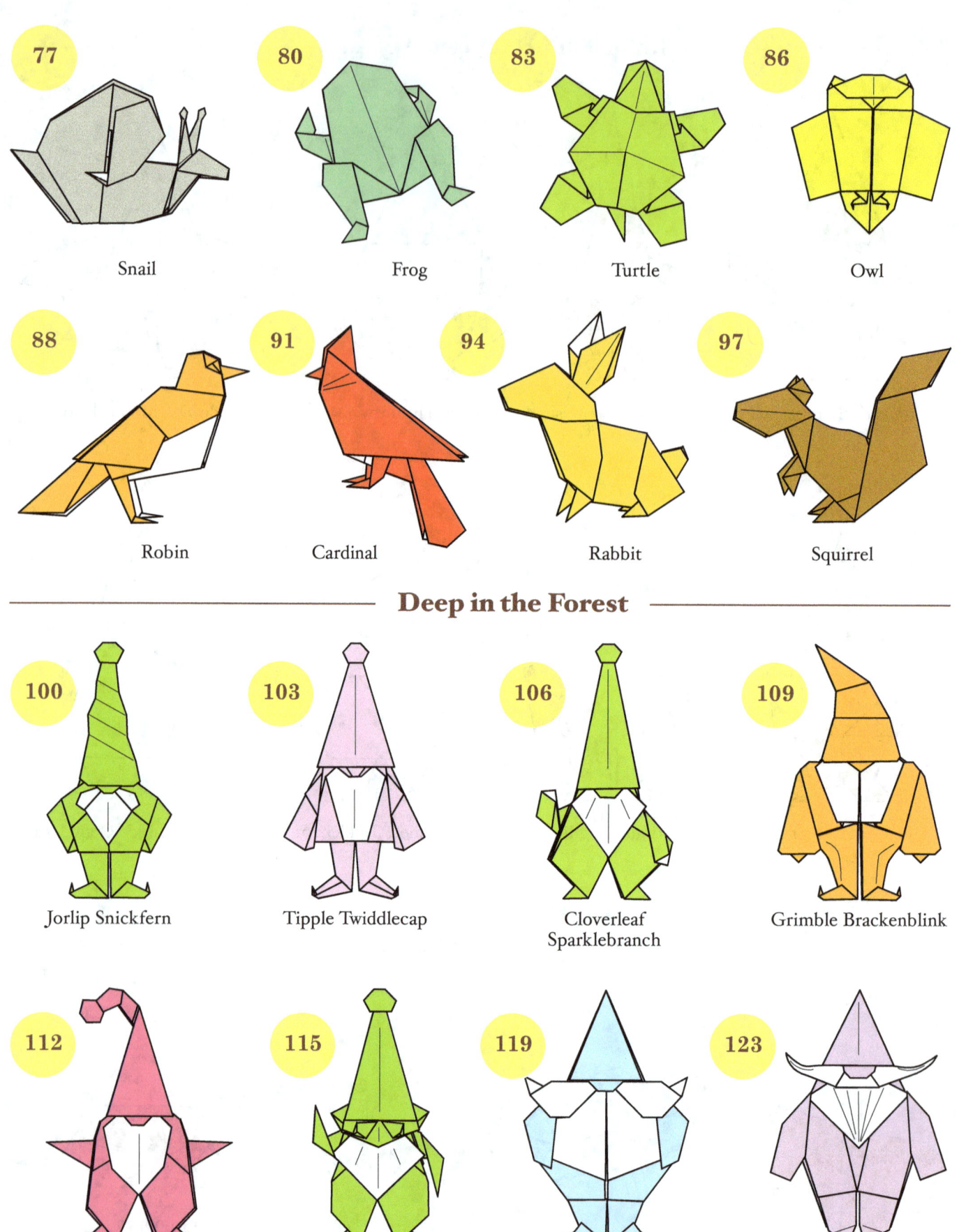

Deep in the Forest

77 Snail
80 Frog
83 Turtle
86 Owl
88 Robin
91 Cardinal
94 Rabbit
97 Squirrel
100 Jorlip Snickfern
103 Tipple Twiddlecap
106 Cloverleaf Sparklebranch
109 Grimble Brackenblink
112 Bramblethorn Whistlewind
115 Zindle Bramblewhip
119 Fizzlenip Puddlehopper
123 Tinkerflip Fizzlegear

8 Origami Gnomes of the Forest Wonderland

Symbols

Lines

———————— Valley fold, fold in front.

—··—··—··—··— Mountain fold, fold behind.

——————— Crease line.

················· X-ray or guide line.

Arrows

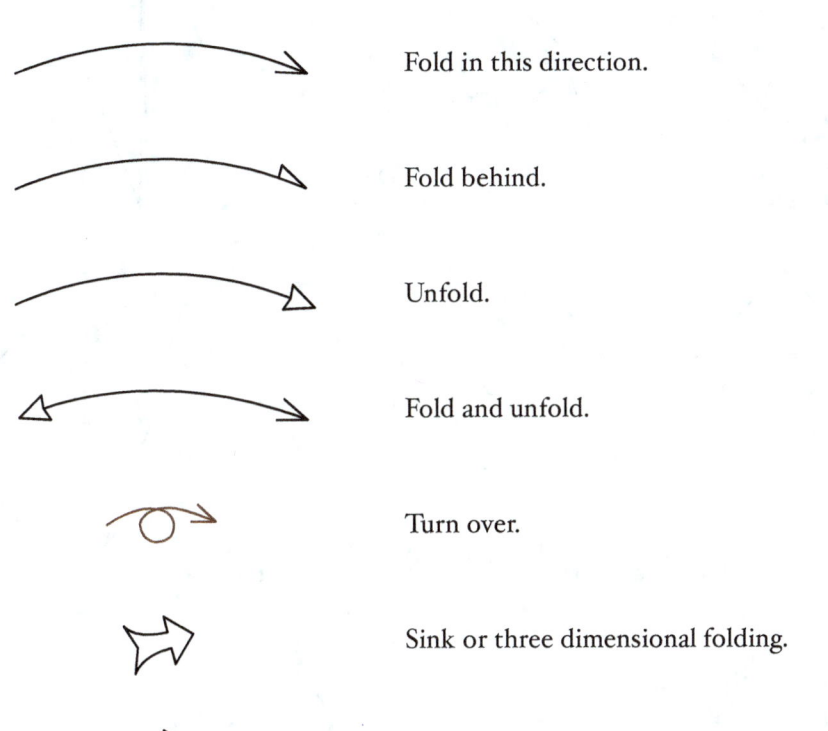

Fold in this direction.

Fold behind.

Unfold.

Fold and unfold.

Turn over.

Sink or three dimensional folding.

Place your finger between these layers.

Basic Folds

Pleat Fold.

Fold back and forth. Each pleat is composed of one valley and mountain fold. Here are two examples.

1 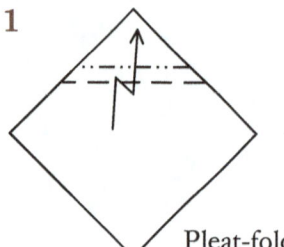 2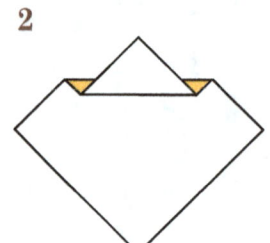

Pleat-fold.

1 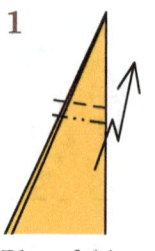 2

Pleat-fold.

Squash Fold.

In a squash fold, some paper is opened and then made flat. The shaded arrow shows where to place your finger.

1 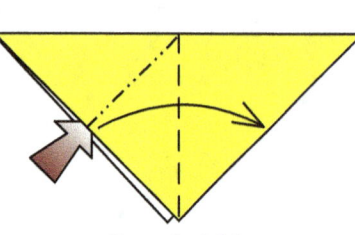 2 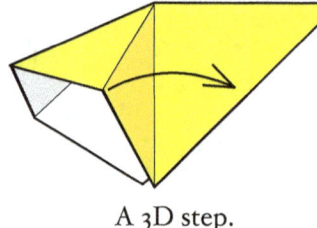 3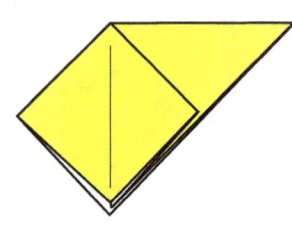

Squash-fold.   A 3D step.

Petal Fold.

In a petal fold, one point is folded up while two opposite sides meet each other.

1 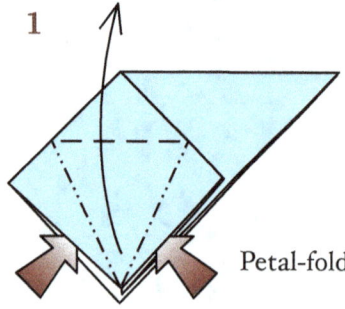 2 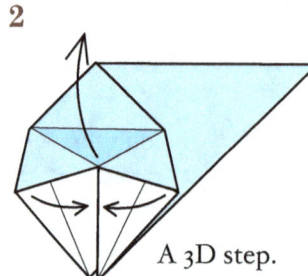 3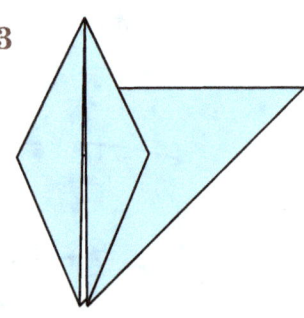

Petal-fold.   A 3D step.

Rabbit Ear.

To fold a rabbit ear, one corner is folded in half and laid down to a side.

1 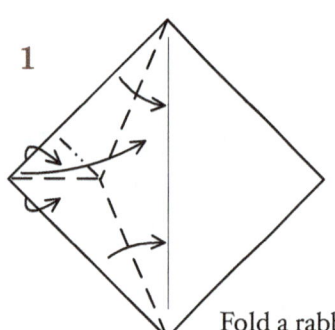 2 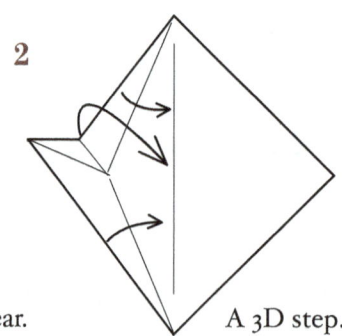 3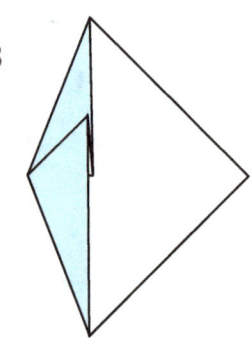

Fold a rabbit ear.   A 3D step.

Double Rabbit Ear.

If you were to bend a straw you would be folding the double rabbit ear.

1 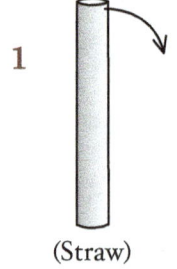 2 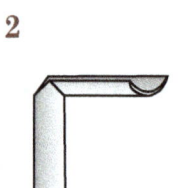 1 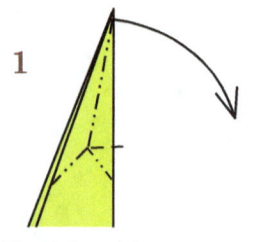 2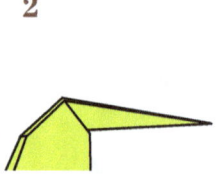

(Straw)   Double-rabbit-ear.

10   *Origami Gnomes of the Forest Wonderland*

Inside Reverse Fold.

In an inside reverse fold, some paper is folded between layers. Here are two examples.

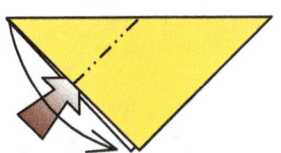

Reverse-fold.

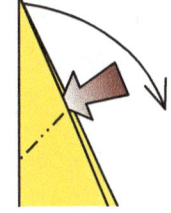 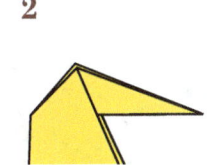

Reverse-fold.

Outside Reverse Fold.

Much of the paper must be unfolded to make an outside reverse fold.

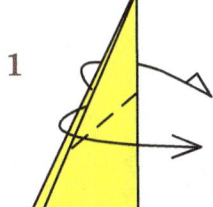

Outside-reverse-fold.

Crimp Fold.

A crimp fold is a combination of two reverse folds. Open the model slightly to form the crimp evenly on each side. Here are two examples.

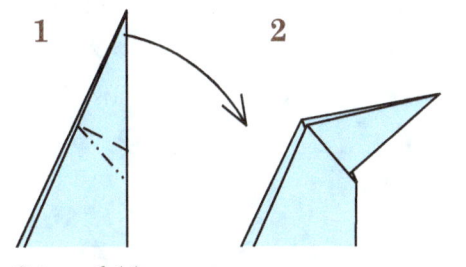

Crimp-fold.

 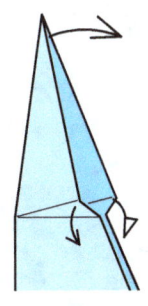 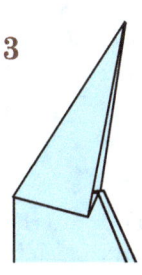

Crimp-fold. A 3D step.

Sink.

For a sink, some of the paper without edges is folded inside. To do this fold, much of the model must be unfolded.

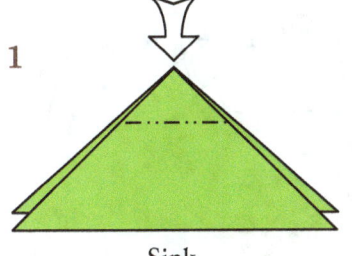 

Sink.

Spread Squash Fold.

A cross between a squash fold and sink fold, some paper in the center is spread apart and then made flat.

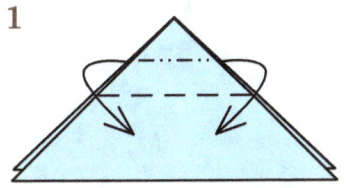 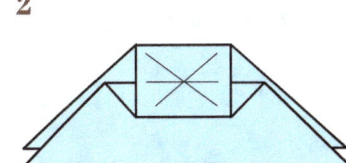

Spread-squash-fold.

Basic Folds 11

Sink Nose Fold.

The sink nose fold is used in many gnomes, as a way to create the hat and nose. The diagrams will be shown as in step 8. To do this fold, the steps below show more detail.

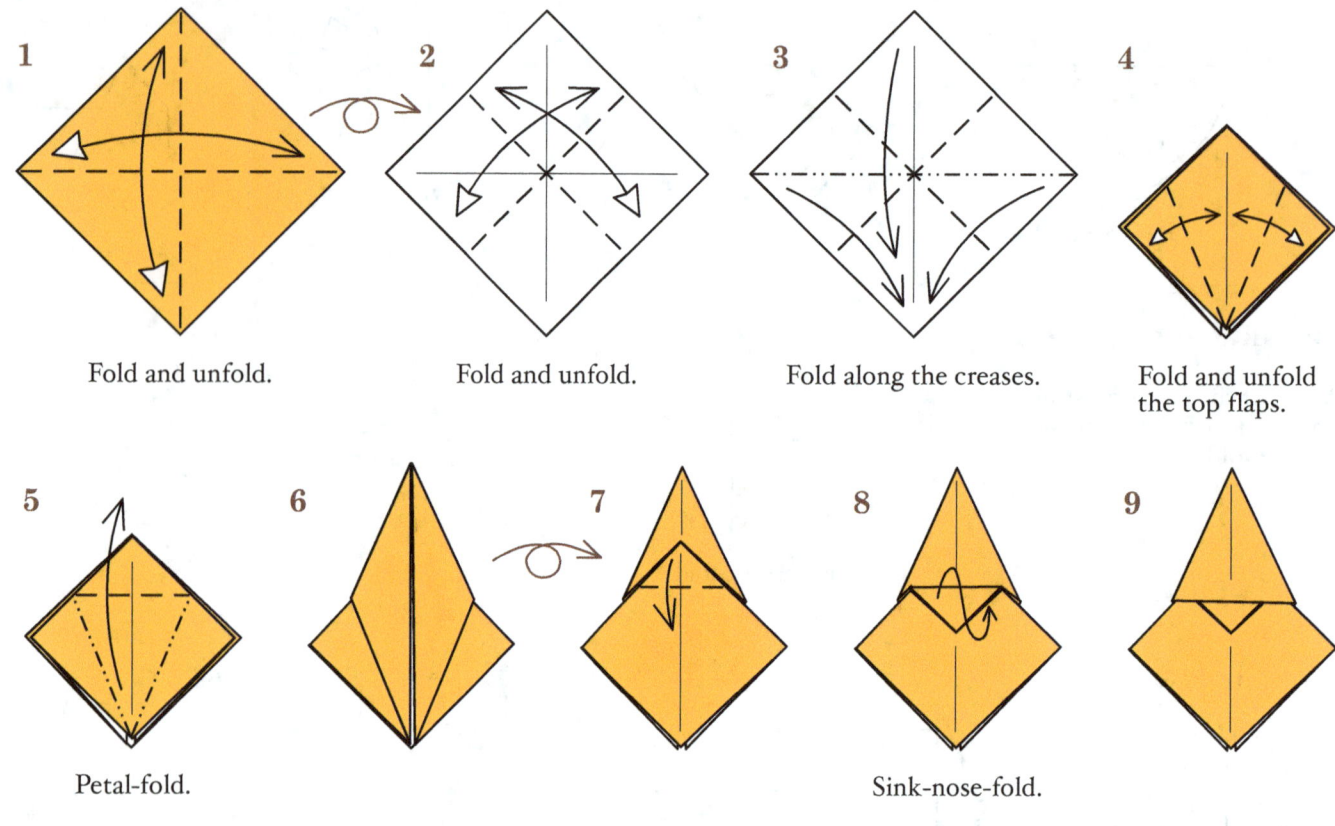

Here are the details for the sink nose fold. Begin with step 8.

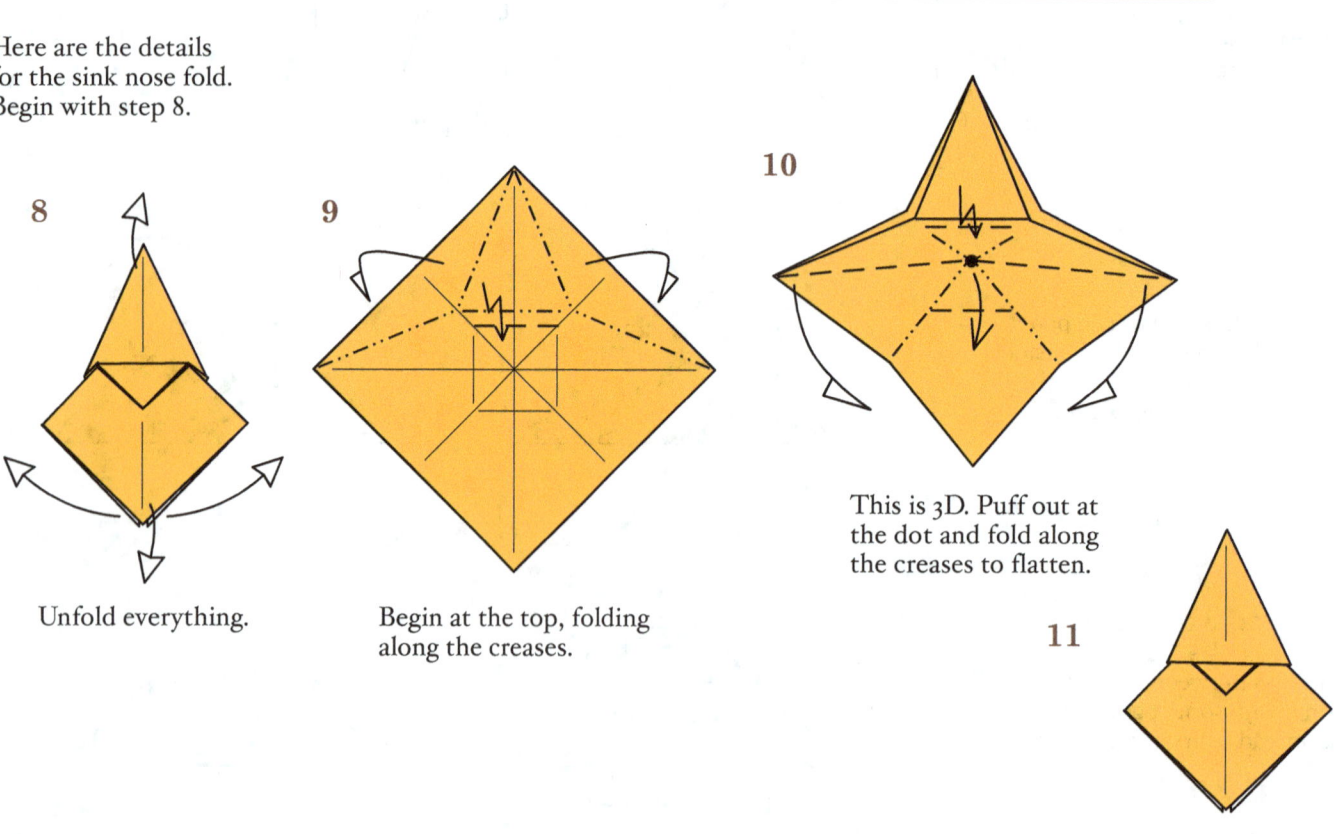

12 *Origami Gnomes of the Forest Wonderland*

Blintz Frog Base.

This uses the double unwrap fold which is shown in detail below.

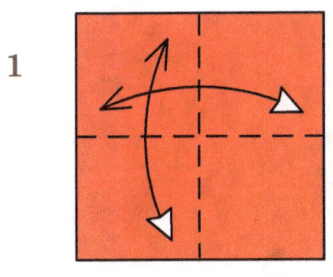

1. Fold and unfold.

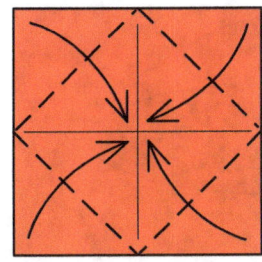

2. Blintz fold: Fold the four corners to the center.

3.

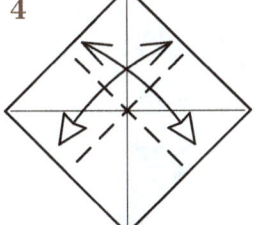

4. Fold and unfold.

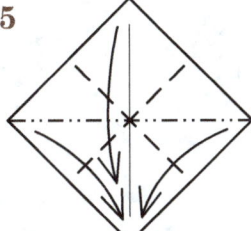

5. This is similar to the Preliminary Fold.

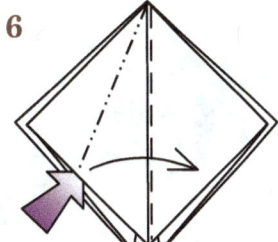

6. (Diagram enlarged.) Squash-fold.

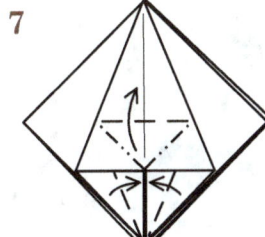

7. Petal-fold.

8. Double-unwrap-fold.

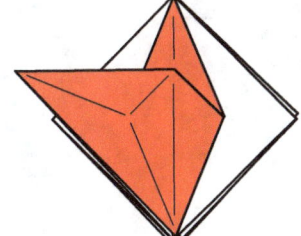

9. Repeat steps 6–8 three more times, on the back and sides.

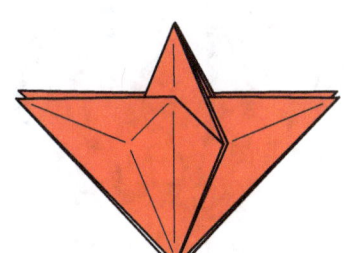

10. Blintz Frog Base

Double Unwrap Fold.

In the double unwrap fold, locked layers are unwrapped and refolded. Much of the folding is 3D. The diagrams are depicted as shown in steps 8 and 9 of the Blintz Frog Base.

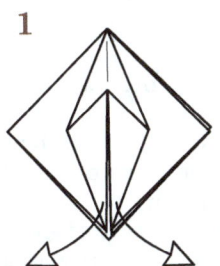

1. Begin with step 8 of the Blintz Frog Base. Spread at the bottom.

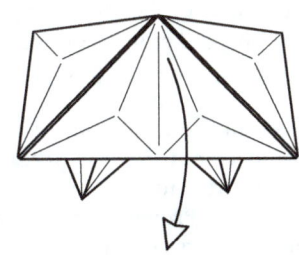

2. Unfold the top layer.

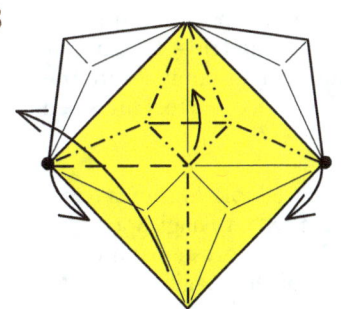

3. Refold along the creases. The dots will meet at the bottom.

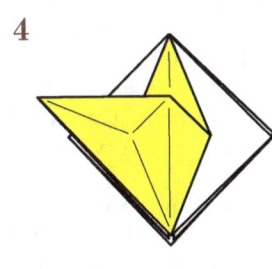

4.

Basic Folds 13

Appreciating Gnomes of the Forest Wonderland

Bright, friendly, clever, and just a bit mischievous, the forest gnomes are eager to lead us on a spectacular adventure. At the edge of the woodland they wave us in, and soon we find ourselves wandering among enchanting mushrooms, cheerful gnomes tucked along mossy paths, and a lively host of woodland creatures who scamper, flutter, and hop beside us as we journey deeper.

As we step beneath the trees, a group of gnomes is ready to greet us with gifts to make the adventure even more delightful. Among them is a charming trio—the son, papa, and grandpa of the Bramblebright family. With the enchanted trinkets and heartfelt advice, we feel prepared to explore every magical nook ahead.

Mushrooms appear everywhere we look. Gnomes have given them whimsical names like Skyfloat Fungi, Sporevine Jellyshrooms, and Sparklecaps. In this forest, mushrooms aren't just plants—they are part of the magic.

Farther along, we meet gnomes who show us how they enjoy the woodlands and all the playful antics they perform for their animal neighbors. Tinker gnomes demonstrate the gadgets they've invented to make forest life even more fun. The wizard Wizzlewick Moonwhistle teaches those who seek it the shimmering secrets of forest magic.

Throughout the journey, a delightful parade of animals crosses our path. Butterflies and dragonflies guide us forward with fluttering grace. Spiders and grasshoppers reveal that even the smallest creatures have big personalities. Snails, frogs, and turtles wander through streams and along wooded trails. A rabbit, squirrel, and some birds add color and music to the forest around us.

Deep in the forest, more gnomes await. Some bring music, or noise, while others craft sparkly surprises. Our adventure ends at the wonder-filled amusement park of Tinkerflip Fizzlegear, whose marvelous rides send gnomes and creatures spinning, swooshing, and soaring with joy.

By combing origami with forest gnomes, enchanting mushrooms, and friendly woodland animals, we can fold scenes that remind us the world is filled with magic.

Greetings at the Edge of the Forest

Greeting gnomes are cheerful, often wearing bright caps and boots made for tiptoeing along mossy paths. Their eyes sparkle with curiosity, and their voices carry soft timbre of forest wind or babbling brooks. Known for their playful antics and unusual talents, these gnomes blend charm with enchantments—leaving tiny gifts, glowing lights, or magical notes to prepare visitors for all the forest's wonders, leading into wild adventures among the trees.

Flint Oakentoe

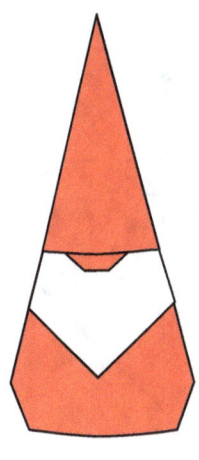

Flint lives under an old wooden bridge where a brook hums all day. When someone crosses, Flint pops up to offer safe passage, bridge trivia, and sometimes a fish that jumped into his hands by accident. He hands out sprig and thyme like greeting cards.

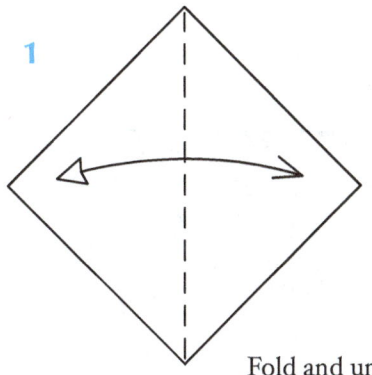

1. Fold and unfold.

2. Fold and unfold on the edge.

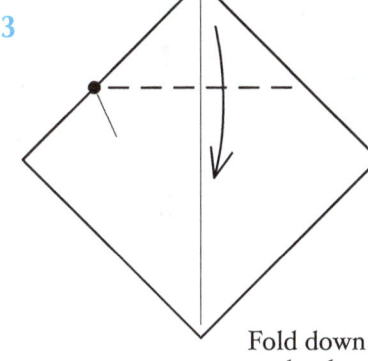

3. Fold down at the dot.

Flint Oakentoe 15

4

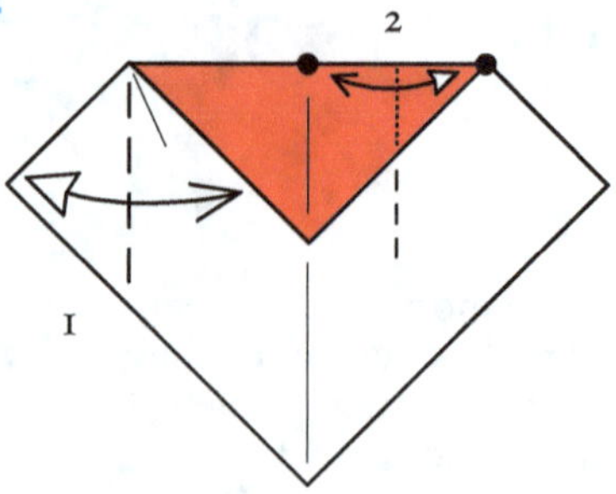

Fold and unfold at 1 and 2.

5

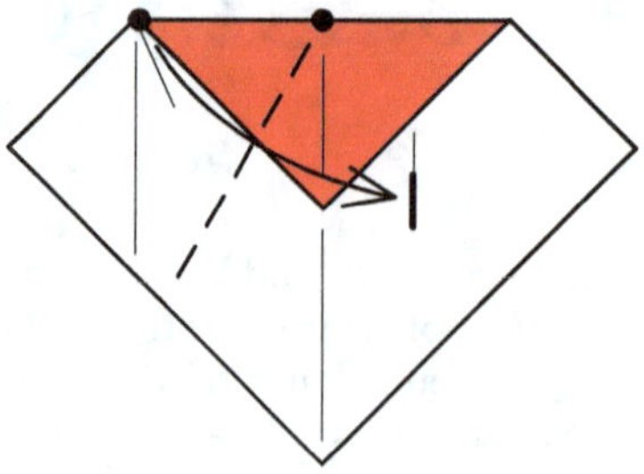

Bring the dot on the left to the crease.

6

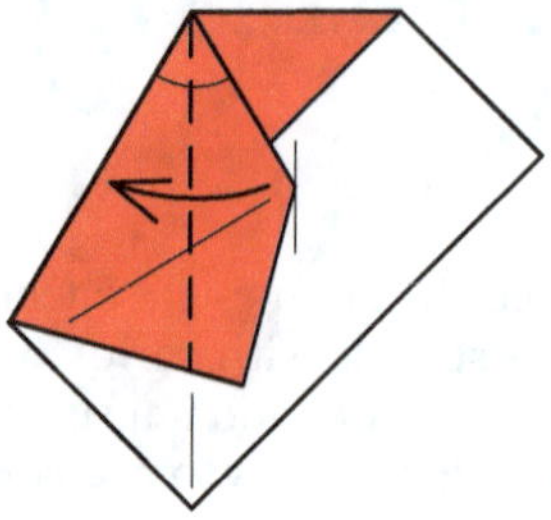

7

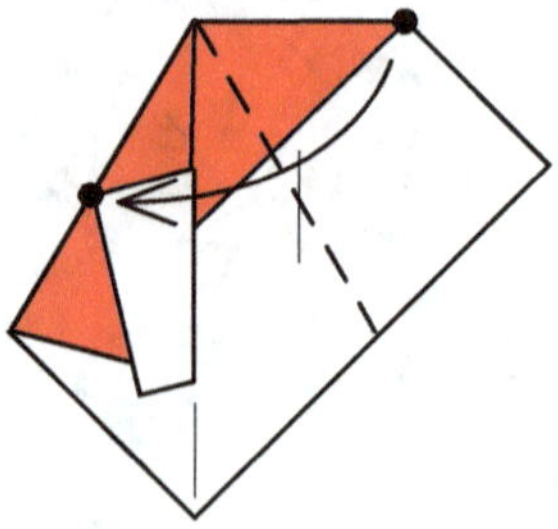

Repeat steps 5–6 on the right.

8

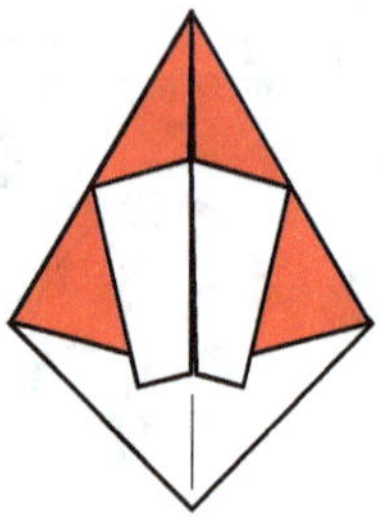

9

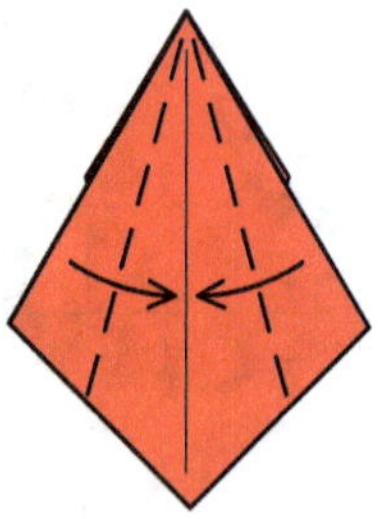

Fold all the layers to the center.

10

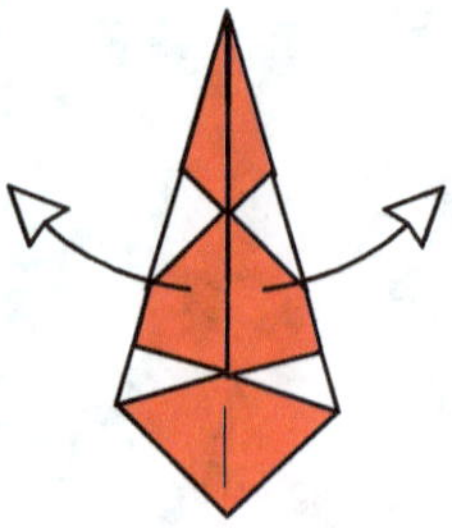

Unfold everything.

11

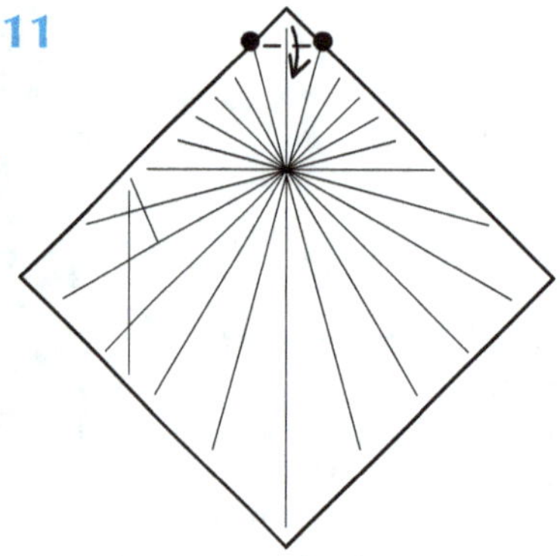

12

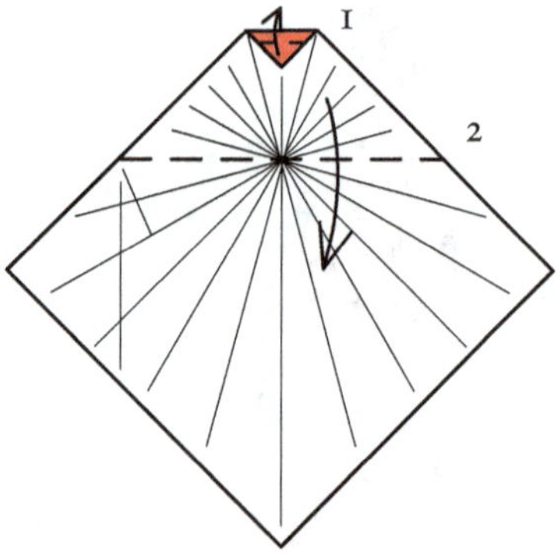

1. Fold up.
2. Fold down along the crease.

13

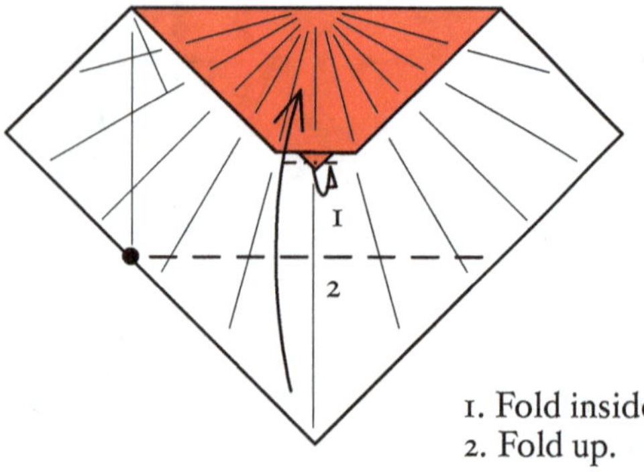

1. Fold inside.
2. Fold up.

14

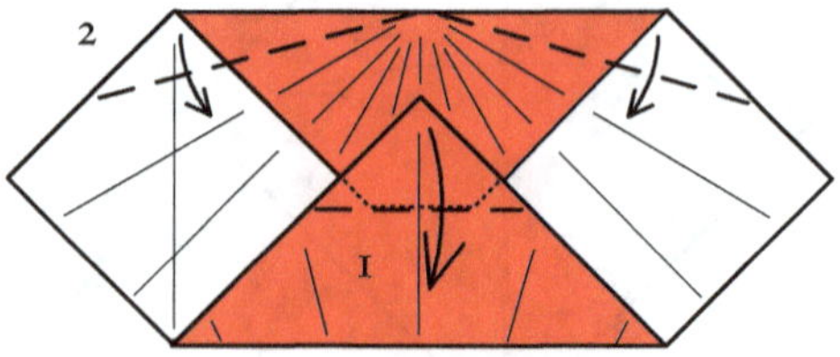

1. Fold along the hidden edge.
2. Fold along the creases.

16 *Origami Gnomes of the Forest Wonderland*

15

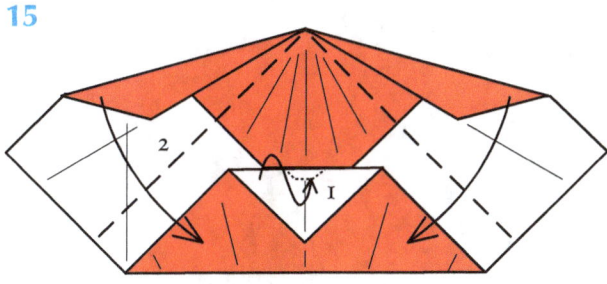

1. Tuck inside.
2. Fold along the creases.

16

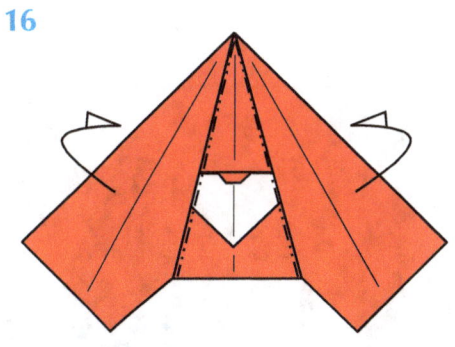

Fold behind along the creases.

17

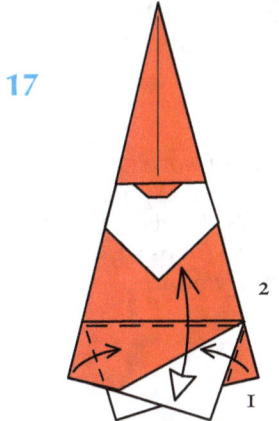

1. Fold on the left and right.
2. Fold and unfold.

18

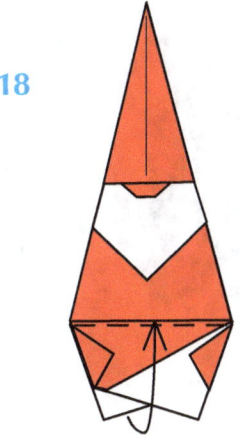

Tuck inside.

19

1. Make small reverse folds.
2. Puff out to make the model round.

20

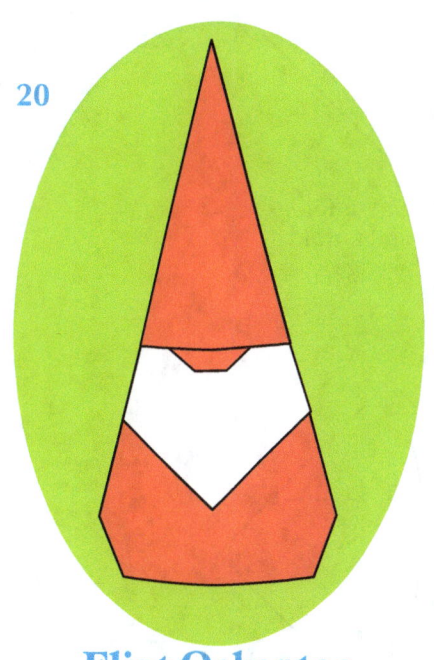

Flint Oakentoe

Dandelion Pipwhistle

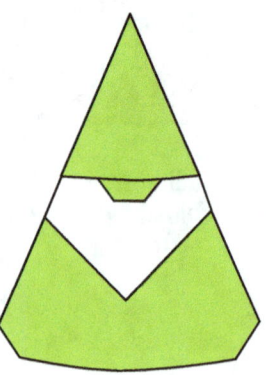

Pipwhistle wears a hat made of woven dandelion stems, and every time someone approaches he hands them a stem. He tells the visitor to use the stem as a magic wand so tulips appear, leading the path to more adventures.

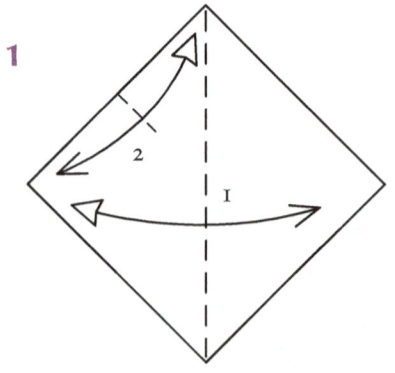

1. Fold and unfold.
2. Fold and unfold on the edge.

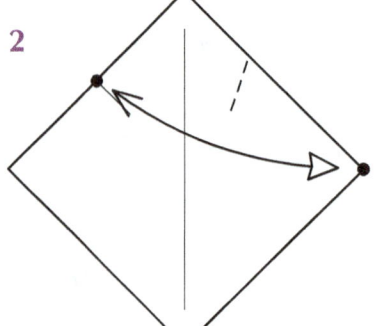

Fold and unfold.

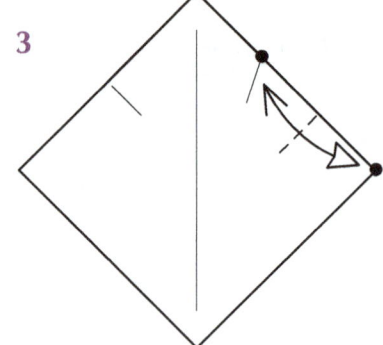

Fold and unfold.

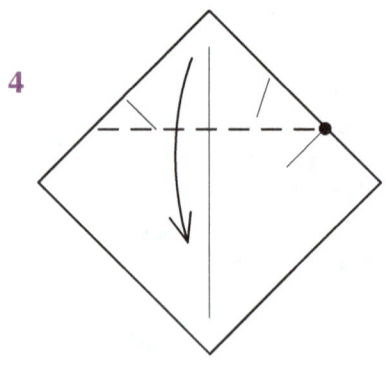

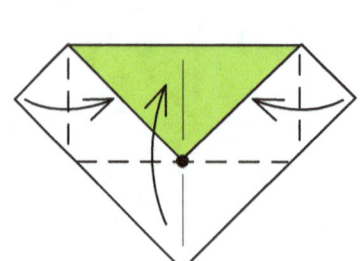

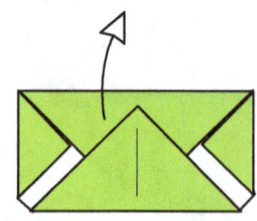

Unfold.

18   *Origami Gnomes of the Forest Wonderland*

7

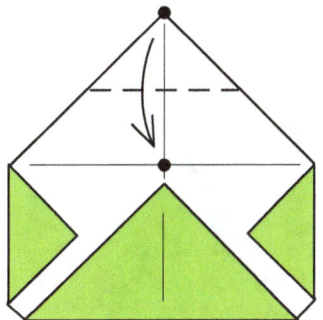

8

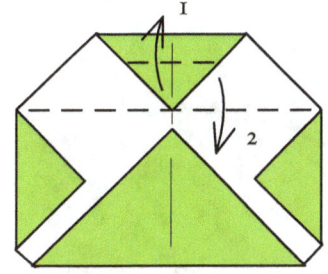

1. Fold up.
2. Fold down along the crease.

9

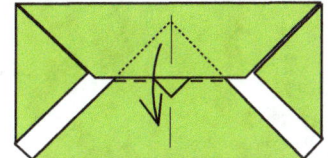

Fold down from inside.

10

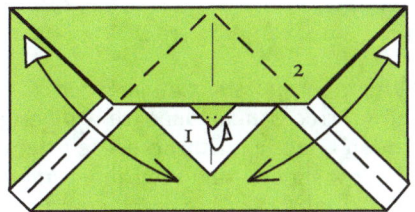

1. Fold inside.
2. Fold to the center and unfold.

11

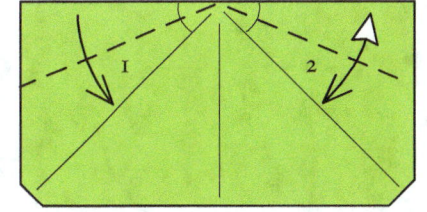

1. Fold to the crease.
2. Fold and unfold.

12

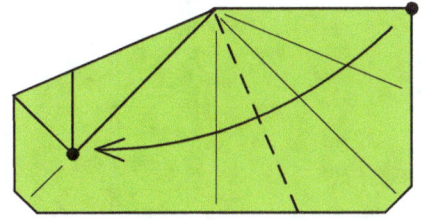

13

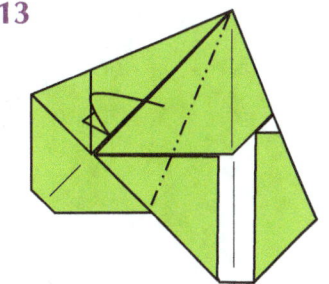

Fold inside along the crease.

14

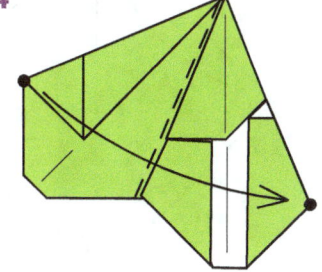

15

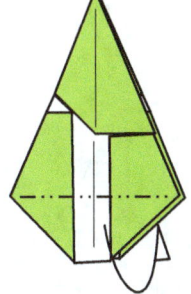

Tuck both flaps inside.

16

1. Make small reverse folds.
2. Puff out to make the model round.

17

Dandelion Pipwhistle

Dandelion Pipwhistle 19

Murk Hollowpocket

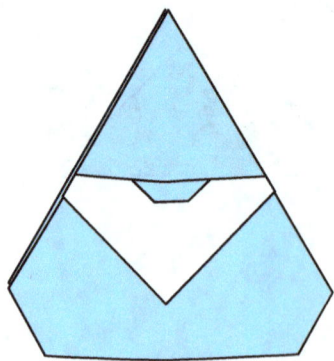

Murk greets guests from unexpected places: behind tree trunks, beneath bridges, or hidden under a mushroom. He offers "shadow slips"—small swirling scraps of enchanted shade that can be used to hide, cool off, or block the glare of trolls.

1 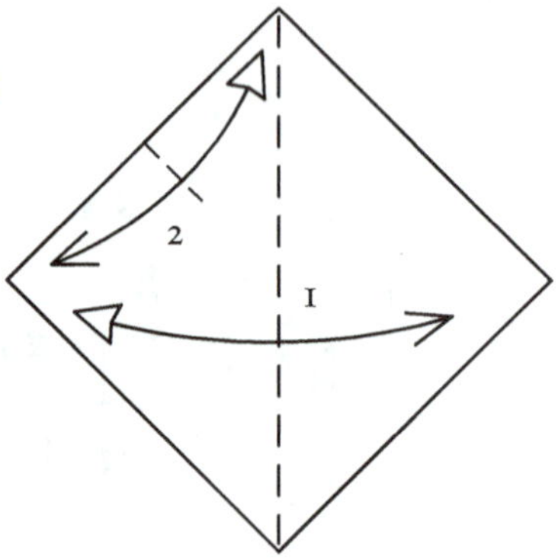
1. Fold and unfold.
2. Fold and unfold on the edge.

2 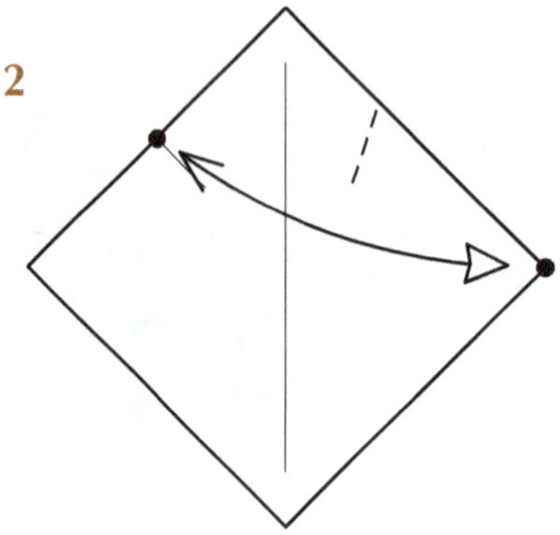
Fold and unfold.

3 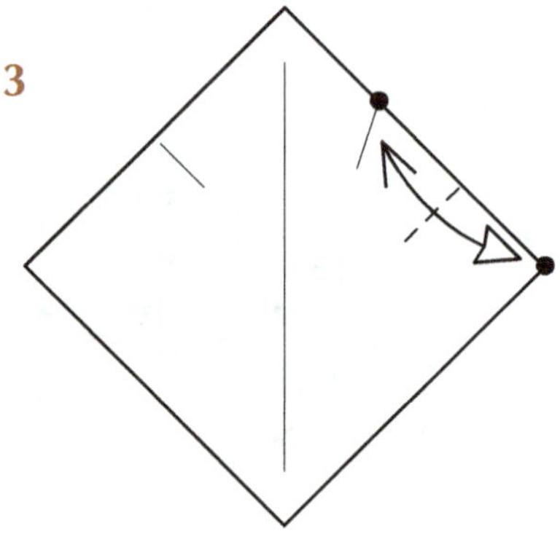
Fold and unfold.

4

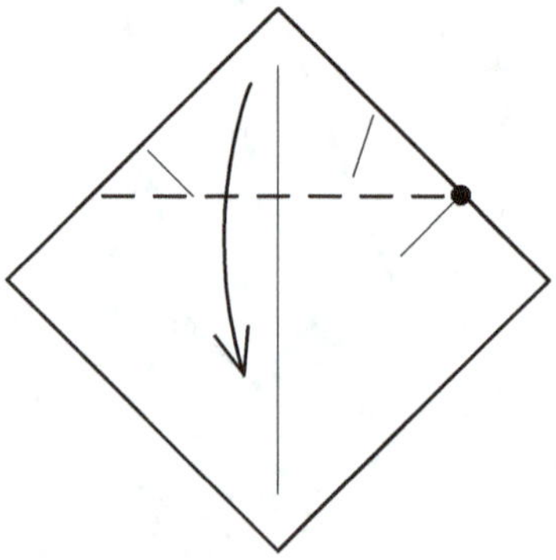

5
Fold and unfold. 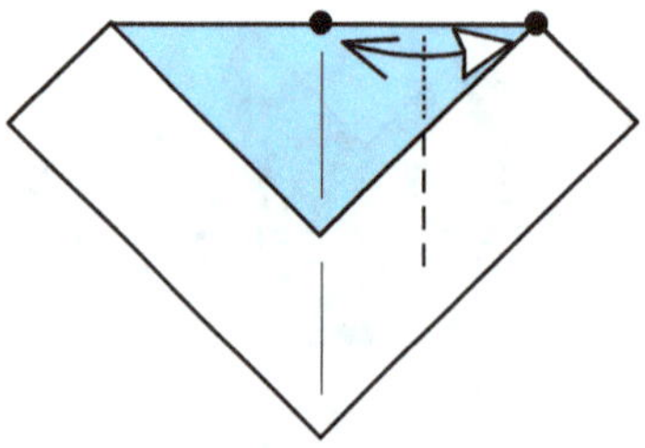

6 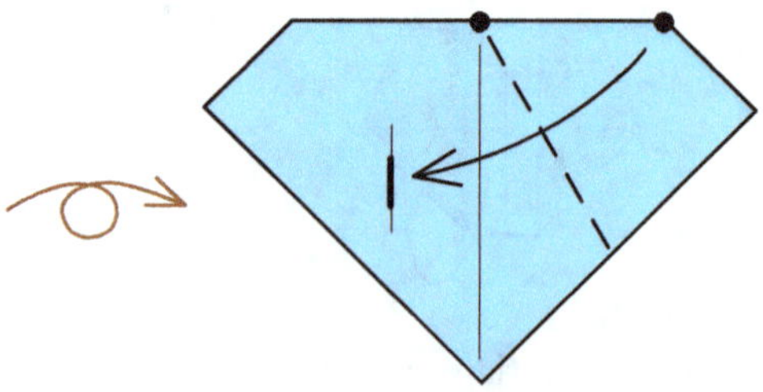
Bring the dot on the right to the crease.

20 *Origami Gnomes of the Forest Wonderland*

7

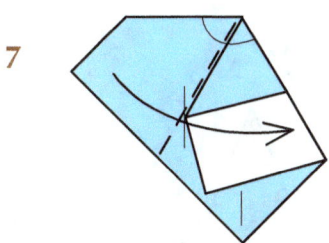

8

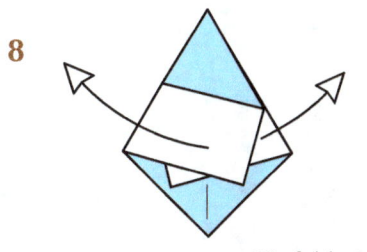 

Unfold.

9

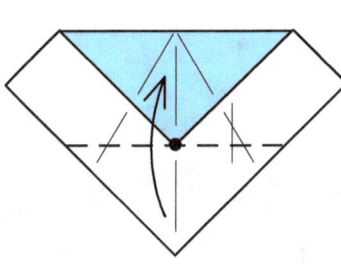

10

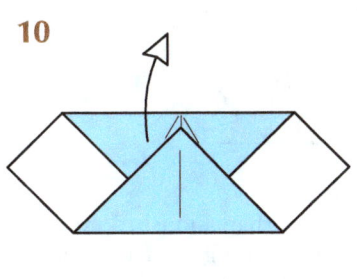

Unfold.

11

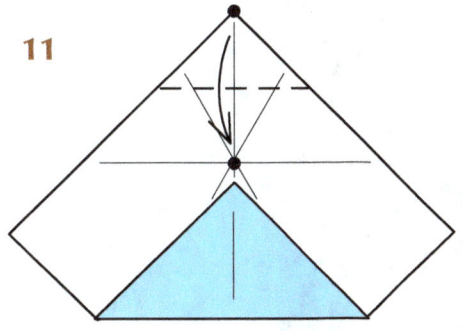

12

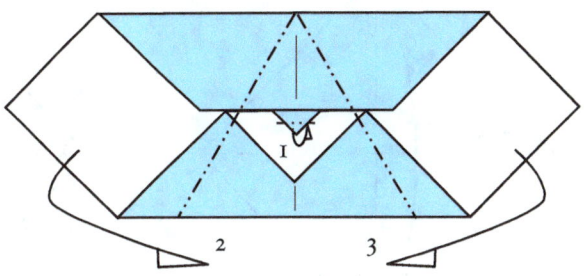

1. Fold up.
2. Fold down along the crease.

13

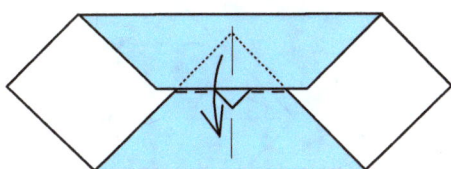

Fold down from inside.

14

1. Fold inside.
2 and 3. Fold along the creases.

15

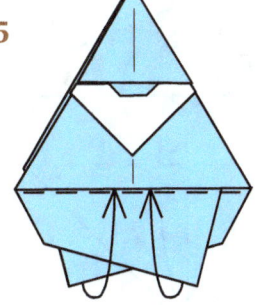

Tuck both flaps inside.

16

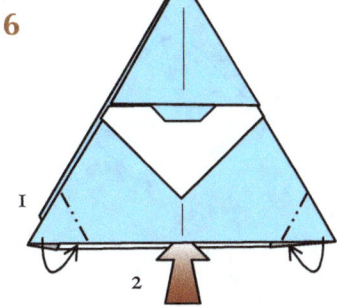

1. Make small reverse folds.
2. Puff out to make the model round.

17

Murk Hollowpocket

Murk Hollowpocket 21

Son: Sprigley Bramblebright

Sprigley is barely taller than a mushroom cap. He greets visitors by popping out from behind roots. He offers carved wooden animals made from small branches and hats filled with blueberries. He instructs the visitors to eat quickly so they can wear the hats.

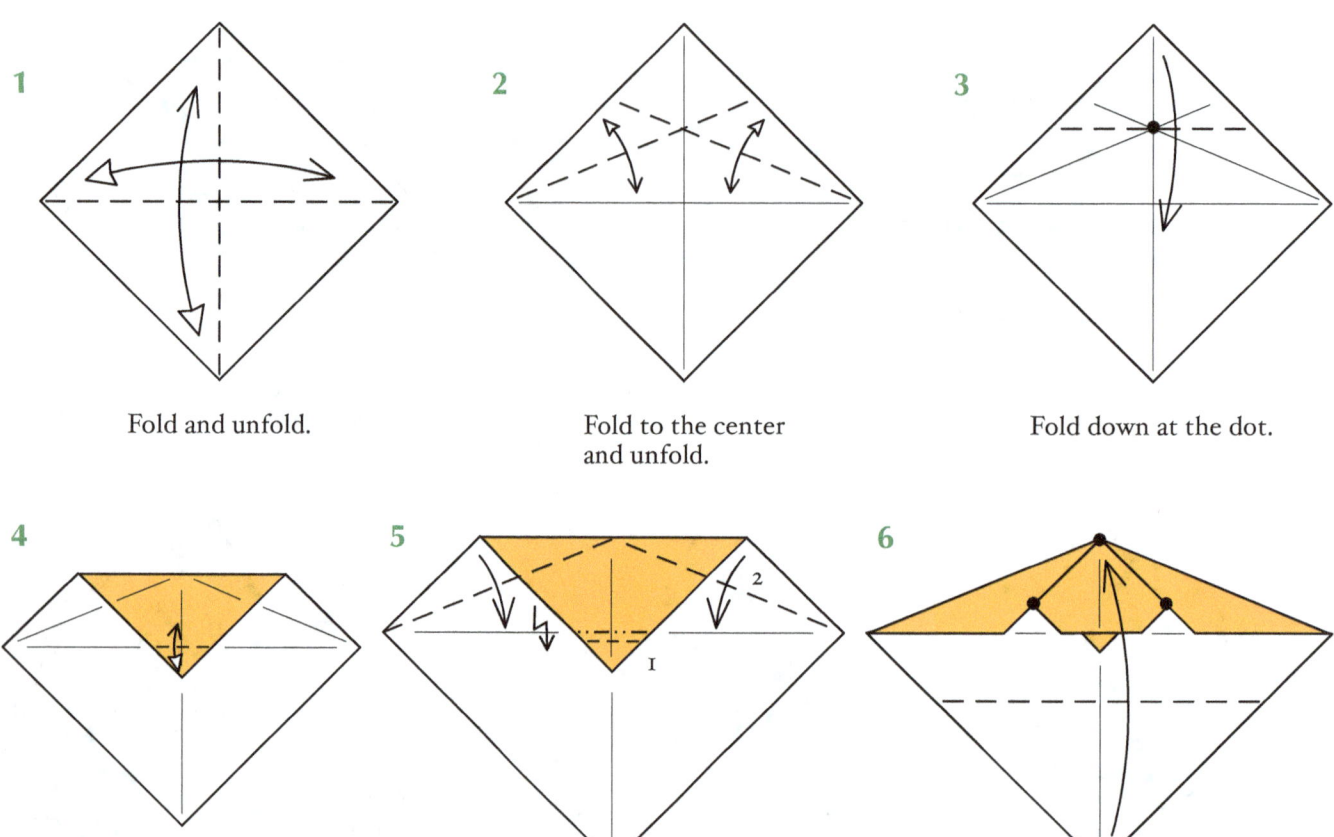

1. Fold and unfold.

2. Fold to the center and unfold.

3. Fold down at the dot.

4. Fold and unfold along the hidden crease.

5. 1. Mountain-fold along the crease for this pleat fold.
   2. Fold along the creases.

6. Note the dots on the left and right, which will be used for the next step.

22 *Origami Gnomes of the Forest Wonderland*

7

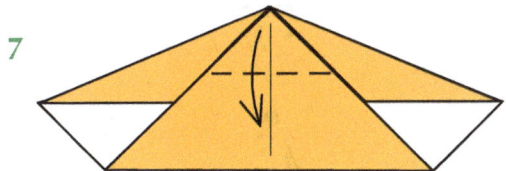

Fold at the dots from step 6.

8

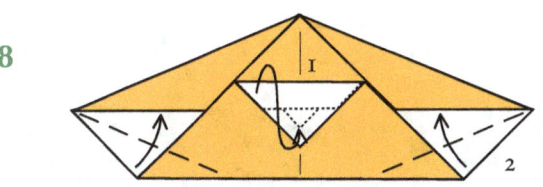

1. Tuck inside.
2. Fold on the left and right.

9

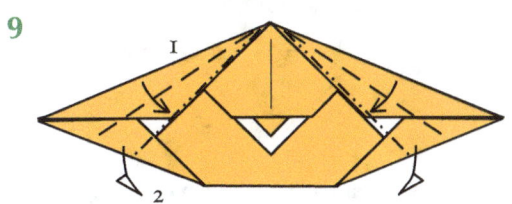

Make pleat folds.

10

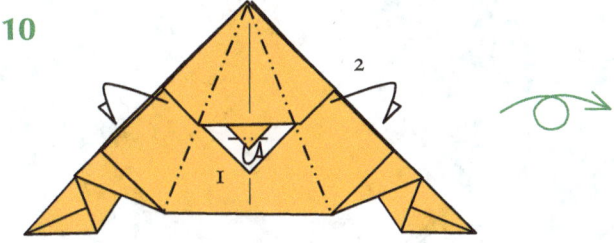

1. Fold inside.
2. Fold to the center.

11

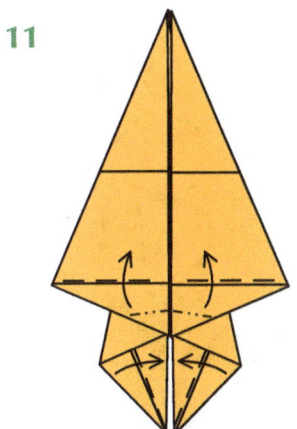

This is a combination of squash folds.

12

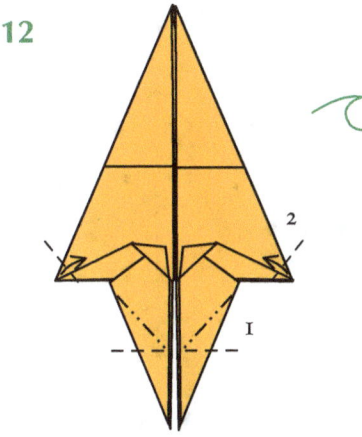

1. Make crimp folds.
2. Fold up on the left and right.

13

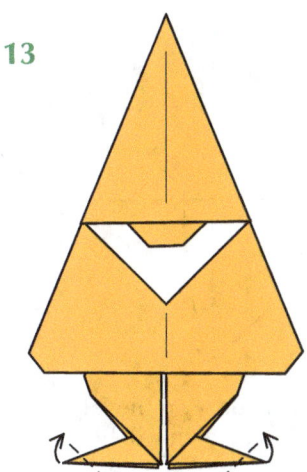

Make outside reverse folds. Spread the bottom of the feet so the Gnome can stand.

14

Sprigley Bramblebright

Sprigley Bramblebright 23

Papa: Thornwick Bramblebright

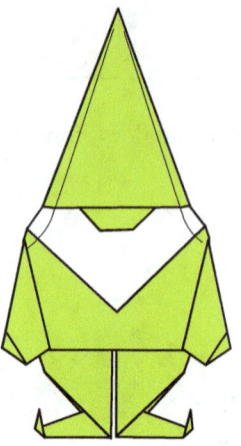

Thornwick wears a hat filled with overlapping pine needles. He welcomes visitors and assures them that everything here already knows they will be wandering through. He offers glowlight maps that warn of muddy patches, thorny bushes, and heavy fog. He places a frog on the visitor's shoulder and suggest they find the best spot for the frog to leap into.

1. Fold and unfold.

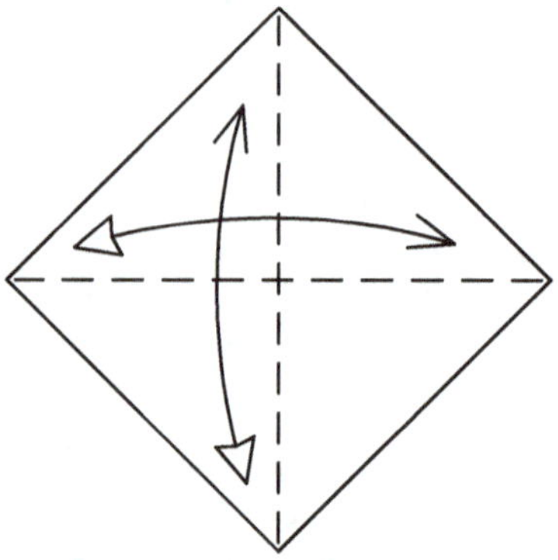

2. Fold to the center and unfold.

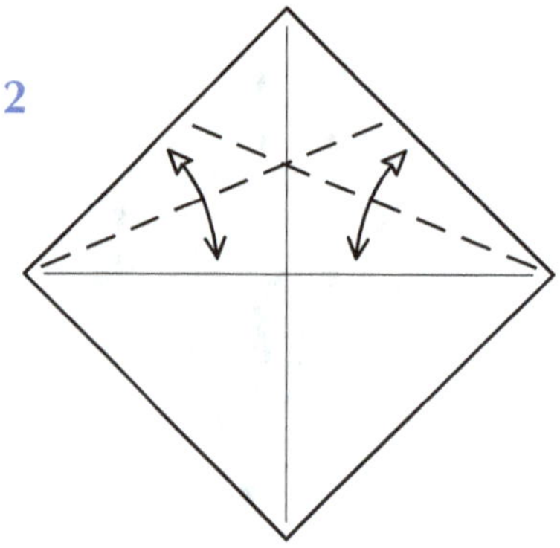

3. Fold down at the dot.

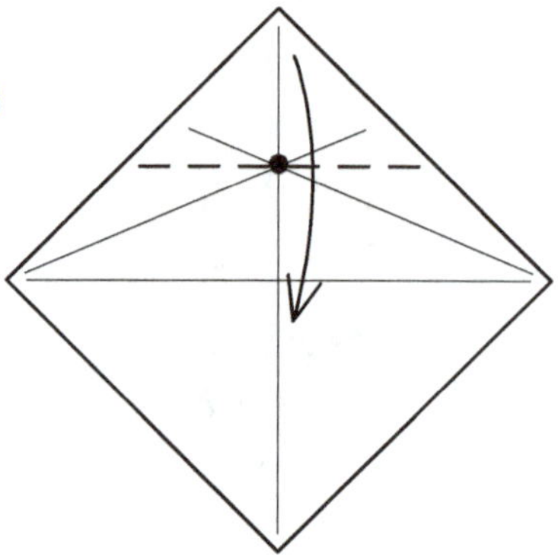

4. Fold and unfold along the hidden crease.

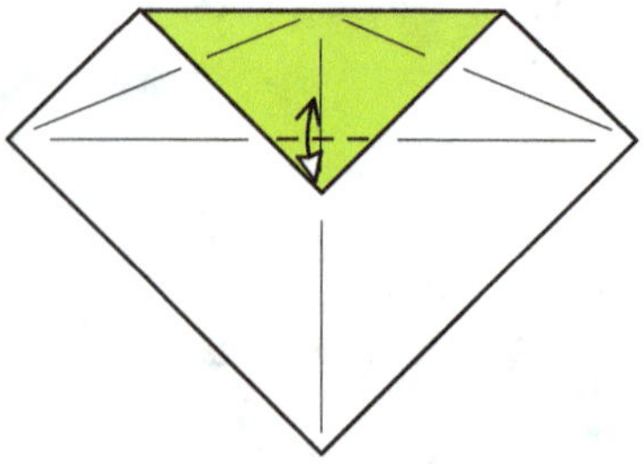

5. 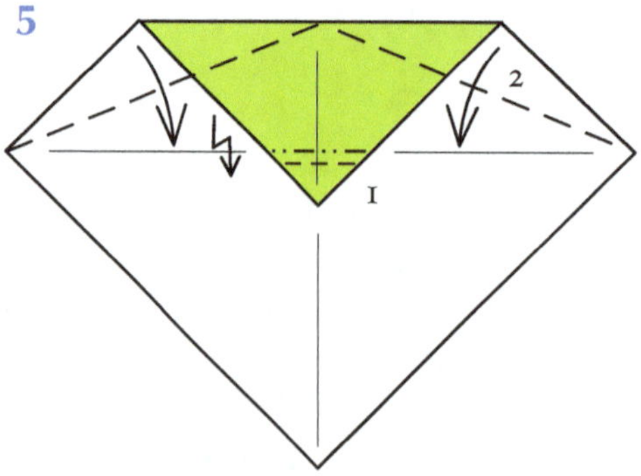
   1. Mountain-fold along the crease for this pleat fold.
   2. Fold along the creases.

6. Note the dots on the left and right, which will be used for the next step.

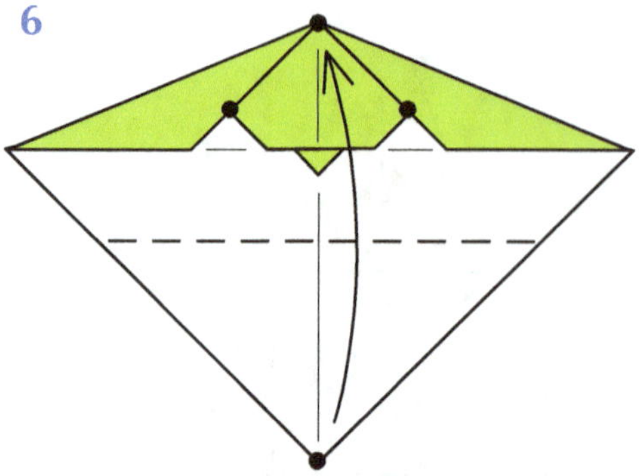

24   *Origami Gnomes of the Forest Wonderland*

7

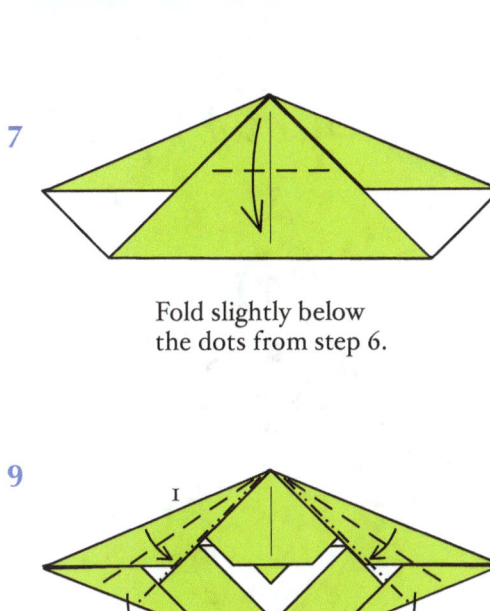

Fold slightly below the dots from step 6.

8

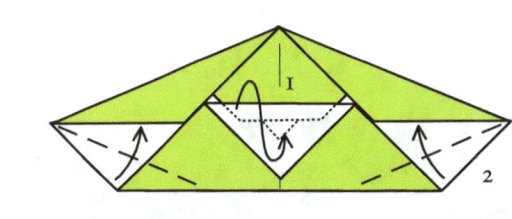

1. Tuck inside.
2. Fold on the left and right.

9

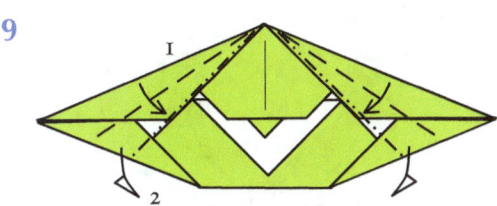

Make pleat folds.

10

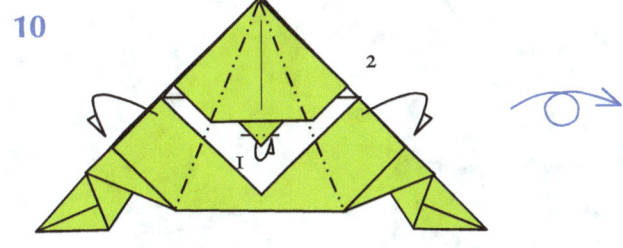

1. Fold inside.
2. Fold to the center.

11

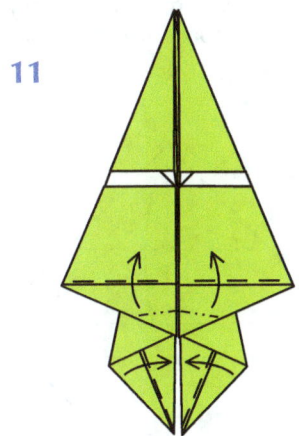

This is a combination of squash folds.

12

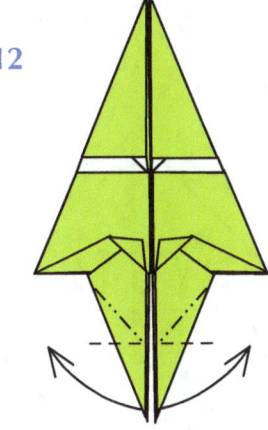

Make crimp folds.

13

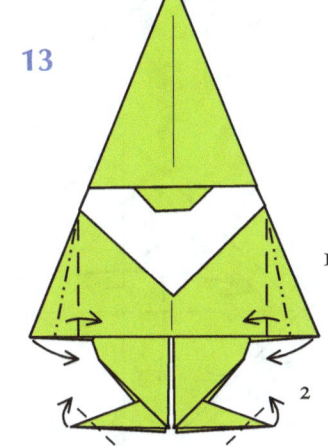

1. Make squash folds.
2. Make outside reverse folds.

14

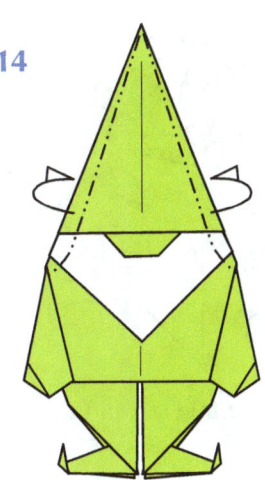

Shape the top with 3D folds. Spread the bottom of the feet so the Gnome can stand.

15

Thornwick Bramblebright

Thornwick Bramblebright 25

Grandpa: Elder Mossroot Bramblebright

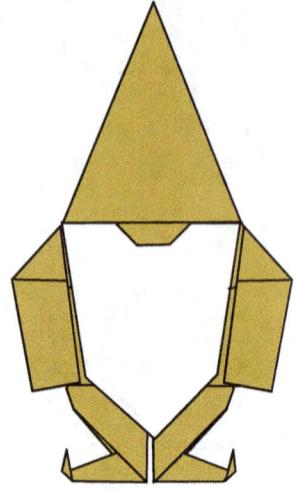

Elder Mossroot's hat is full of tiny mushrooms because he forgets to brush off the spores. He gifts travelers with his handcrafted wise cloaks. The cloaks wisely stay silent throughout their journeys while keeping them comfortably warm. Elder reminds travelers that they will not get lost in the forest as all roads lead to Gnome.

1. Fold and unfold.

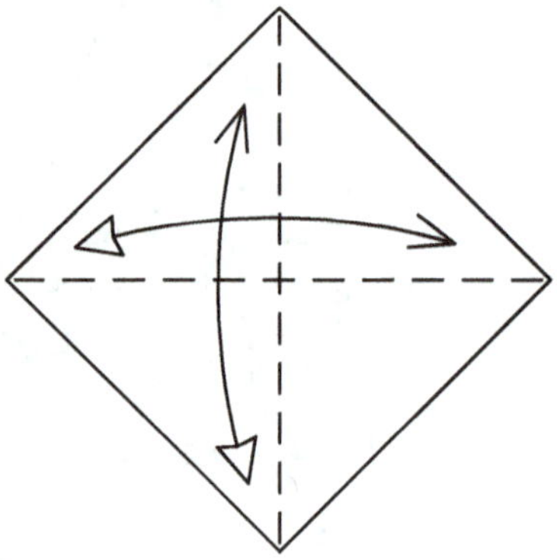

2. Fold to the center and unfold.

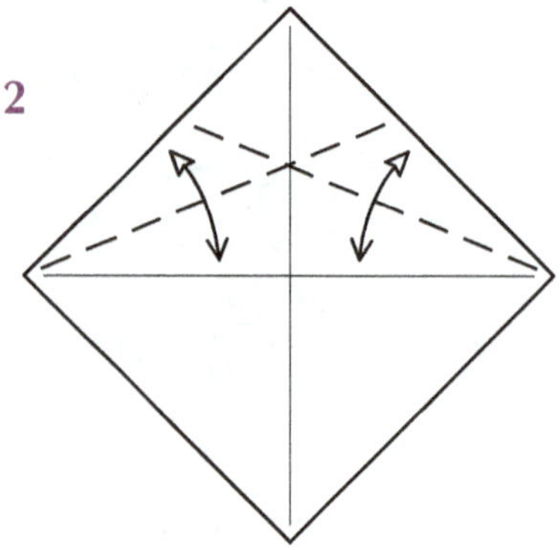

3. Fold down at the dot.

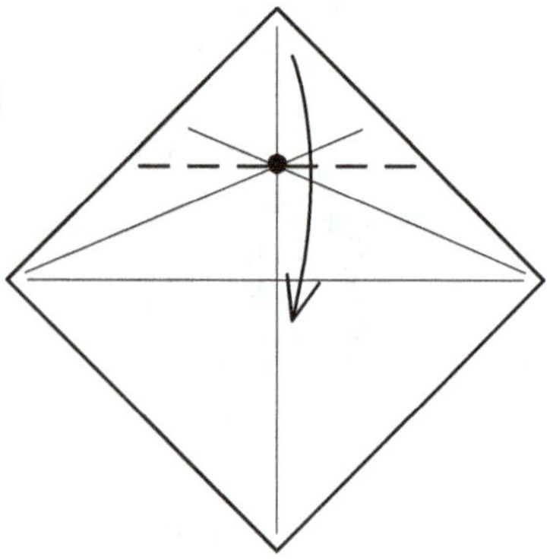

4. Fold and unfold along the hidden crease.

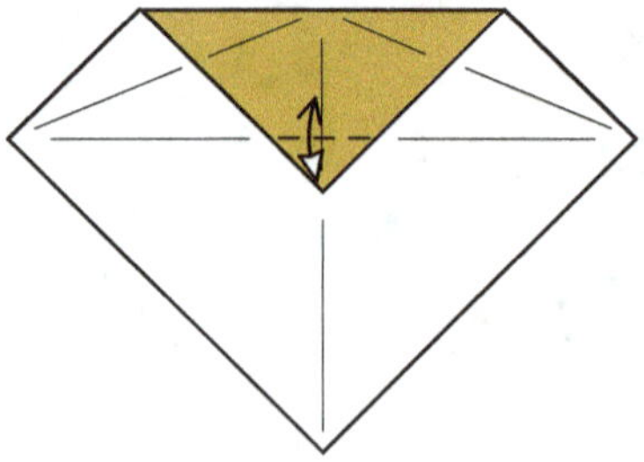

5. 1. Mountain-fold along the crease for this pleat fold.
   2. Fold along the creases.

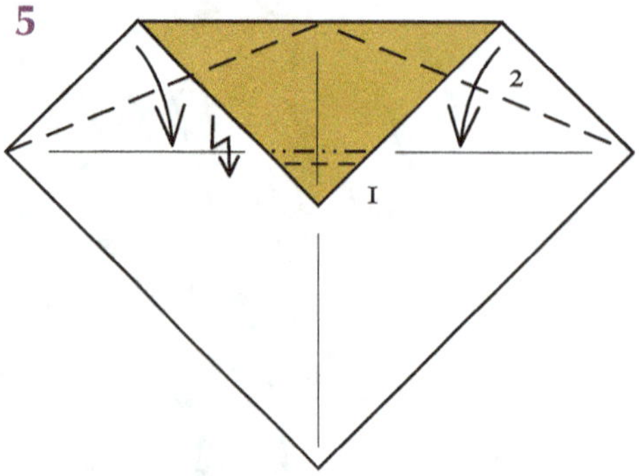

6. Fold and unfold at 1 and 2.

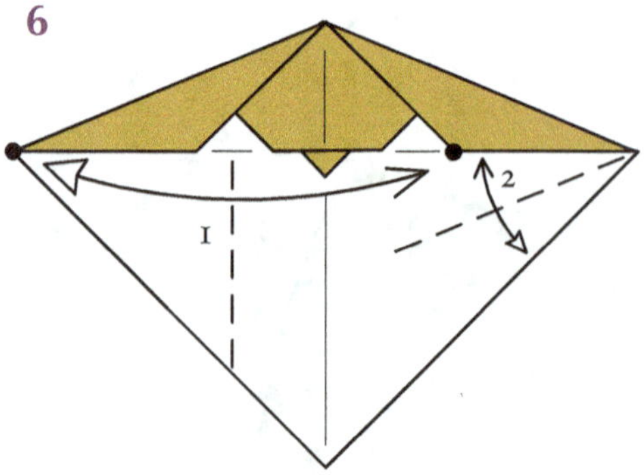

26 *Origami Gnomes of the Forest Wonderland*

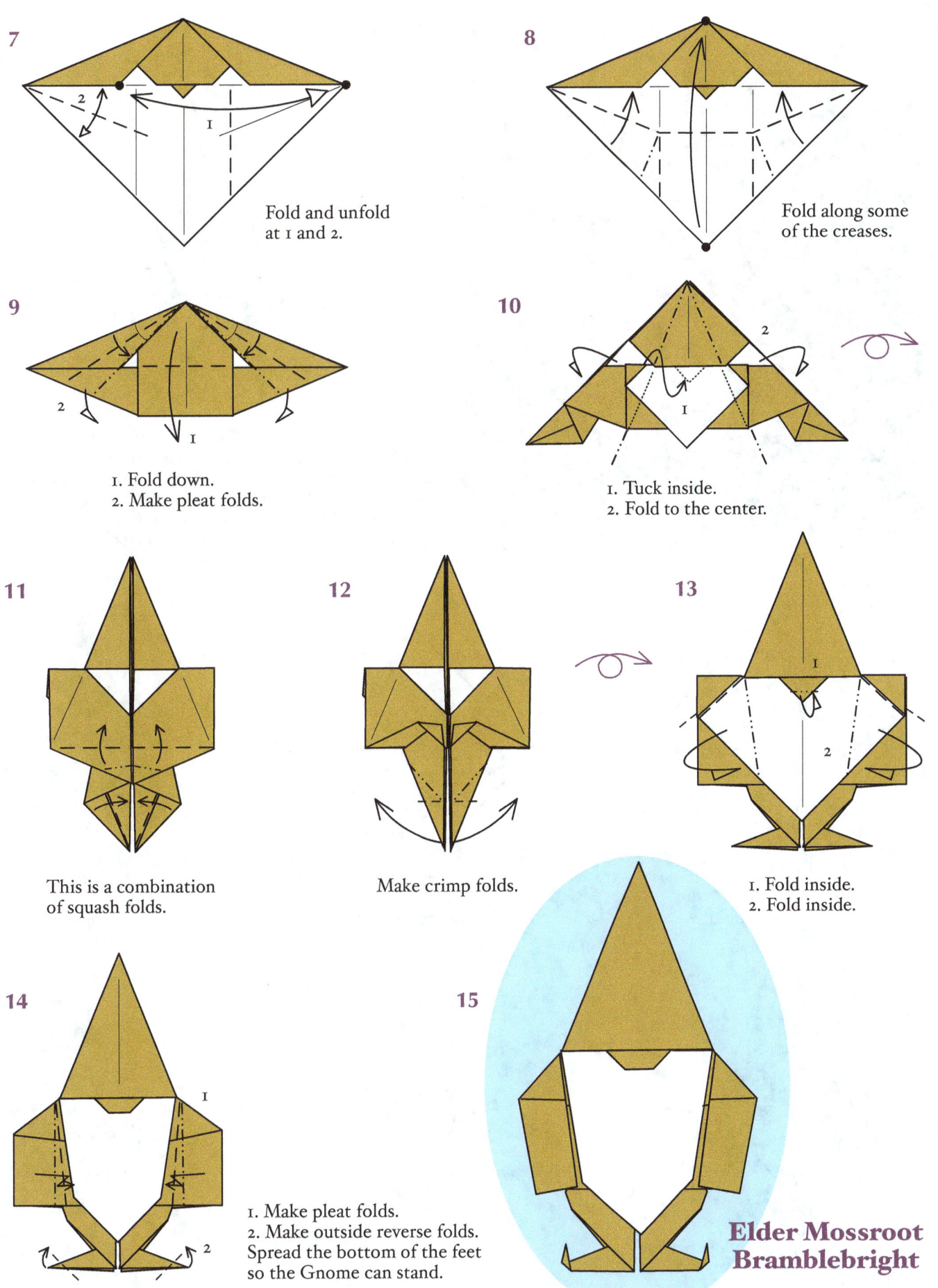

Elder Mossroot Bramblebright 27

Elmwick Driftstone

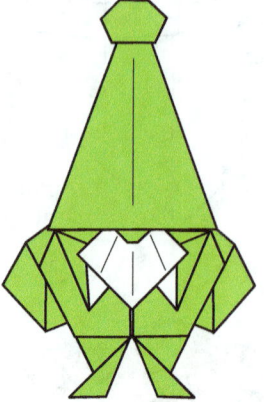

Elmwick rarely touches the ground. He drifts at ankle-height, humming a tune that make stones rise and float in the air. When he greets a visitor, he offers floating stones that lead the way to the best treats in the area. When asked how he learned how to make stones float he shrugs, "Gravity and I had a disagreement."

1 Fold and unfold.

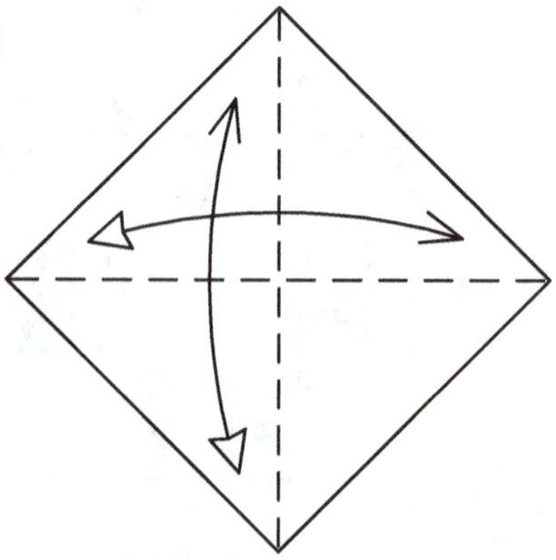

2 Fold to the center.

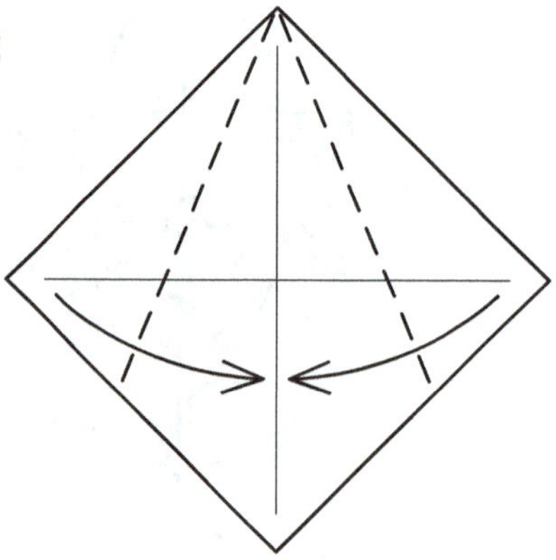

3 1. Fold inside.
   2. Spread.

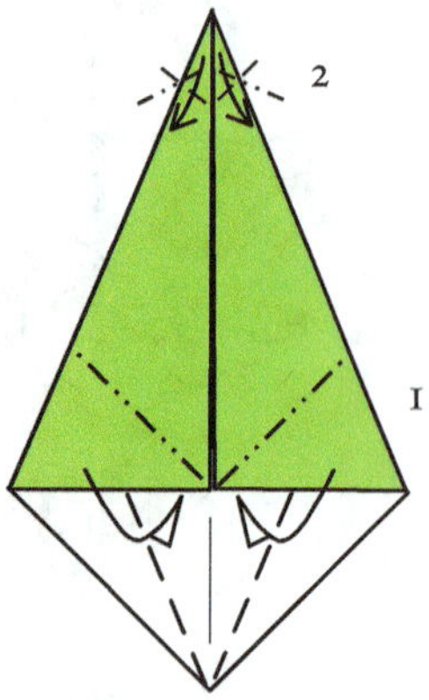

4 Fold behind.

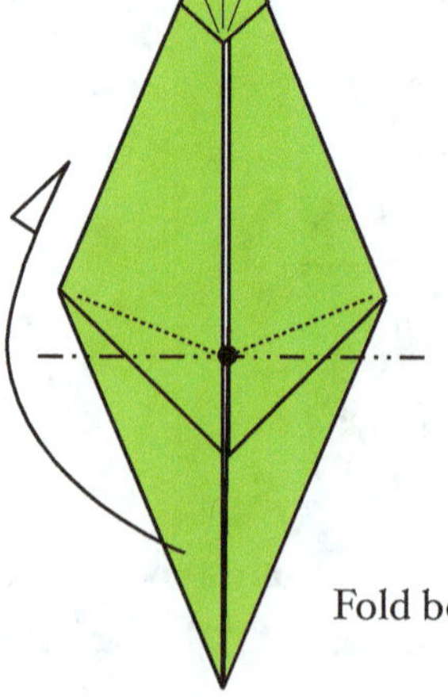

5

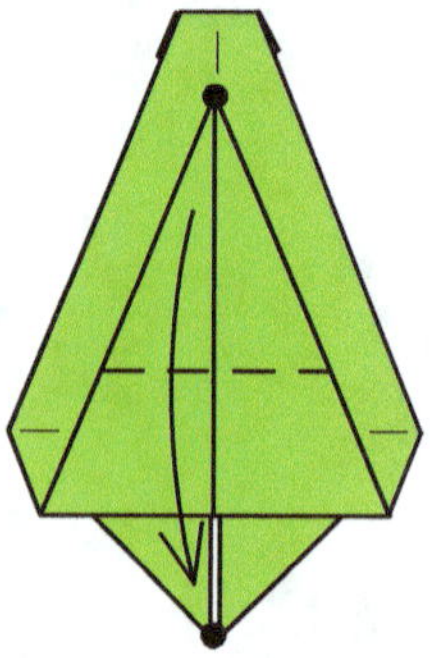

6 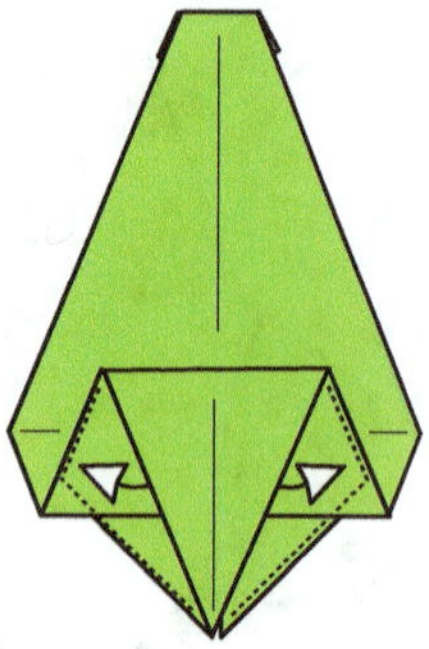 Pull out to the dotted lines.

28   *Origami Gnomes of the Forest Wonderland*

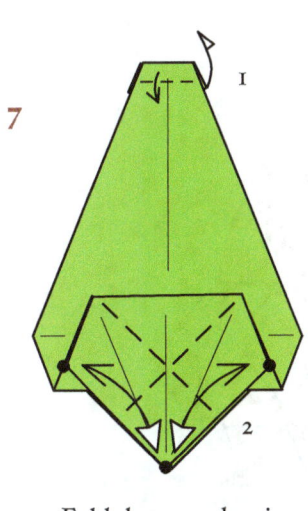

7

1. Fold down and swing out from behind.
2. Fold and unfold.

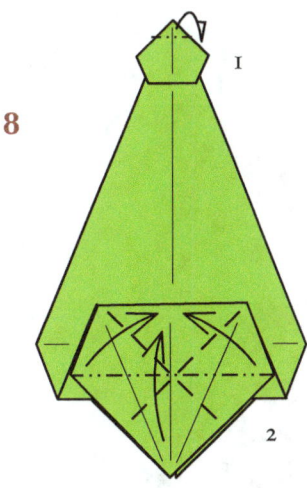

8

1. Fold behind.
2. Fold along the creases.

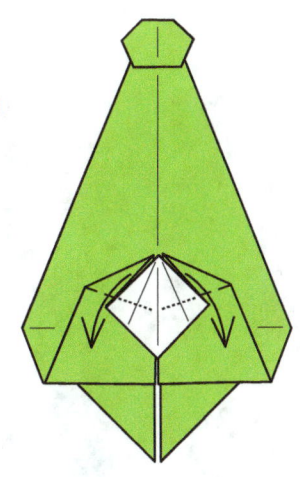

9

Make reverse folds.

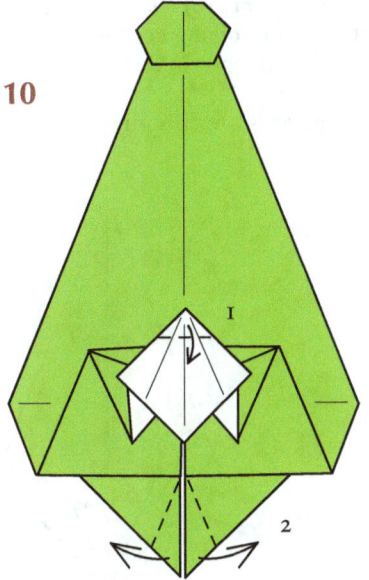

10

1. Fold down.
2. Fold on the left and right.

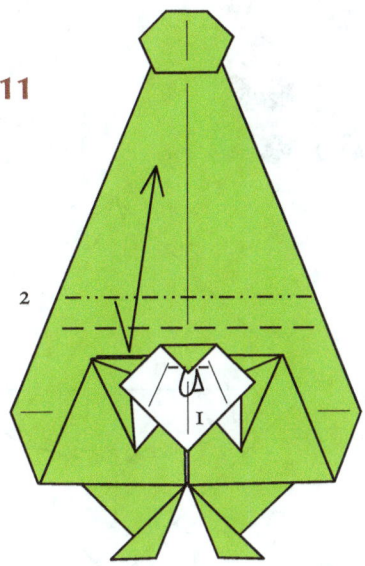

11

1. Fold inside.
2. Pleat-fold to the bold line.

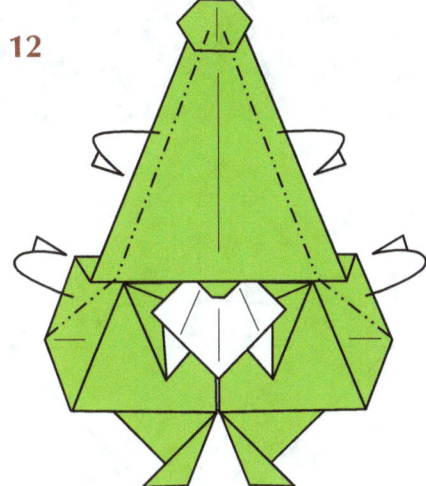

12

Make squash folds. It is easier to turn to model over to do this.

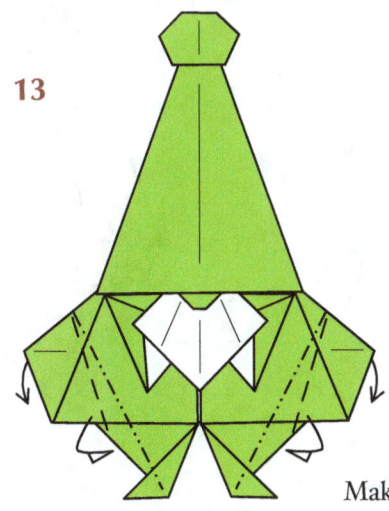

13

Make pleat folds.

14

Elmwick Driftstone

Elmwick Driftstone 29

Pebblecrest Underbough

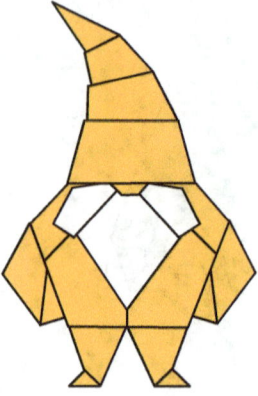

Visitors usually hear Pebblecrest before they see him, as he attempts to juggle stones that mostly land with a clang. He offers a handful of enchanted pebbles that change color depending on what lies deeper in the forest.
Blue means "river ahead."
Gold means "the squirrels are friendly today."
Red means "berries nearby."

1

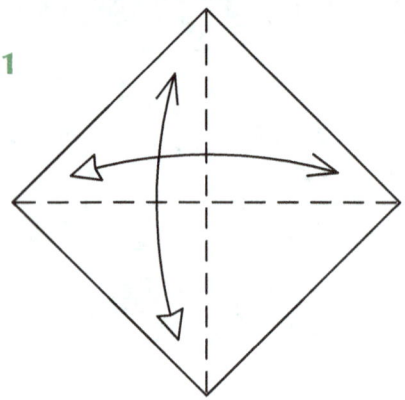

Fold and unfold.

2

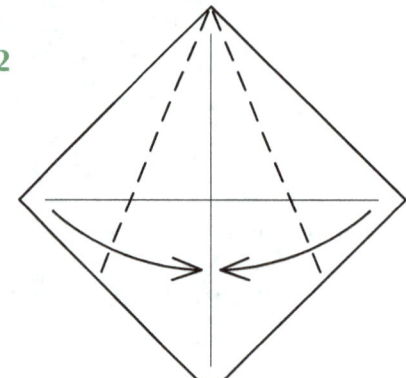

Fold to the center.

3

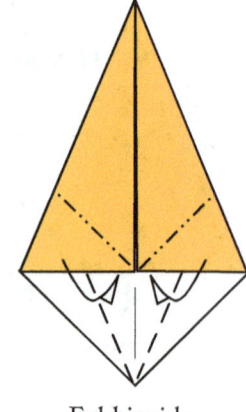

Fold inside.

4

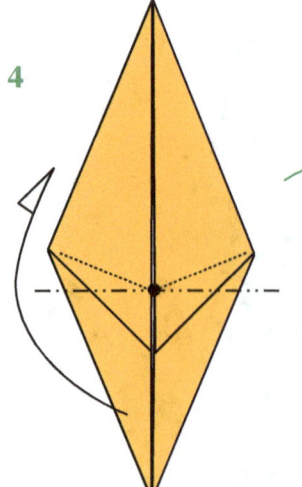

Fold behind.

5

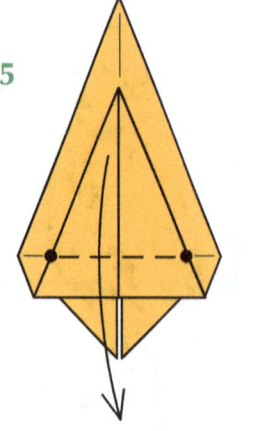

6

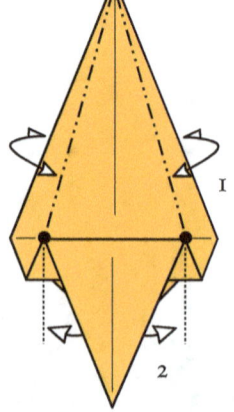

1. Fold and unfold.
2. Pull out to the dotted vertical lines.

7

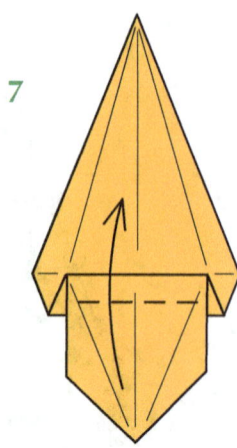

30 *Origami Gnomes of the Forest Wonderland*

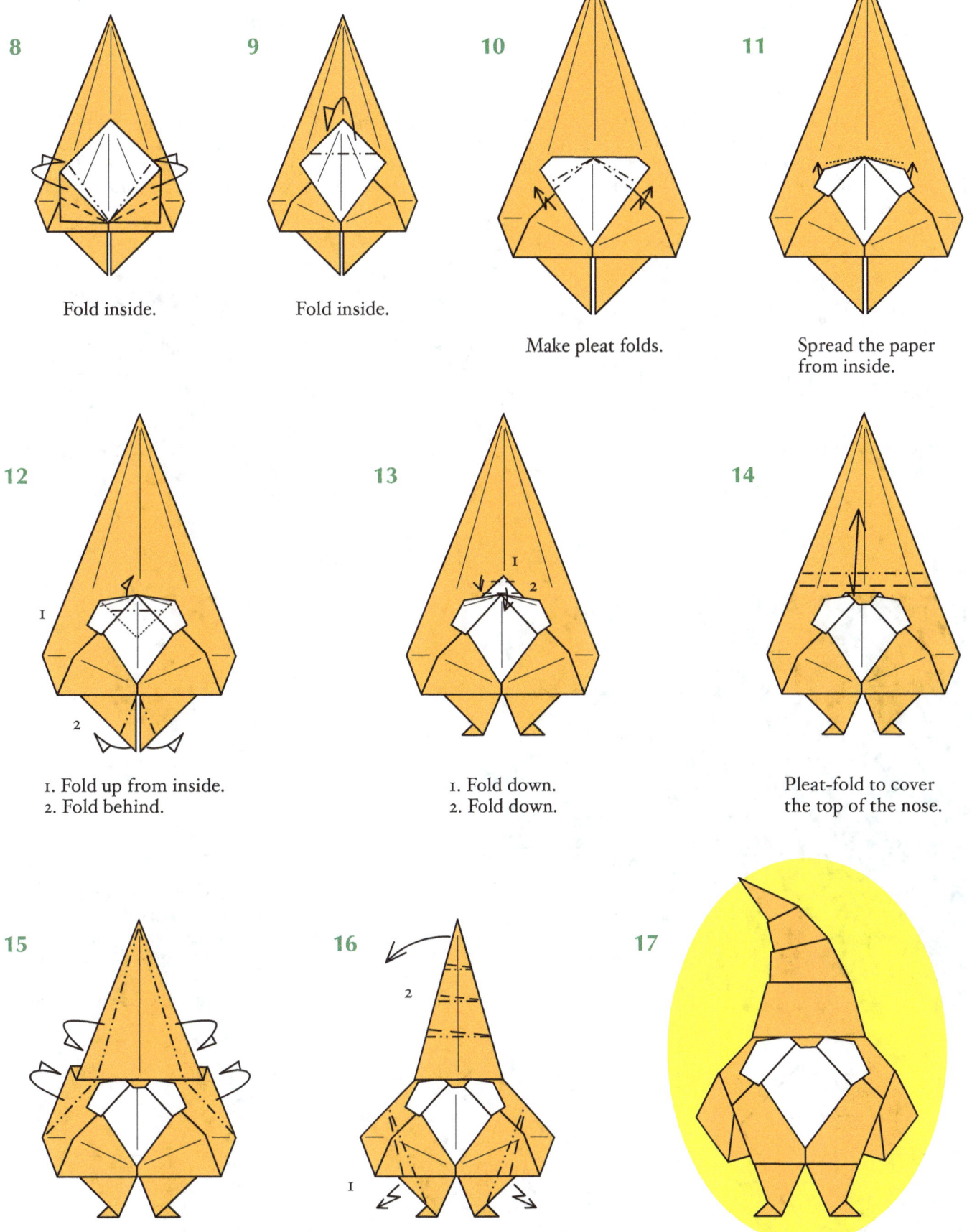

Friendly Forest Mushrooms

Mushrooms fill the forest floor with beauty and roof coverings. Mistakes are the mushrooms of life: unexpected, sometimes poisonous yet sometimes delicious. When a mushroom is silent, it's plotting, ever so slowly. If you carry a mushroom, expect curious squirrels and maybe curious raccoons, or possibly both at the same time. If you can't fix it with spores, you're not using enough spores.

Skyfloat Fungi

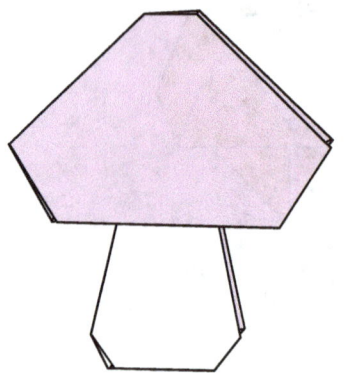

These buoyant mushrooms float like balloons. They predict the weather by rising if it will get warmer or fall if cold air is on the way. These decorative mushrooms are found on paths and near river shallows. Gnomes make sky lanterns by attaching them to threads. If they drift in circles, ignore it... or else you will chase it for hours.

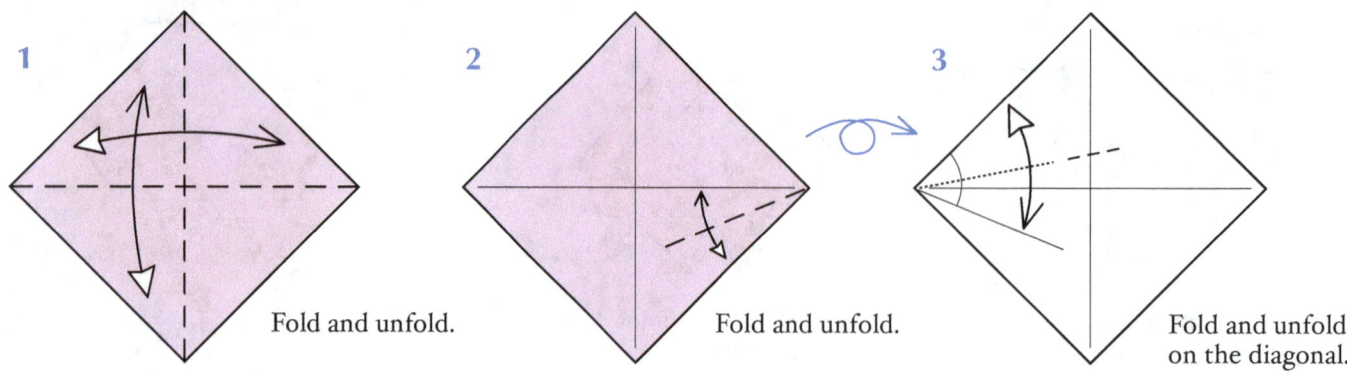

1. Fold and unfold.
2. Fold and unfold.
3. Fold and unfold on the diagonal.

32   *Origami Gnomes of the Forest Wonderland*

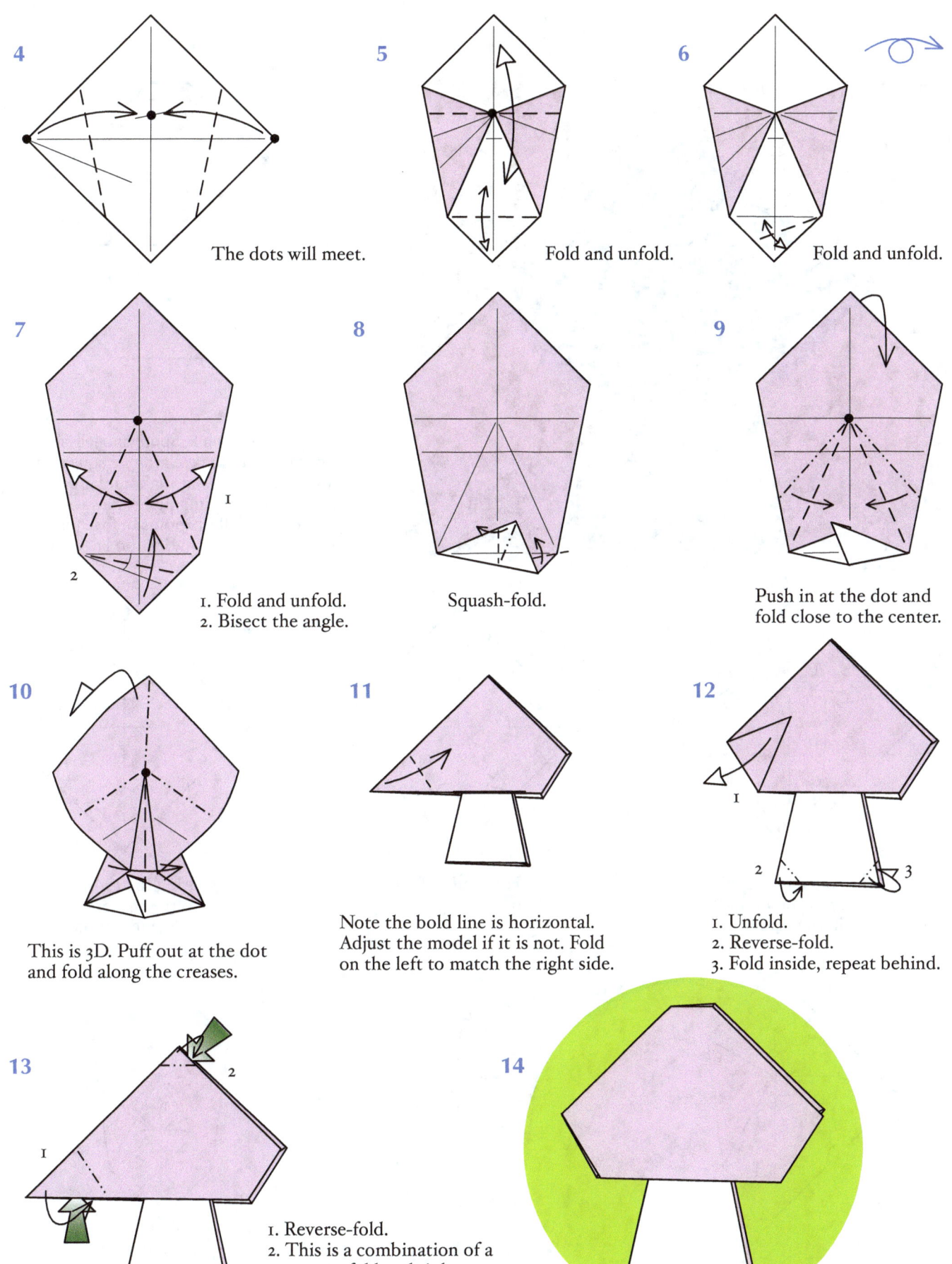

Skyfloat Fungi

Sporevine Jellyshrooms

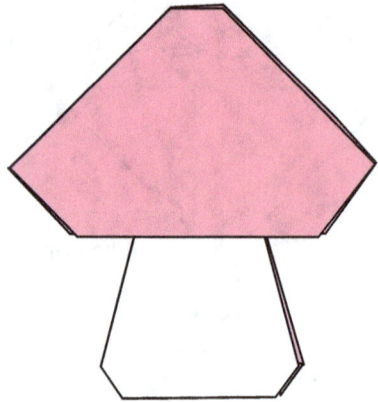

Purple and soft pink, Sporevine Jellyshrooms are wobbly and make strange squeaking noises. They glow at night and are used as lanterns and reading lights. Always check your hat for jellyshrooms before putting it on. If it feels squishy, it's too late.

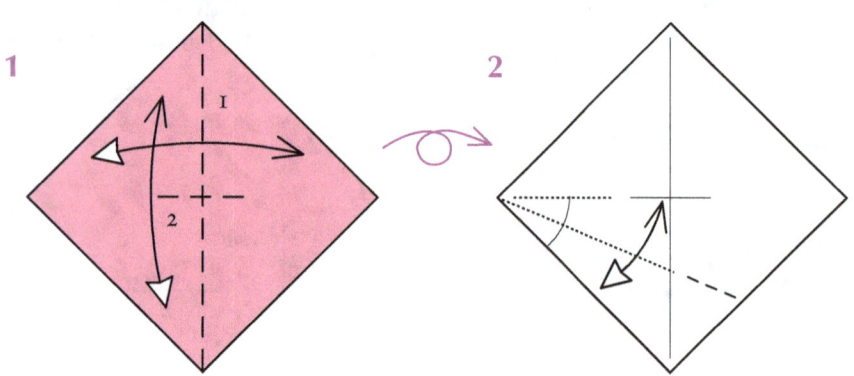

1
1. Fold and unfold.
2. Fold and unfold in the center.

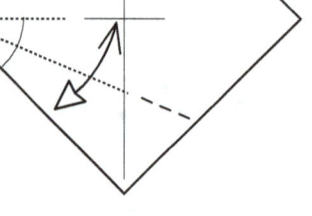

2
Fold and unfold on the edge.

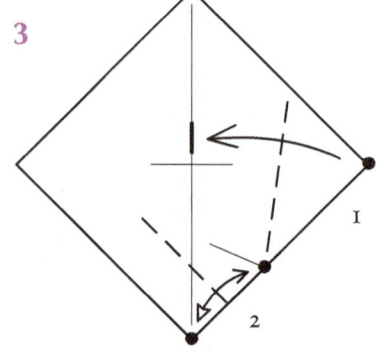

3
1. Bring the right corner to the center line.
2. Fold and unfold.

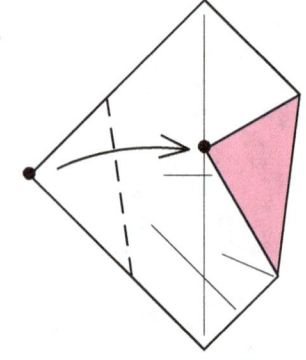

4

5
1. Fold and unfold.
2. Fold and unfold on the left and right.

6
Fold and unfold.

34 *Origami Gnomes of the Forest Wonderland*

7

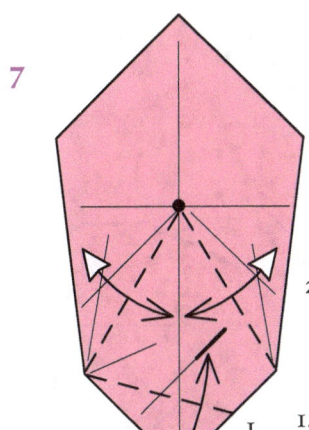

1. Bring the bottom corner up to the line.
2. Fold and unfold.

8

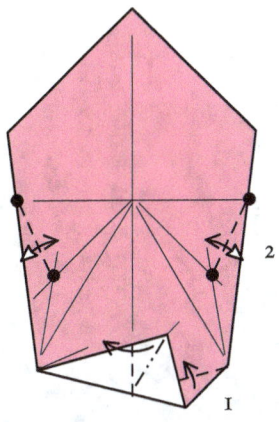

1. Squash-fold.
2. Fold and unfold.

9

Push in at the dot and fold along the creases.

10

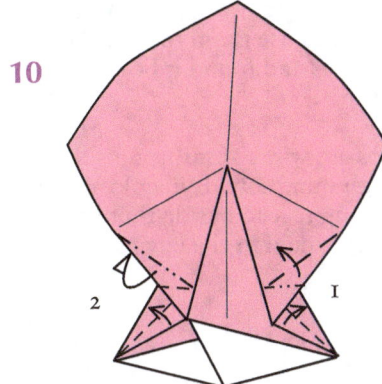

This is 3D. Fold along the creases.
1. Squash-fold.
2. Fold inside.

11

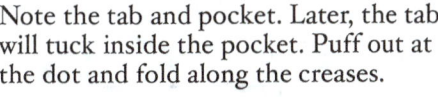
pocket 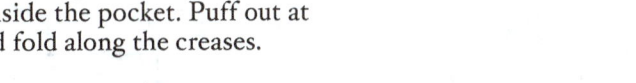 tab

Note the tab and pocket. Later, the tab will tuck inside the pocket. Puff out at the dot and fold along the creases.

12

Fold and unfold.

13

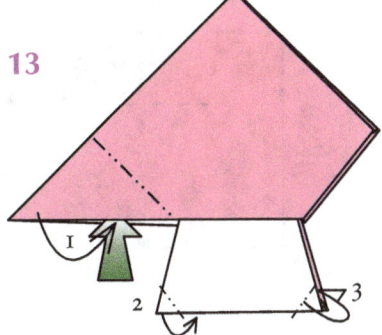

1. Reverse-fold.
2. Reverse-fold.
3. Fold inside, repeat behind.

14

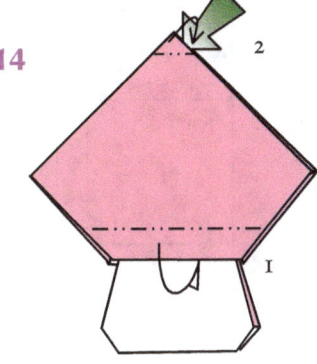

1. Fold inside, repeat behind.
2. This is a combination of a reverse fold and sink.

15

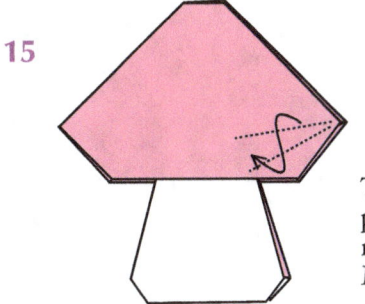

Tuck the tab inside the pocket to lock the model. See step 11. The Mushroom can stand.

16

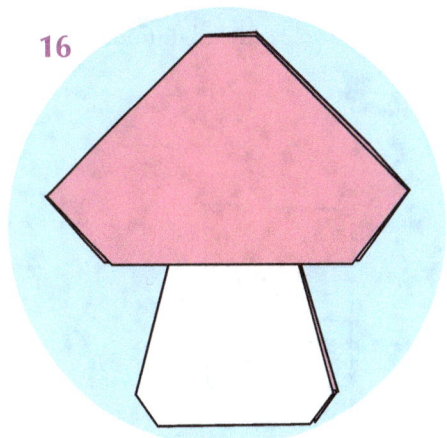

Sporevine Jellyshrooms

Sporevine Jellyshrooms 35

Embercaps & Frostbell Caps

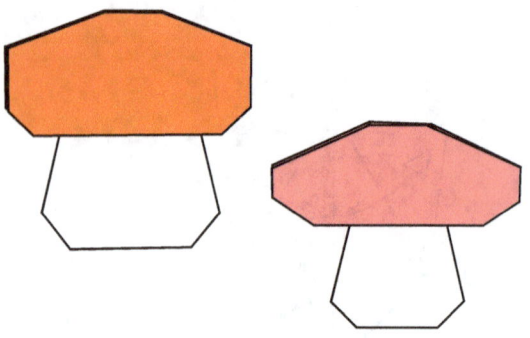

Embercaps are deep red. They can heat tea or twig soup. Gnomes use them to heat the gears in their inventions and found it best to keep away from beards.

Frostbell Caps are winter mushrooms that produce soft chiming sounds in cold air. They can cool anything placed beside them. They feed by absorbing cold in the environment.

Embercap

1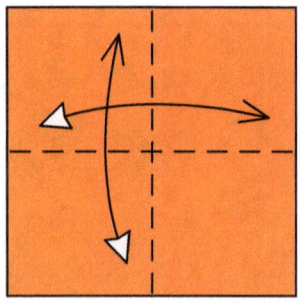
Fold and unfold.

2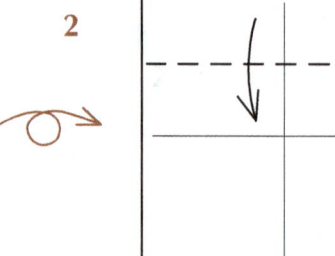

3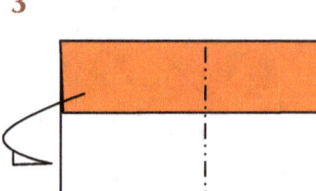

4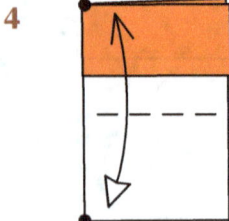

5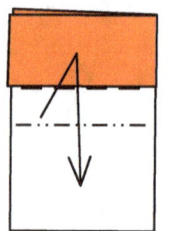
Pleat-fold along the creases.

6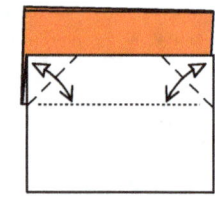
Fold and unfold.

36 *Origami Gnomes of the Forest Wonderland*

7

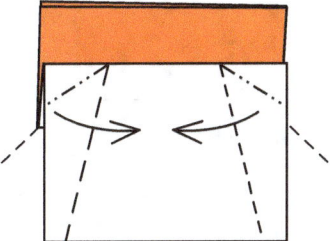

Make squash folds.

8

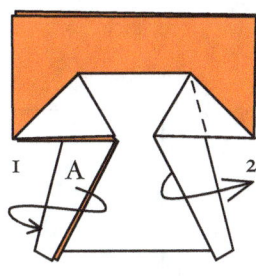

1. Tuck region A, the top layer, inside.
2. Fold to the right.

9

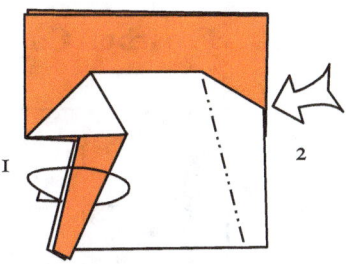

1. Wrap around and tuck inside.
2. Open the model to sink.

10

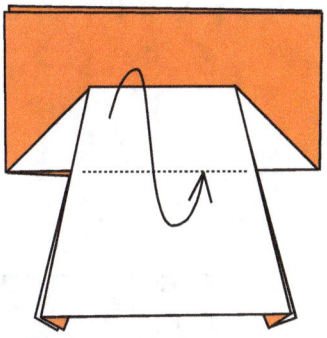

Tuck inside.

11

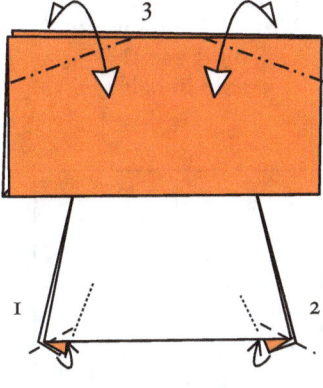

1. Fold both layers together.
2. Fold inside.
3. Fold and unfold.

12

1. Reverse-fold.
2. Fold inside, repeat behind.
3. Fold the hidden white flaps on the left and right.

13

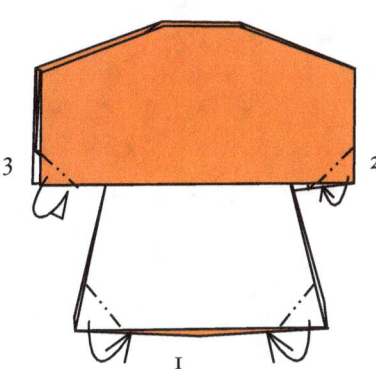

1. Make reverse folds.
2. Reverse-fold.
3. Fold inside, repeat behind. The Mushroom can stand.

14

Embercap

Embercaps & Frostbell Caps 37

Frostbell Cap

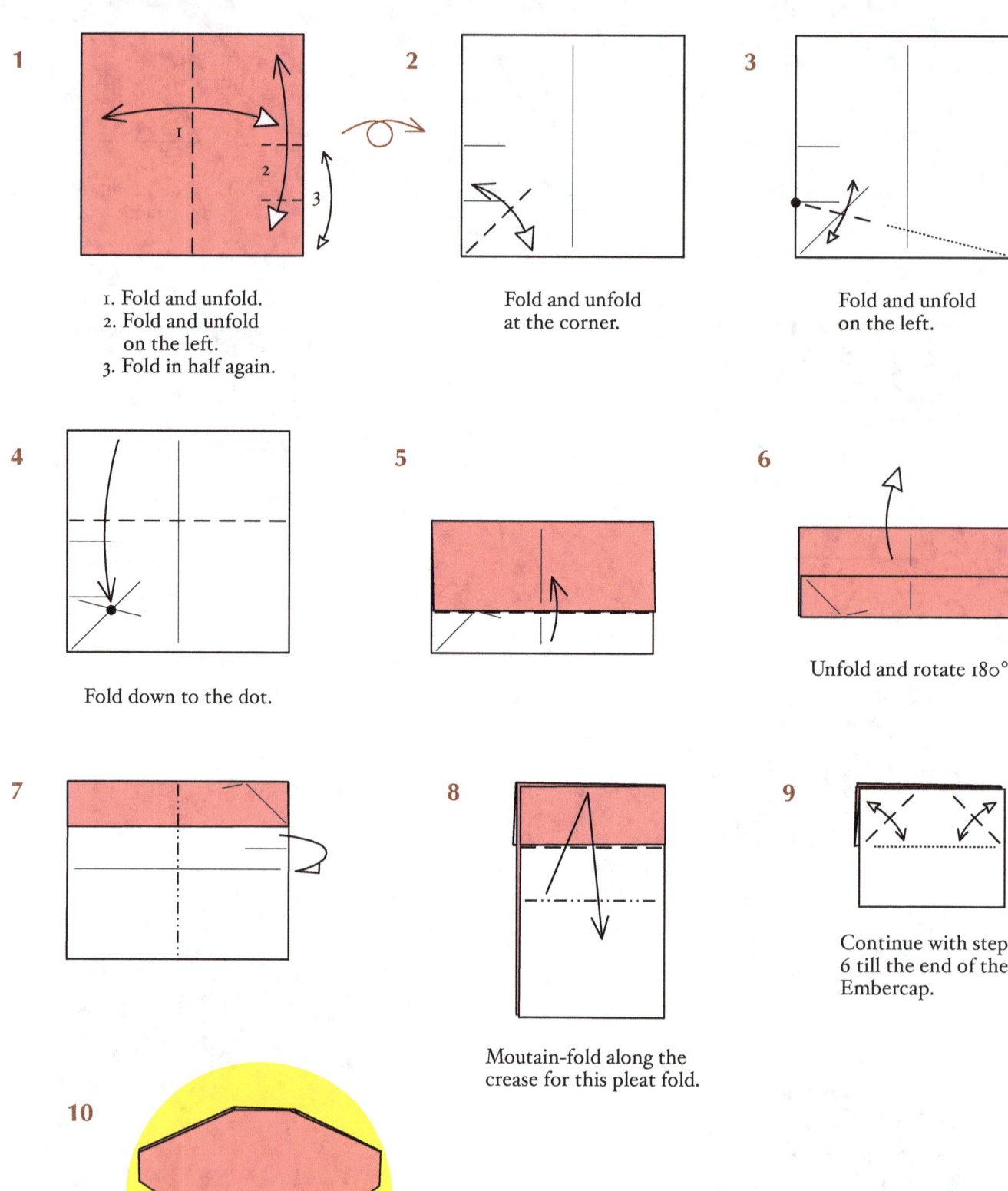

1. Fold and unfold.
2. Fold and unfold on the left.
3. Fold in half again.

Fold and unfold at the corner.

Fold and unfold on the left.

Fold down to the dot.

Unfold and rotate 180°.

Moutain-fold along the crease for this pleat fold.

Continue with steps 6 till the end of the Embercap.

Frostbell Cap

38 *Origami Gnomes of the Forest Wonderland*

Sparklecap

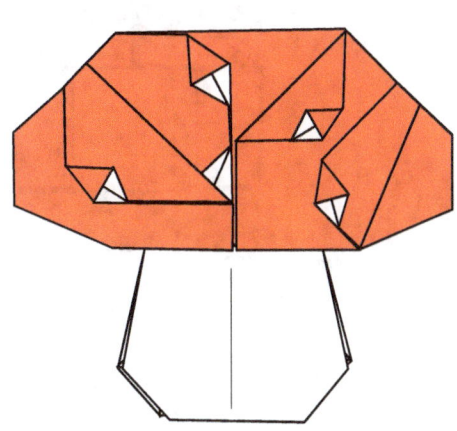

These mushrooms have white caps with small red spots. They glow in moonlight. The small spots hold big secrets. If a spot sings, listen carefully as it often leads to great adventures. These spots attract small insects which fertilize the surrounding soil. Sparklecap villages bring new adventures every day.

1

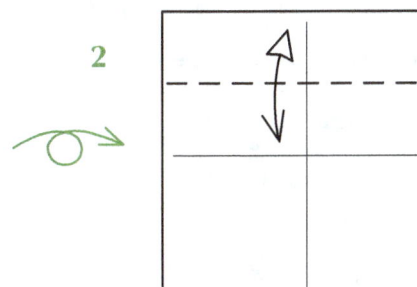

Fold and unfold.

2

Fold and unfold.

3

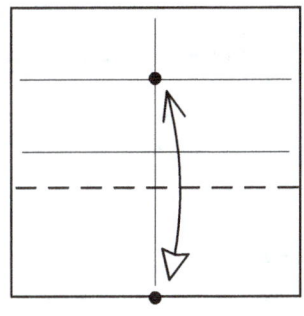

Fold and unfold.

4

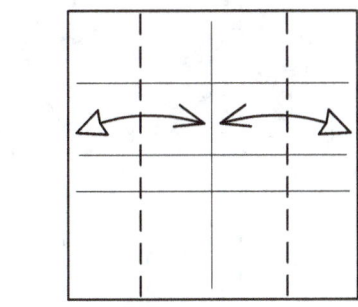

Fold to the center and unfold.

5

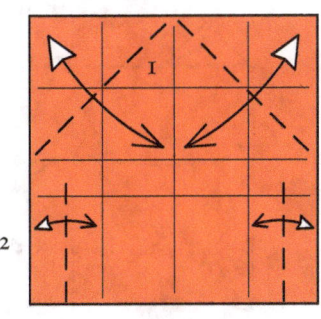

1. Fold and unfold to the center.
2. Fold and unfold on the left and right.

6

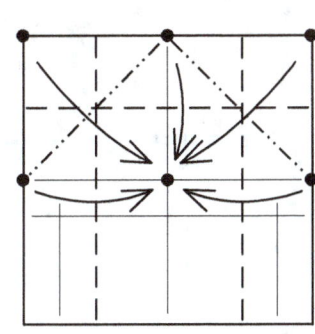

Fold along the creases. All the dots will meet in the center.

Sparklecap 39

7

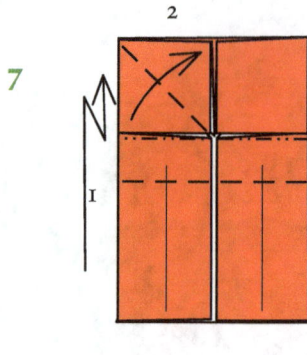

1. Pleat-fold along the creases.
2. Fold the top flap.

8

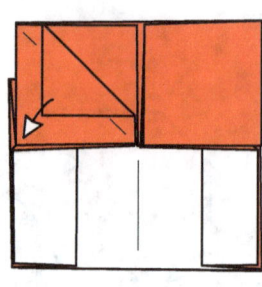

1. Fold the top layers on the left and right, forming hidden squash folds.
2. Fold down.

9

Unfold.

10

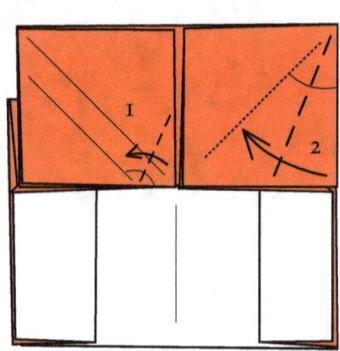

1. Fold the top layer.
2. Fold the top flap.

11

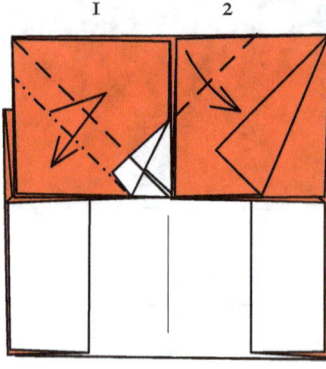

1. Pleat-fold along the creases.
2. Fold the top flap.

12

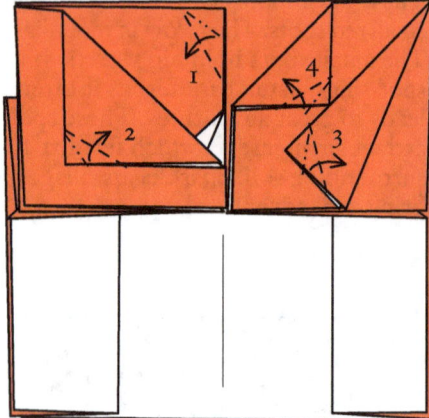

Make four squash folds.

13

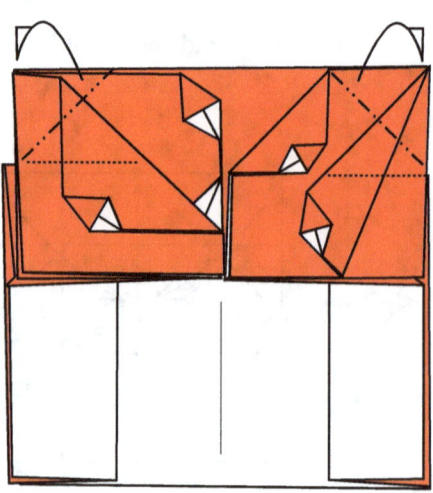

Fold behind.

14

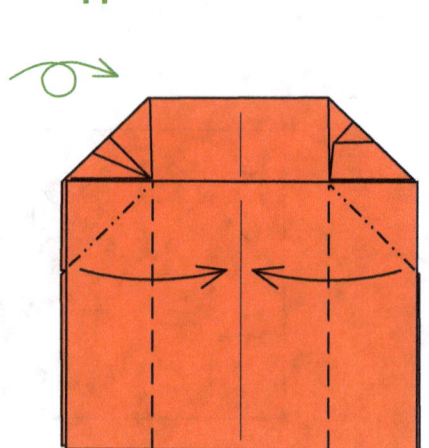

Make squash folds.

15

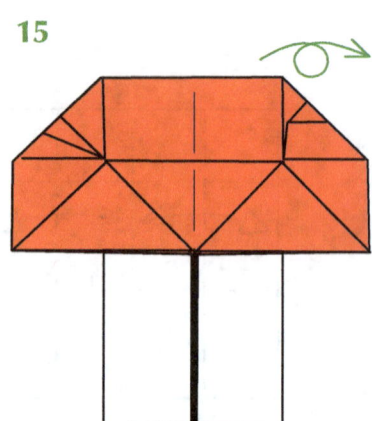

40 *Origami Gnomes of the Forest Wonderland*

16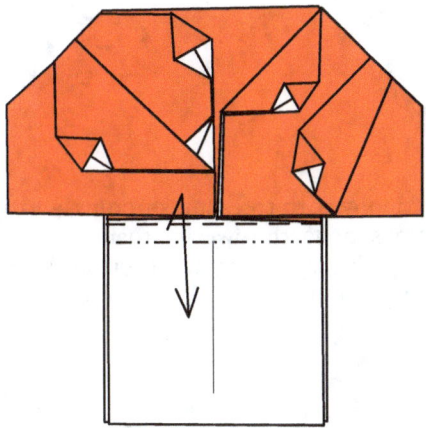

Pleat-fold.

17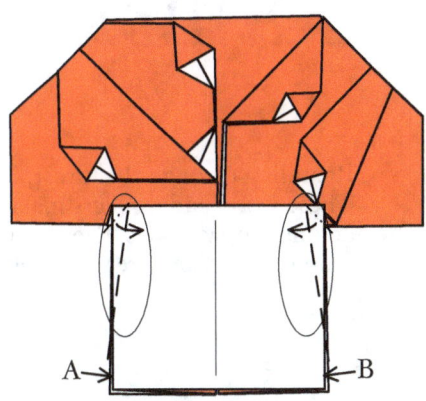

Make squash fold on the hidden layers A and B.

18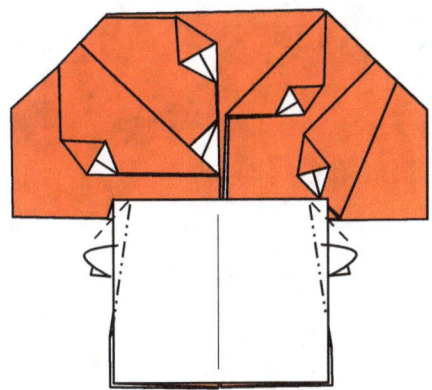

Fold inside.

19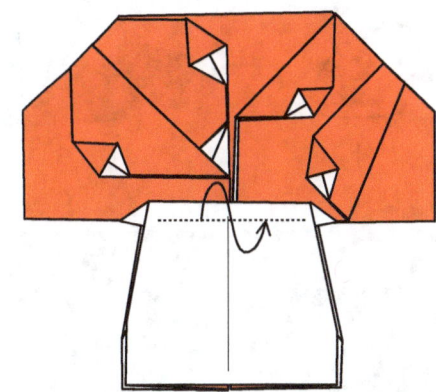

Tuck inside.

20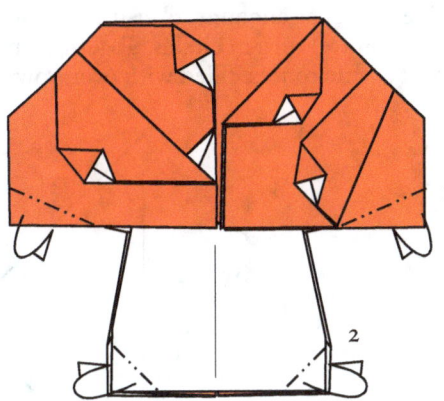

1. Fold behind.
2. Fold inside, repeat behind. Spread at the bottom so the Mushroom can stand.

21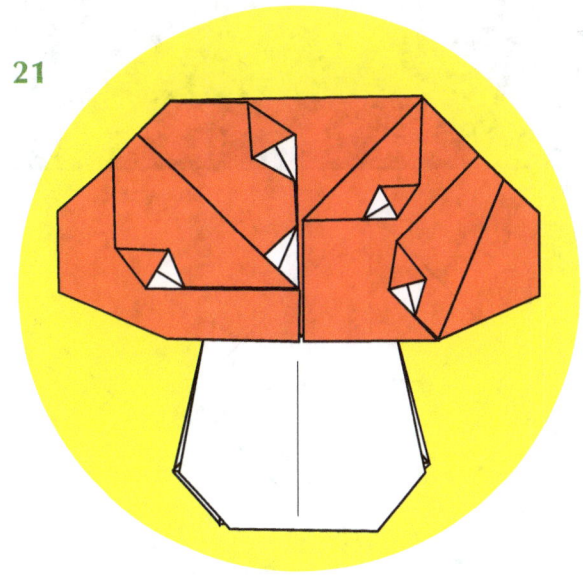

Sparklecap

Rambling Through the Forest

Rambling through the forest, there are gnomes who live in harmony with trees, mushrooms, and animals. These woodland dwellers make their homes in hollow tree trunks, beneath towering toadstools, or nestled among mossy stones. Every corner of the forest serves as both their playground and their workshop. They tend to woodland creatures, blending magic and clever tinkering to nurture life all around them.

Snicket Bramblecoat

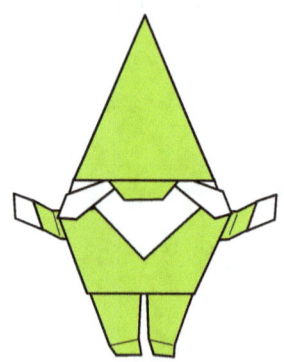

Snicket is a trail-mapper who draws tiny forest maps on mushroom caps. His friendly squirrel rides in his pocket and scouts ahead for new paths. When Snicket encounters visitors, he waves his acorn-ink quill as his squirrel runs in circles. Together, they guide travelers to the most scenic routes, filled with overgrown violets.

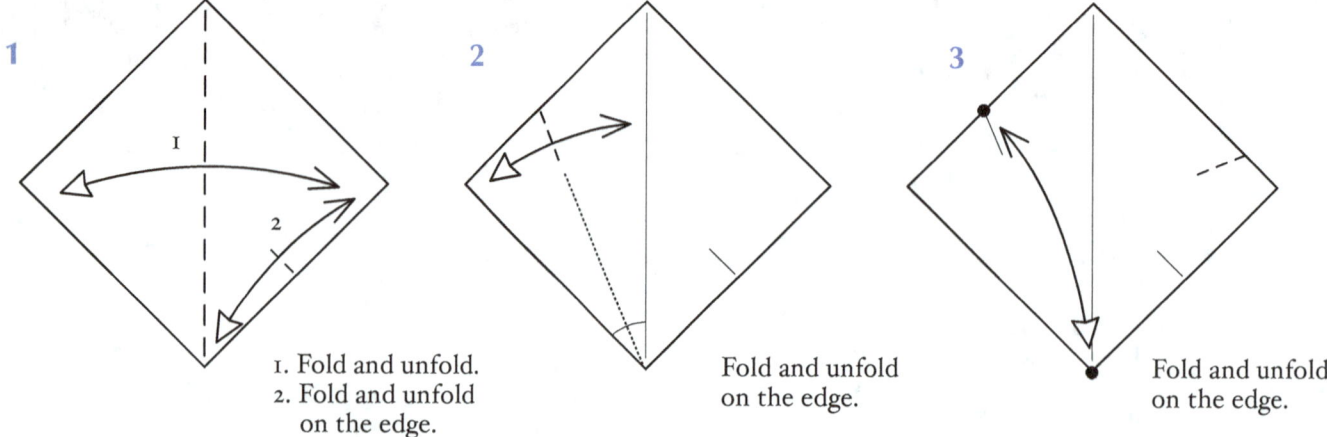

1.
   1. Fold and unfold.
   2. Fold and unfold on the edge.
2. Fold and unfold on the edge.
3. Fold and unfold on the edge.

42 *Origami Gnomes of the Forest Wonderland*

4

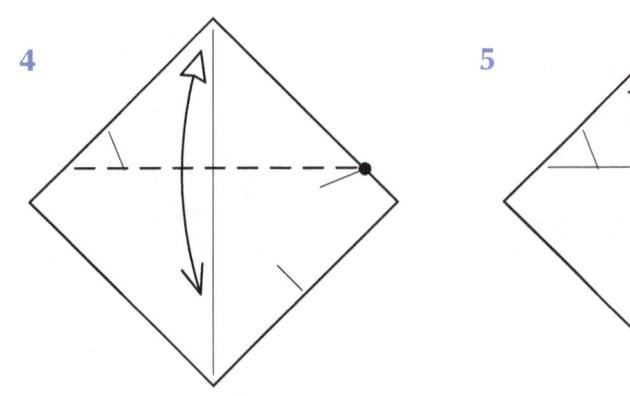

Fold and unfold.

5

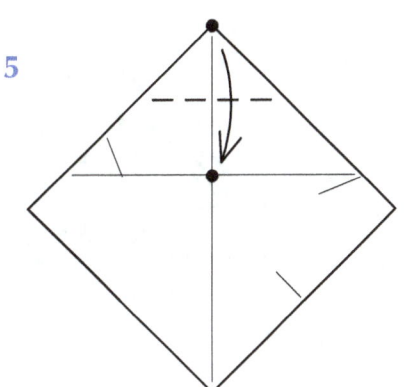

6

1. Fold up.
2. Fold along the crease.

7

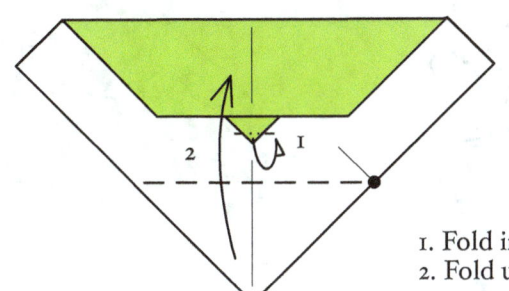

1. Fold inside.
2. Fold up.

8

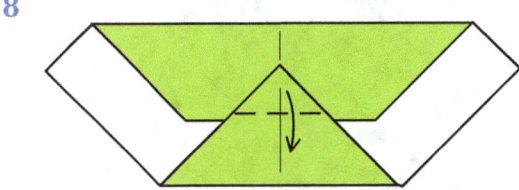

Fold down slightly above the hidden edge.

9

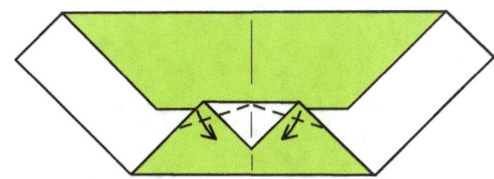

10

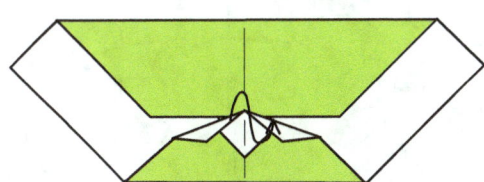

Tuck inside.

11

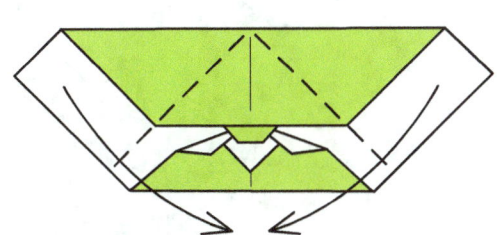

Fold to the center.

12

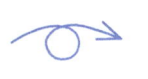
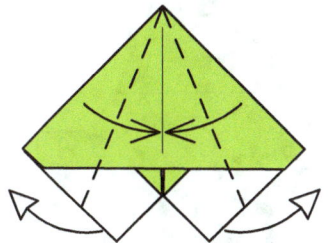

Fold to the center and swing out from behind.

Snicket Bramblecoat 43

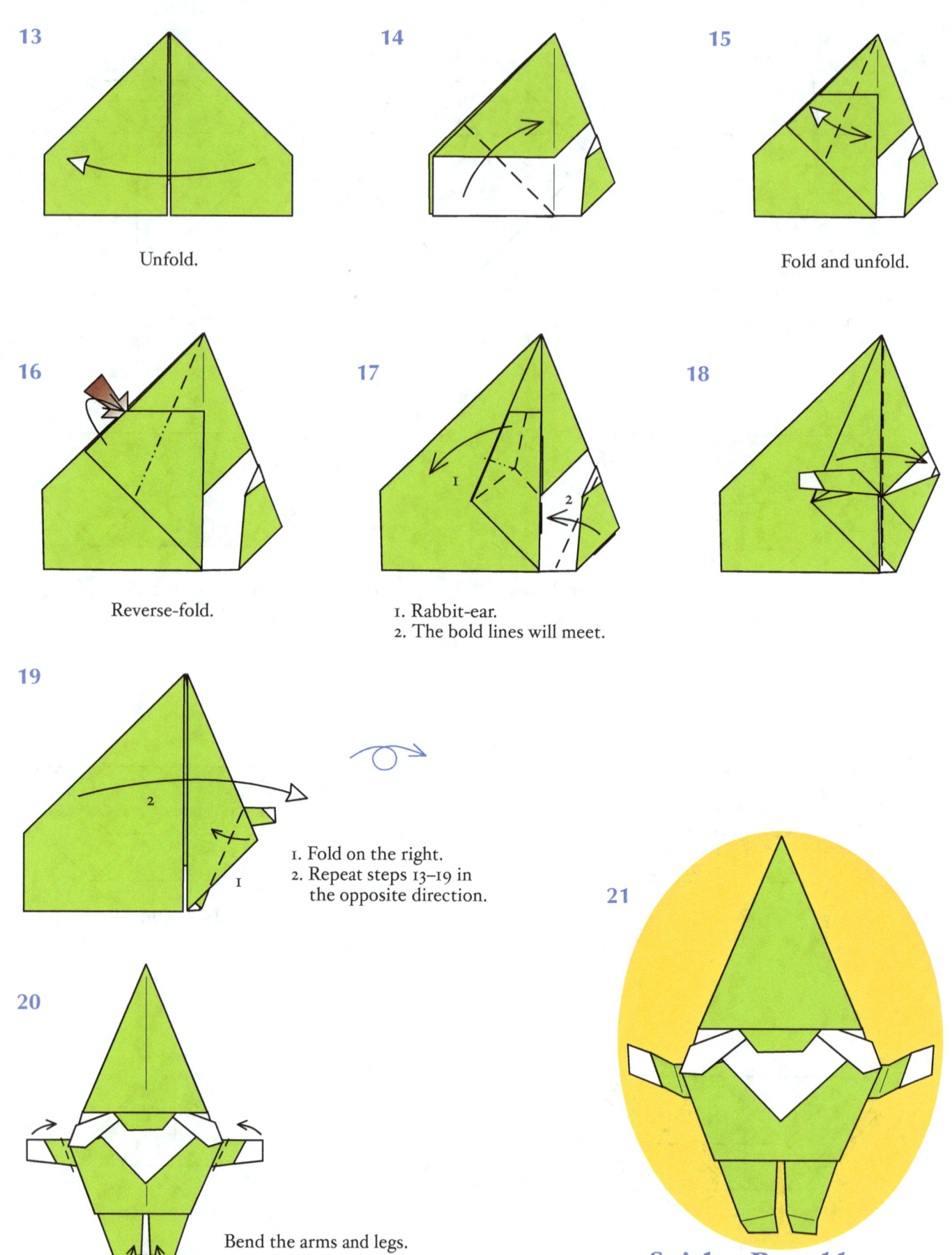

13 Unfold.

14

15 Fold and unfold.

16 Reverse-fold.

17
1. Rabbit-ear.
2. The bold lines will meet.

18

19
1. Fold on the right.
2. Repeat steps 13–19 in the opposite direction.

20 Bend the arms and legs.

21 Snicket Bramblecoat

44 *Origami Gnomes of the Forest Wonderland*

Pompel Oaktwist

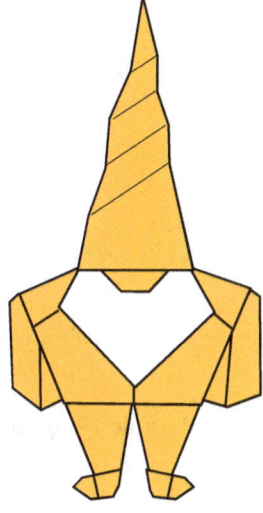

Pompel helps mushrooms sprout in artistic arrangements—circles, spirals, and swirls—while the nearby frogs hop on the mushrooms encouraging them to grow. They create the forest's "mushroom mosaics" which glow at night and guide nocturnal animals.

1.

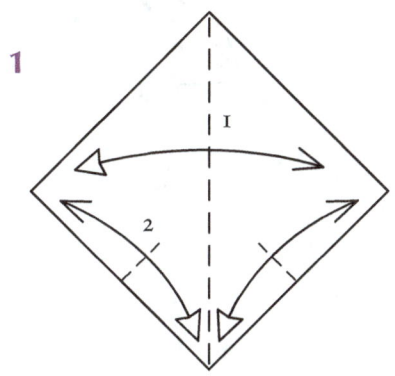

1. Fold and unfold.
2. Fold and unfold on the edges.

2.

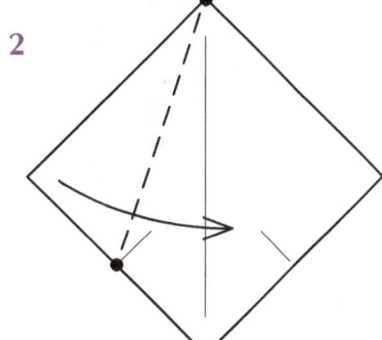

3.

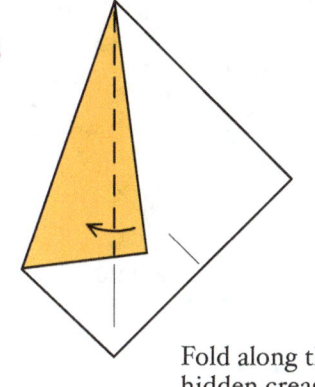

Fold along the hidden crease.

4.

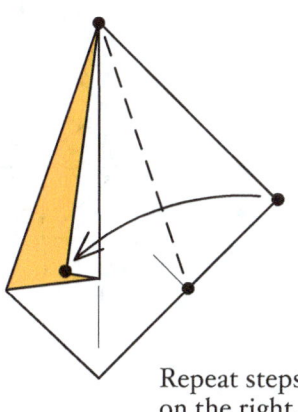

Repeat steps 2–3 on the right.

5.

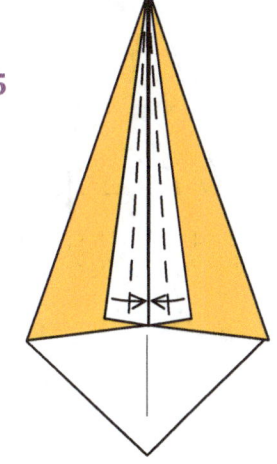

6.

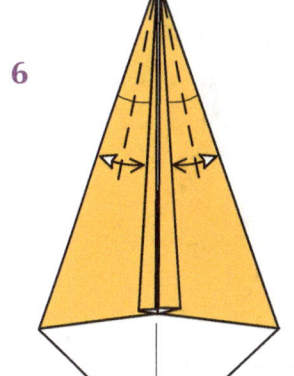

Fold and unfold.

Pompel Oaktwist 45

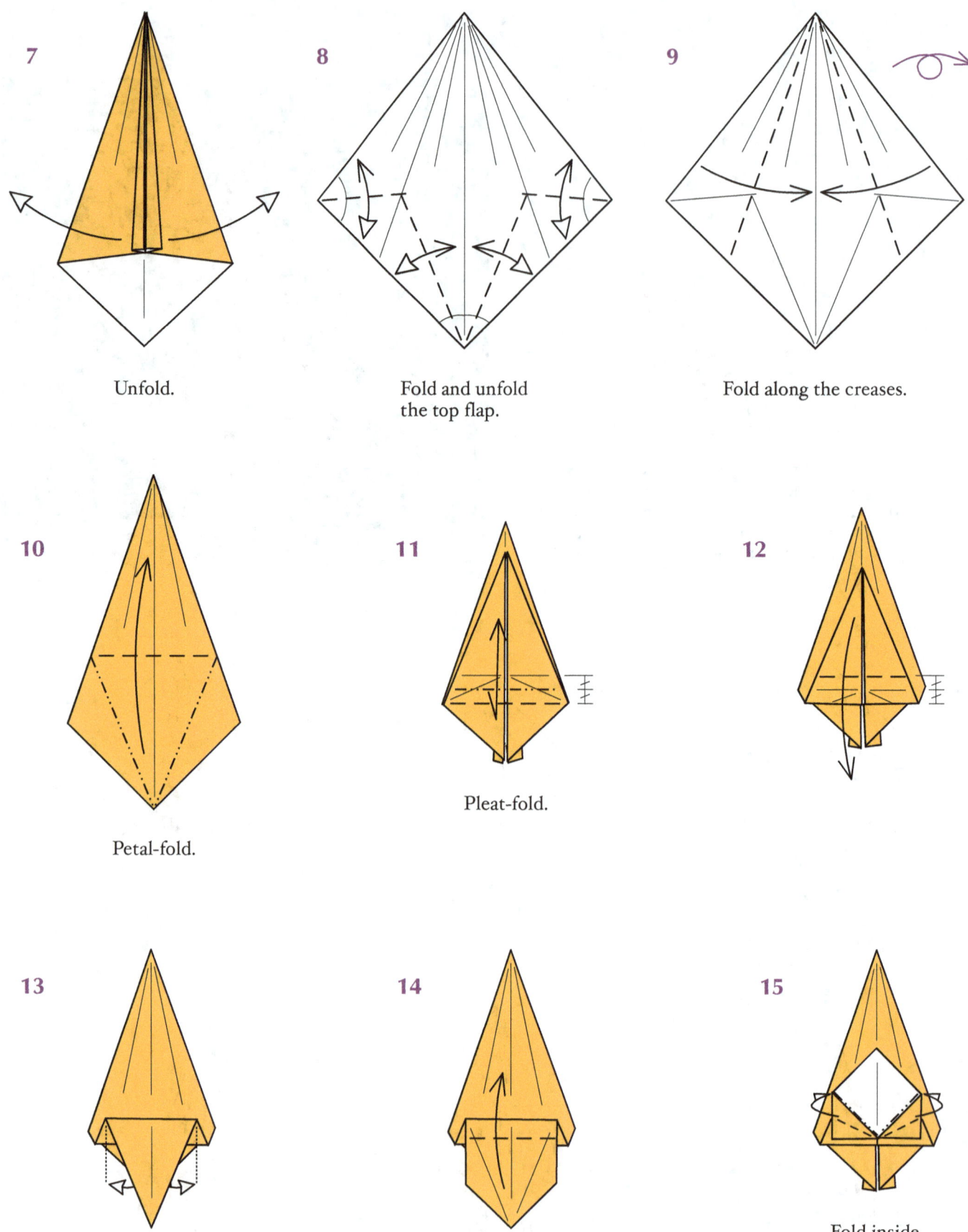

46 *Origami Gnomes of the Forest Wonderland*

16

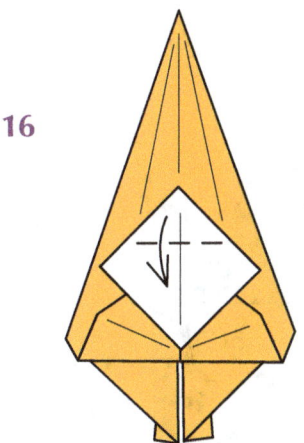

17

Fold inside.

18

1. Pleat-fold.
2. Fold behind.

19

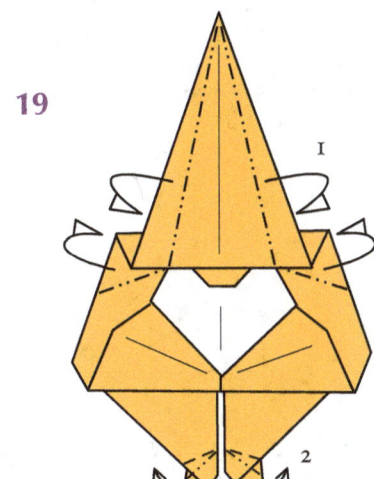

1. Fold behind along the creases at the top.
2. Make pleat folds.

20

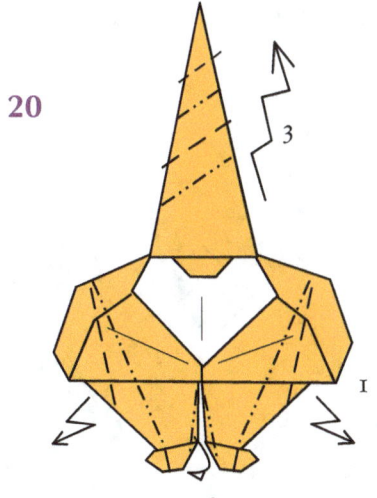

1. Make pleat folds.
2. Fold behind.
3. Pleat-fold.

21

Pompel Oaktwist

Pompel Oaktwist 47

Cobble Thrumtwig

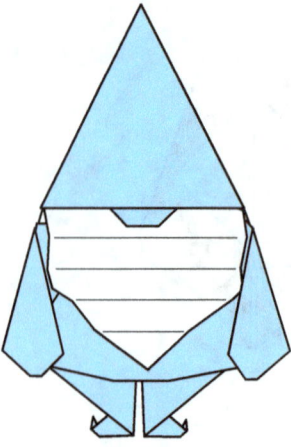

Cobble builds wobbly bridges, ladders, and lookout perches that stretch from treetop to treetop. Thanks to his handiwork, rabbits can hop from oak to pine, bears can wander the canopy hunting for honey, and even turtles can enjoy a bird's-eye view of the forest below. Cobble insists the wobbliness is intentional—because, as he always says, "If it wobbles, it's flexible."

1

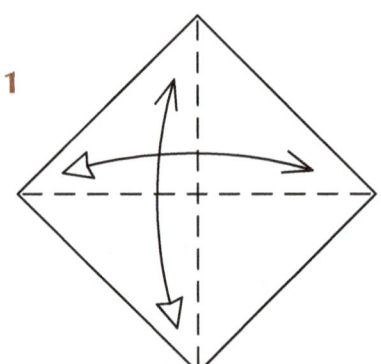

Fold and unfold.

2

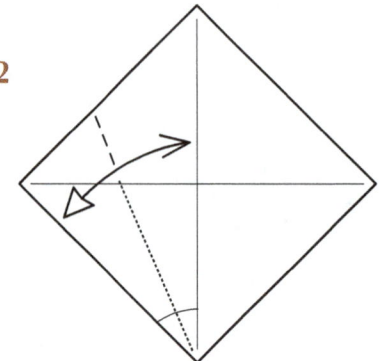

Fold and unfold on the edge.

3

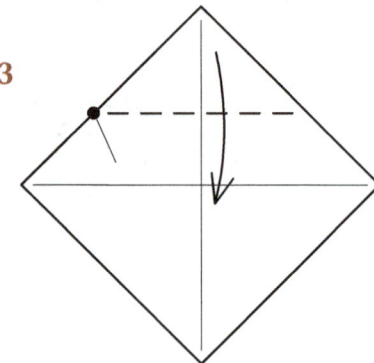

Fold down at the dot.

4

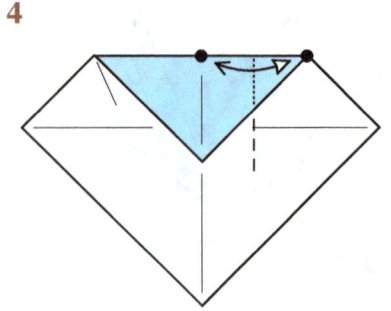

Fold and unfold.

5

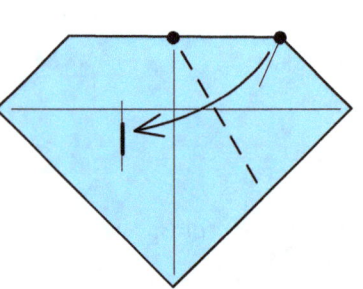

Bring the dot on the right to the crease.

6

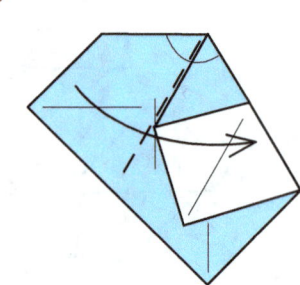

48 *Origami Gnomes of the Forest Wonderland*

7

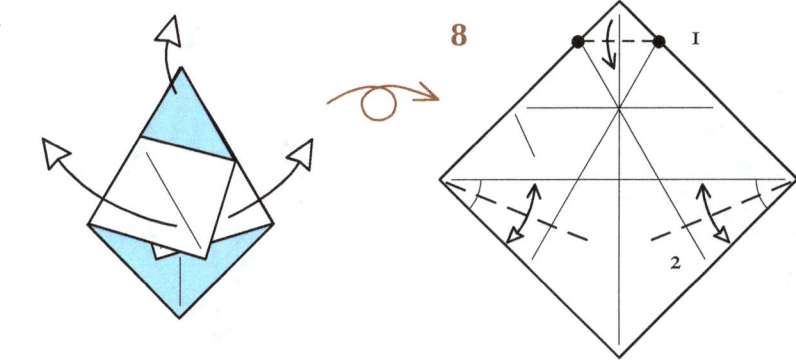

Unfold everything.

8

1. Fold down.
2. Fold and unfold.

9

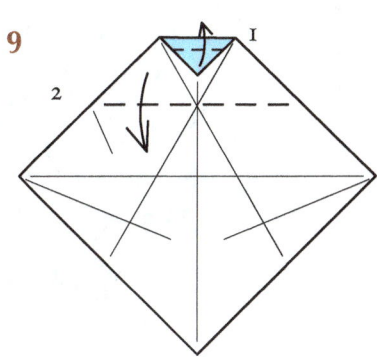

1. Fold up.
2. Fold along the crease.

10

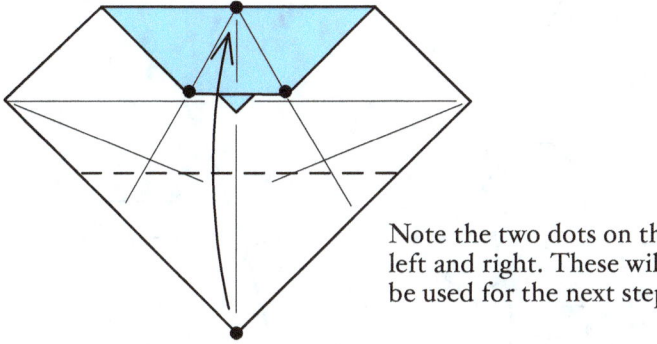

Note the two dots on the left and right. These will be used for the next step.

11

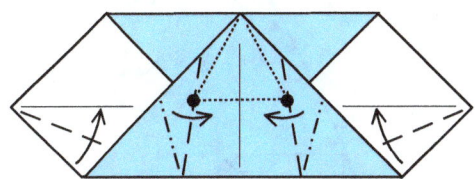

Valley-fold along the dots for these squash folds.

12

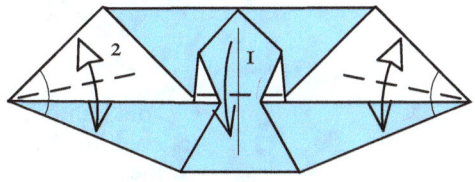

1. Fold along the hidden edge.
2. Fold and unfold on the left and right.

13

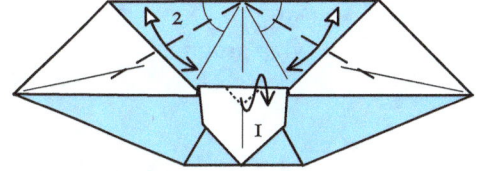

1. Bring the hidden paper to the front.
2. Fold and unfold.

14

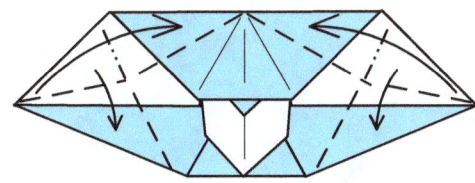

Make rabbit ears.

15

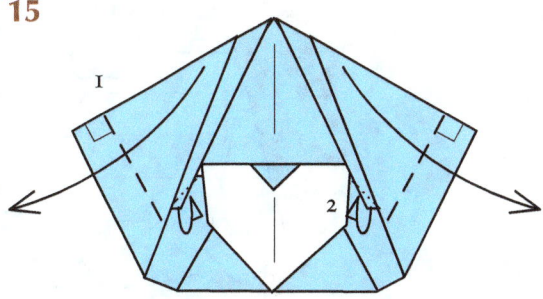

1. Fold at right angles.
2. Fold inside.

Cobble Thrumtwig 49

16

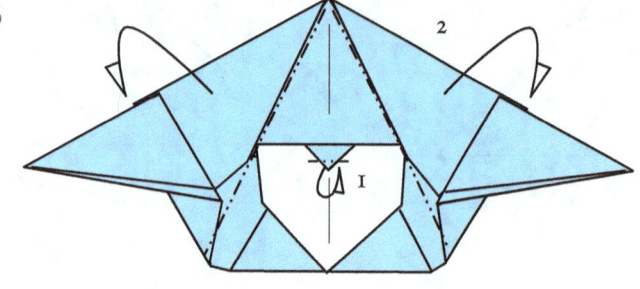

1. Fold inside.
2. Fold to the center.

17

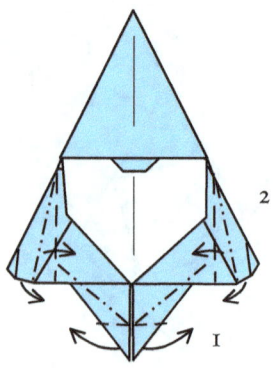

1. Make pleat folds.
2. Make squash folds.

18

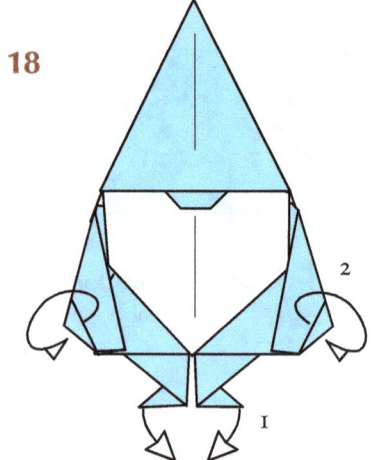

1. Unfold.
2. Wrap around.

19

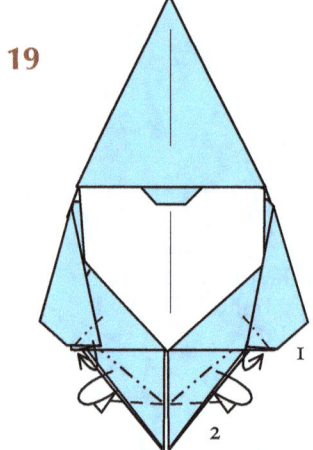

1. Make reverse folds.
2. Make crimp folds.

20

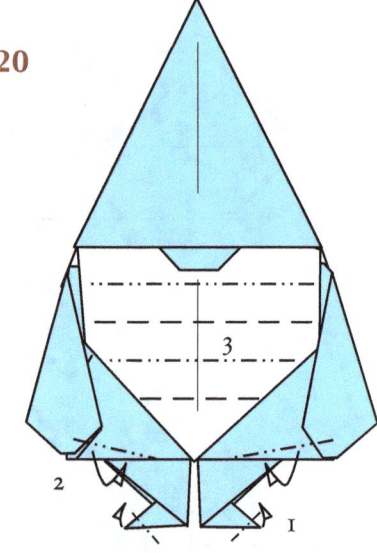

1. Fold behind.
2. Fold inside.
3. Pleat-fold.

21

Cobble Thrumtwig

50 *Origami Gnomes of the Forest Wonderland*

Wizzlewick Moonwhistle

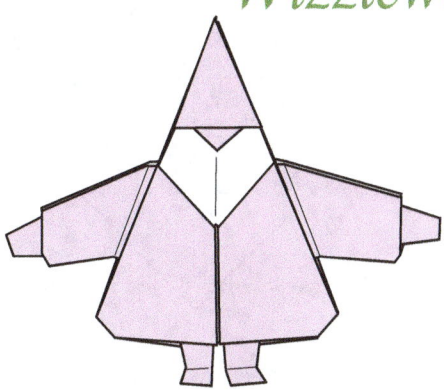

Wizzlewick can magically summon the moon to appear anywhere he wishes. He often gifts tiny glowing moons to gnomes, who perch them atop their hats so they can see clearly in dark caves and underground dwellings. With a flick of his wand, he teaches travelers how to transform branches into wriggling snakes, blades of grass into hopping grasshoppers, and striped leaves into buzzing bumblebees. But his favorite magic trick of all? Showing visitors how to create perfect duplicates of himself—using nothing but paper, nimble fingers, and a touch of deep, concentrated thought.

1
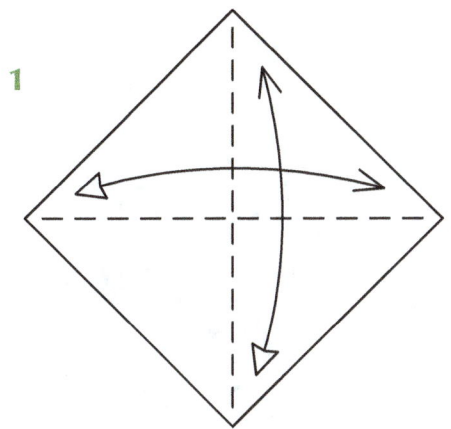
Fold and unfold.

2
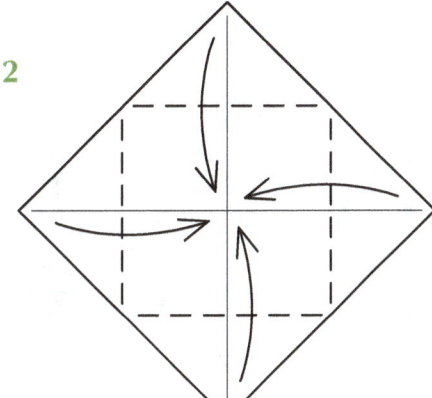
Fold to the center.

3
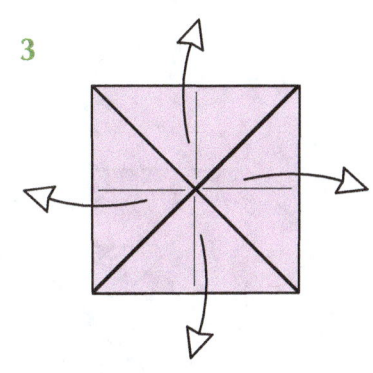
Unfold.

4
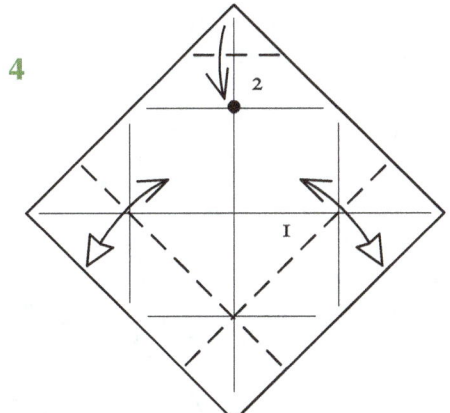
1. Fold and unfold.
2. Fold down.

5
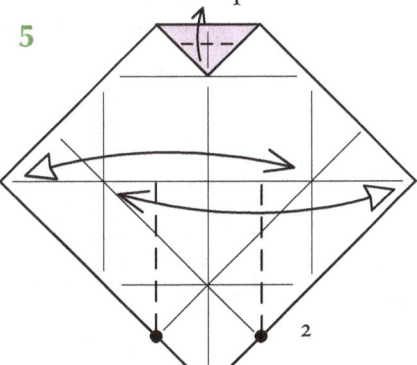
1. Fold up.
2. Fold and unfold.

6
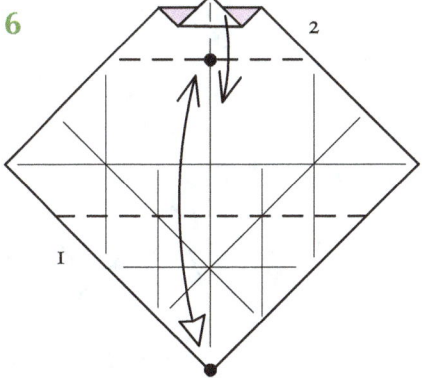
1. Fold and unfold.
2. Fold along the crease.

Wizzlewick Moonwhistle 51

7

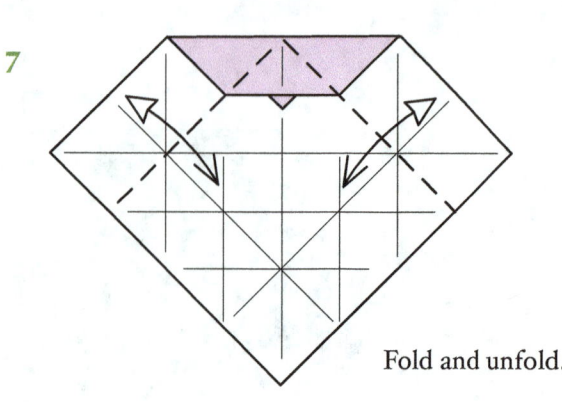

Fold and unfold.

8

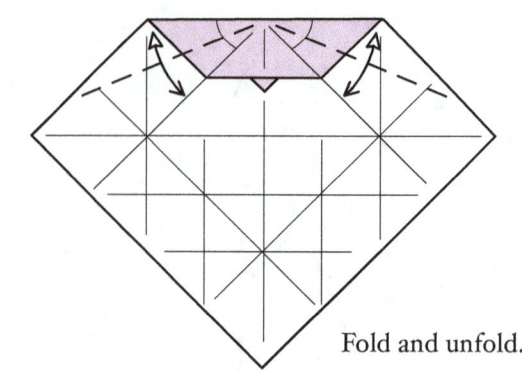

Fold and unfold.

9

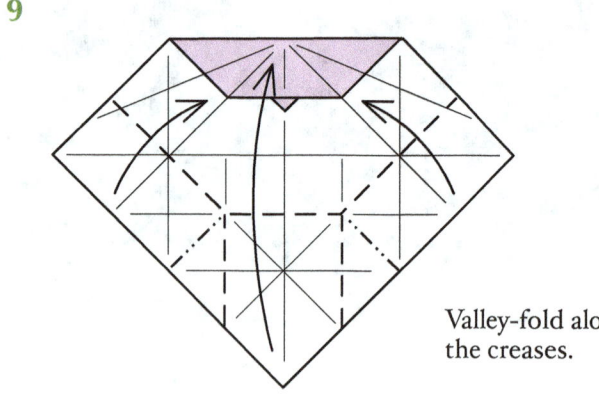

Valley-fold along the creases.

10

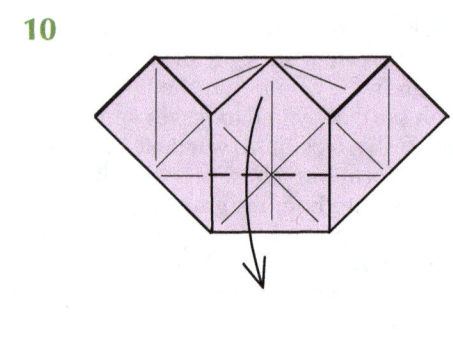

11

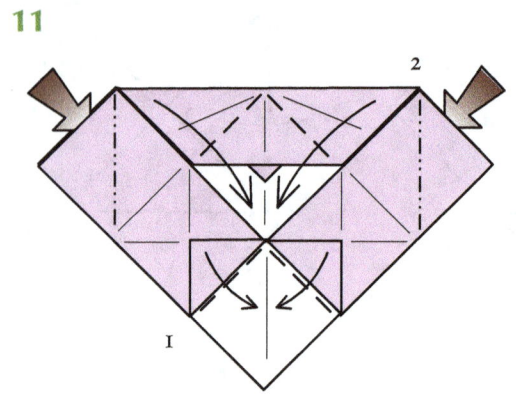

1. Fold to the center.
2. Fold inside.

12

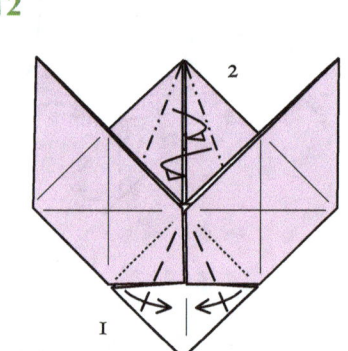

1. Fold close to the center.
2. Fold inside along the creases.

13

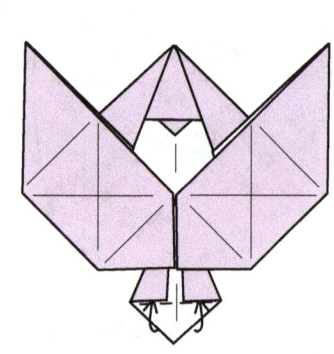

Tuck inside.

14

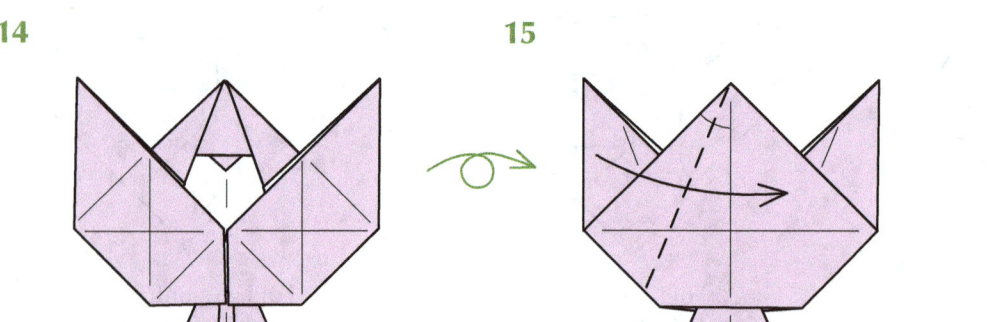

15

16

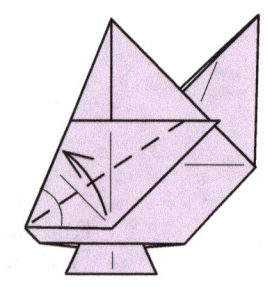

52 *Origami Gnomes of the Forest Wonderland*

17

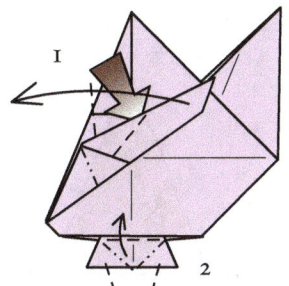

1. Reverse-fold.
2. Petal-fold.

18

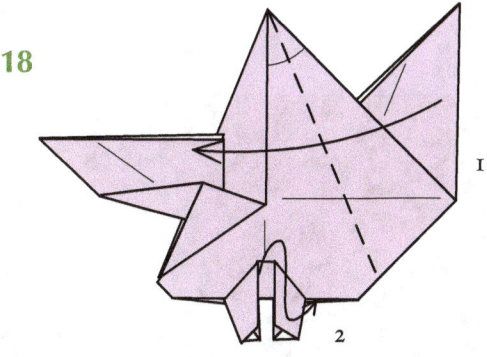

1. Repeat steps 15–17 on the right.
2. Tuck inside.

19

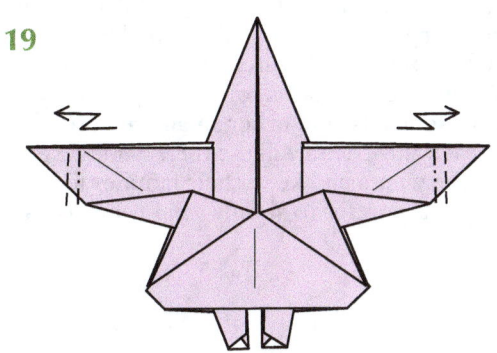

Make reverse folds.

20

1. Spread the hands.
2. Bend the feet.

21

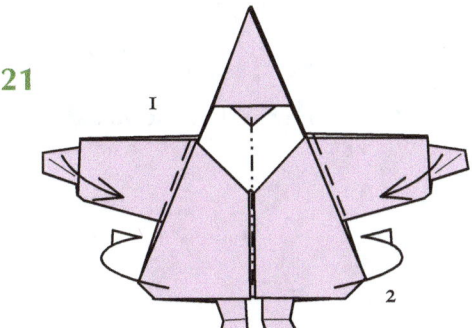

1. Bend the arms.
2. Bend slightly in half so the Wizard can stand.

22

Wizzlewick Moonwhistle

Fennel Fizzbranch

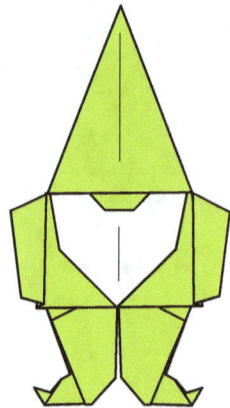

Tinkering with old ballet shoes, wind-dancing branches, bits of string, and clever gears, Fennel has crafted a whole line of colorful Nutcrackers. He wanders the forest with a knapsack full of them, gifting his creations to birds, squirrels, and other small creatures. Fennel hopes each tiny friend will use their Nutcracker to crack open hearty nuts and keep their families fed, though most animals prefer to simply wear them as hats.

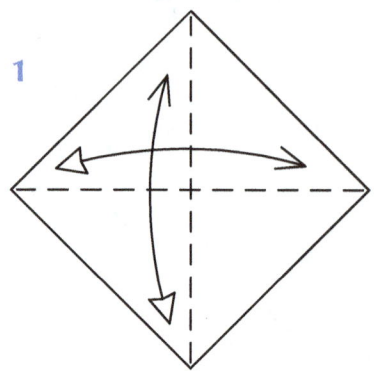

1

Fold and unfold.

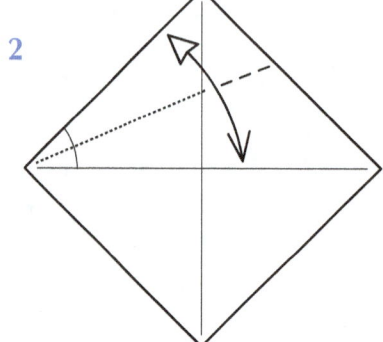

2

Fold and unfold on the edge.

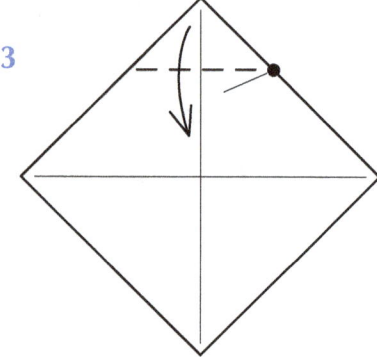

3

Fold down at the dot.

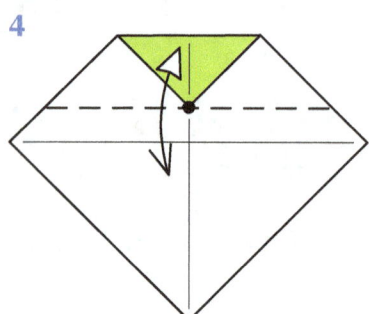

4

Fold and unfold.

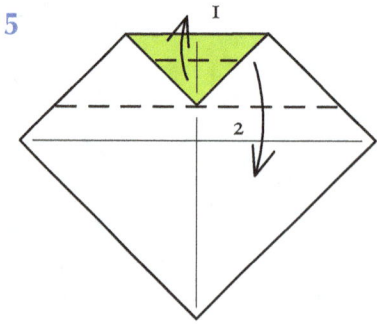

5

1. Fold up.
2. Fold along the crease.

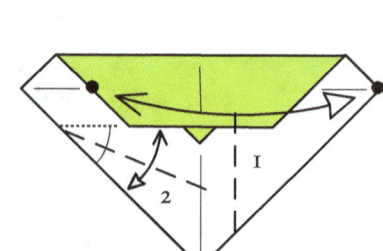

6

Fold and unfold at 1 and 2.

54 *Origami Gnomes of the Forest Wonderland*

7

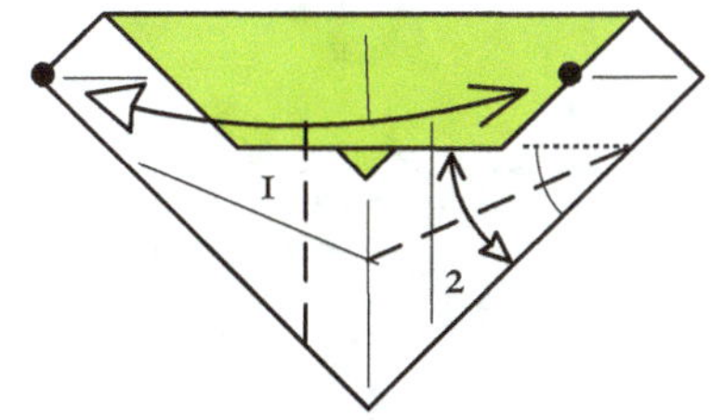

Fold and unfold at 1 and 2.

8

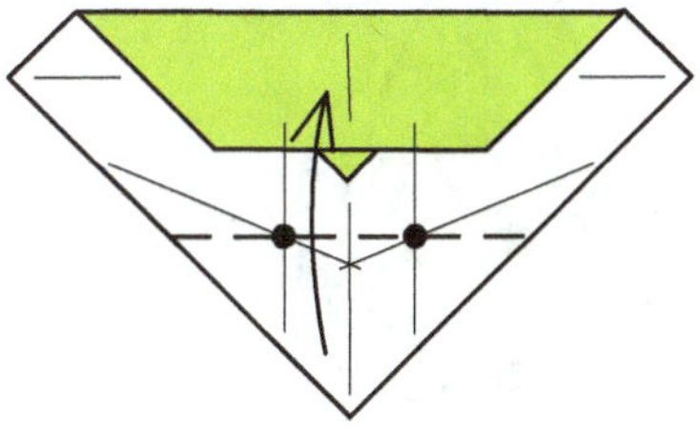

9

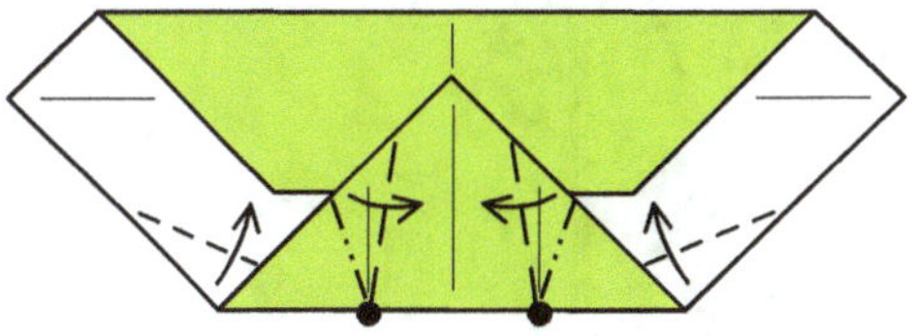

Make squash folds.

10

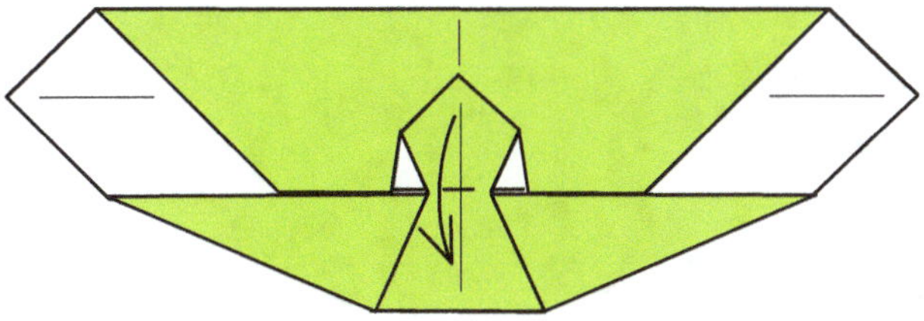

11

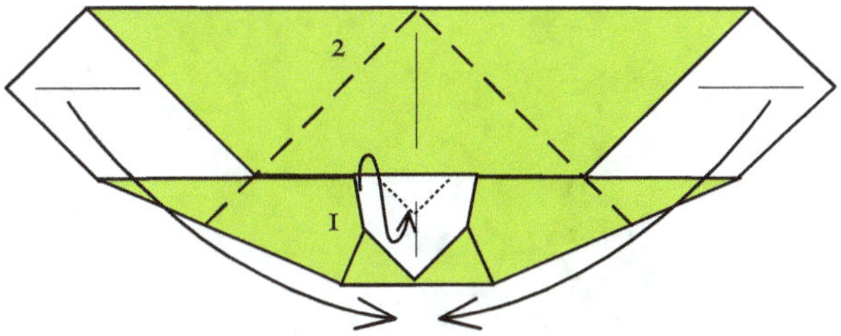

1. Tuck inside.
2. Fold to the center.

12

13

1. Fold inside.
2. Fold to the center.

14

Unfold.

15

Squash-fold.

16

Squash-fold.

17

Fold along the crease.

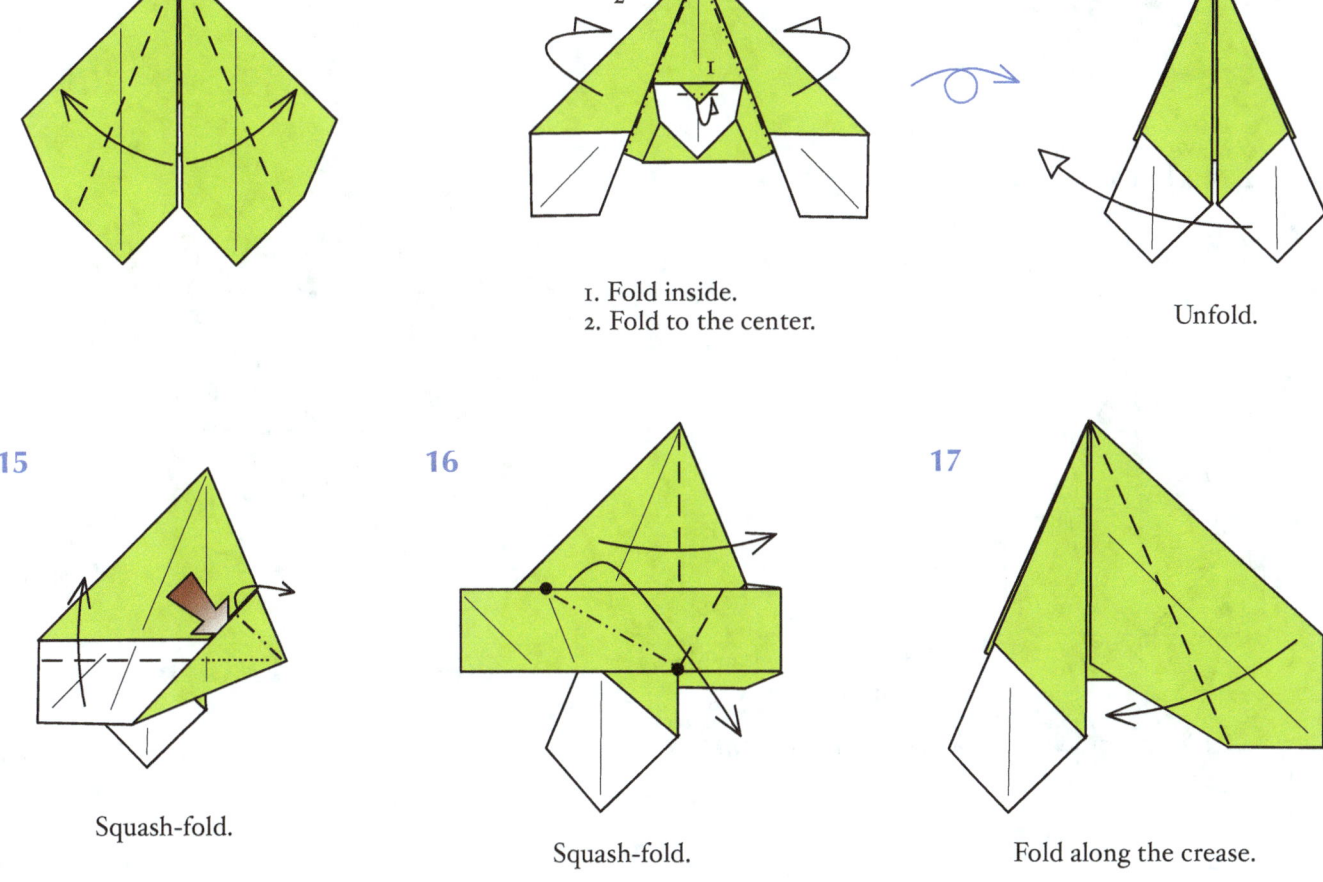

Fennel Fizzbranch 55

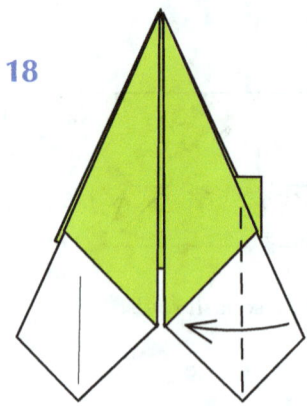

18

Fold along the crease.

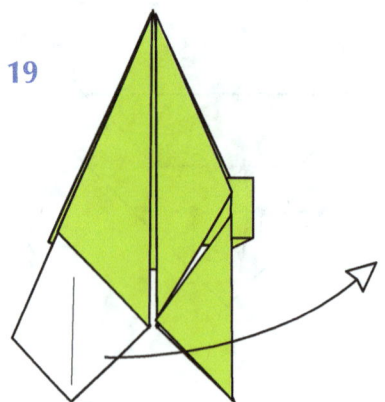

19

Repeat steps 14–18 in the opposite direction.

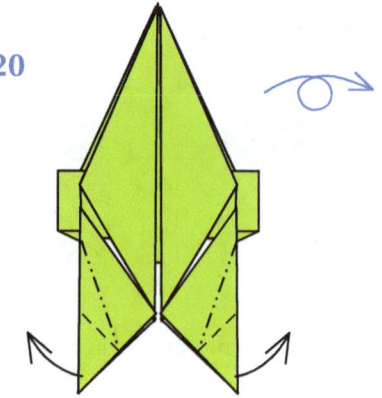

20

Make crimp folds.

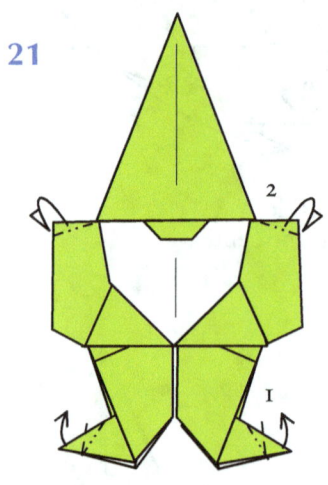

21

1. Make crimp folds.
2. Fold behind.

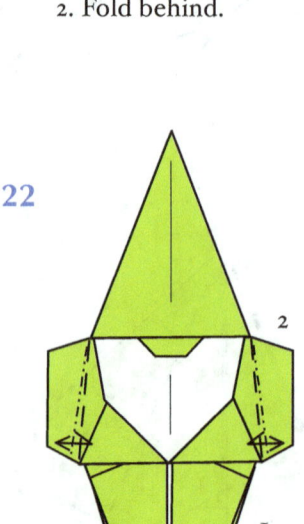

22

1. Fold inside, repeat behind.
2. Make pleat folds.
Spread the feet at the bottom so the Gnome can stand.

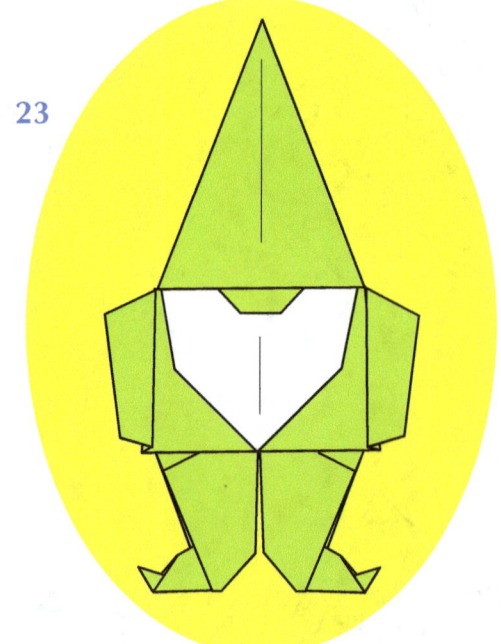

23

Fennel Fizzbranch

56 *Origami Gnomes of the Forest Wonderland*

Grindle Cogflick

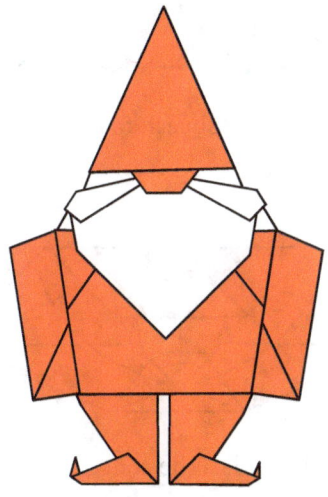

Using crystals and puddles as lenses, Grindle set out to build telescopes, periscopes, and all manner of spyglasses for observing the forest at night. Unfortunately, when one of his telescope flipped upside down, the entire forest appeared to flip with it. Startled, Grindle lost his footing, tumbled headfirst into the moss—followed promptly by every wobbling invention he had perched around him.

1
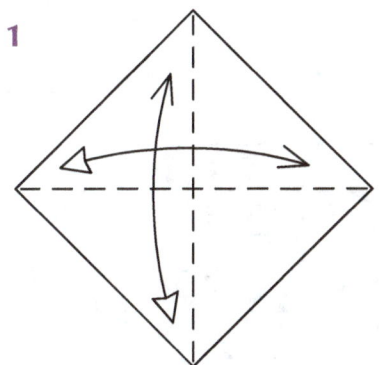
Fold and unfold.

2
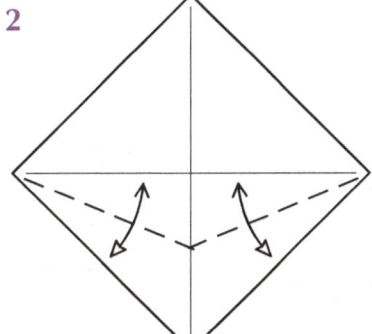
Fold to the center and unfold. Rotate 180°.

3
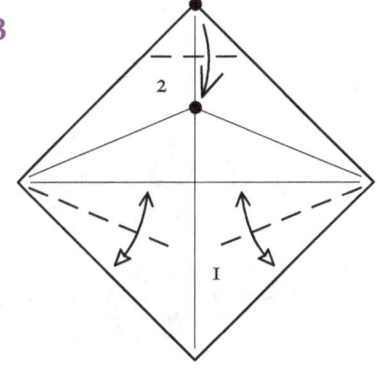
1. Fold and unfold.
2. Fold down.

4
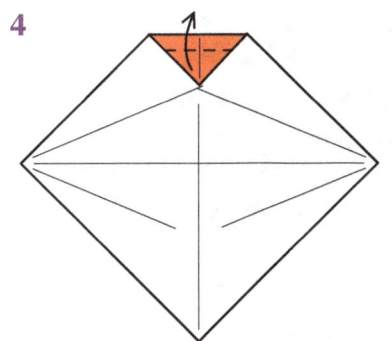

5
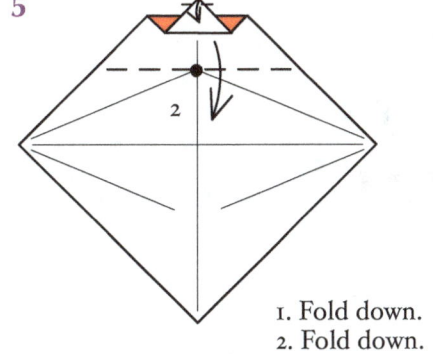
1. Fold down.
2. Fold down.

6
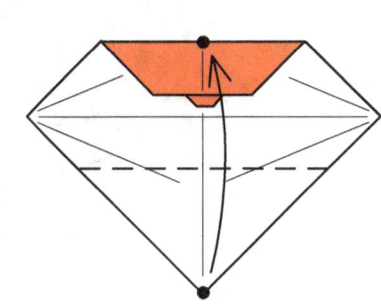

Grindle Cogflick 57

7

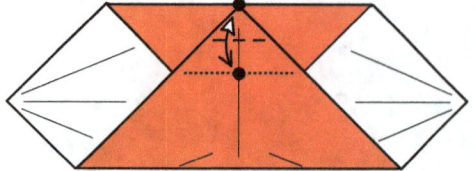

Fold and unfold.

8

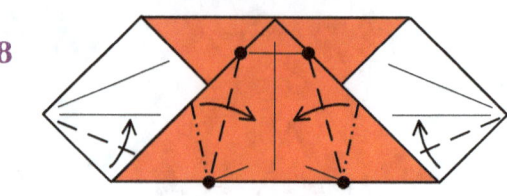

Make squash folds.

9

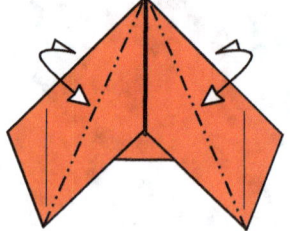

10

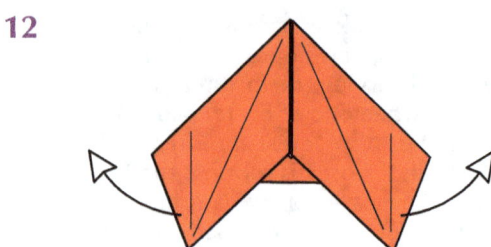

Fold to the center.

11

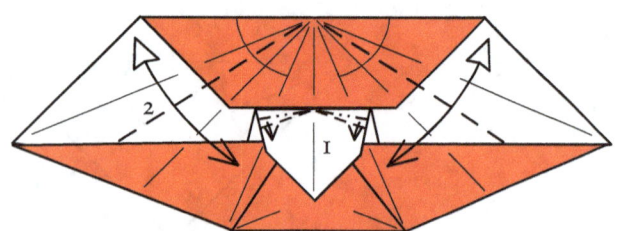

Fold and unfold all the layers along the creases.

12

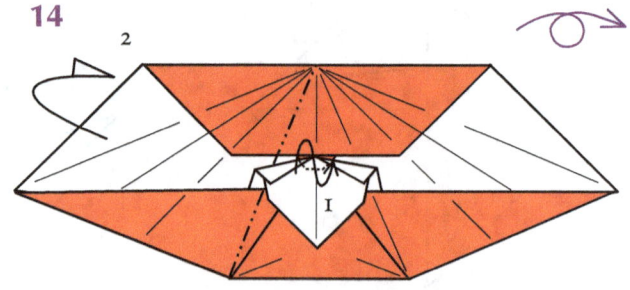

Unfold.

13

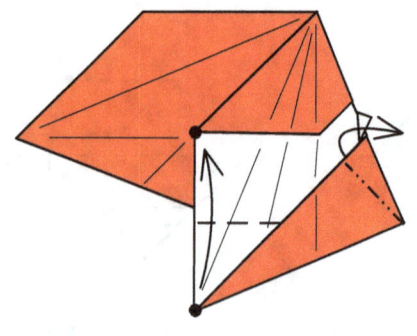

1. Make squash folds.
2. Fold and unfold.

14

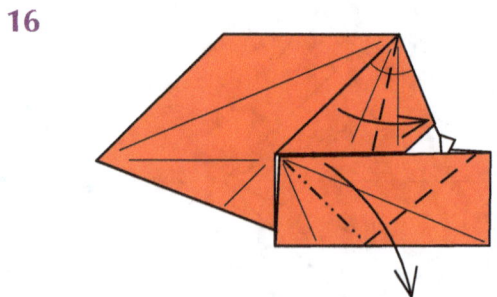

1. Tuck inside.
2. Fold along the crease.

15

Slide the paper up.

16

Squash-fold along some of the creases.

58 *Origami Gnomes of the Forest Wonderland*

17

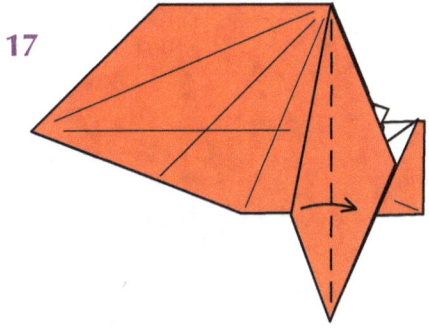

18

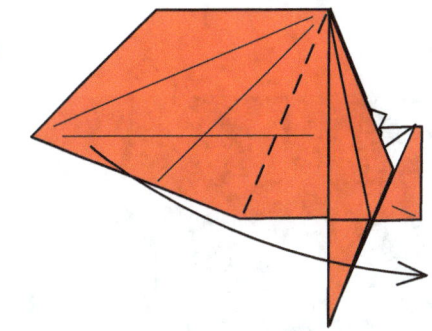

Fold along the crease.

19

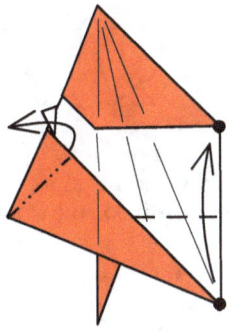

Repeat steps 15–17 in the opposite direction.

20

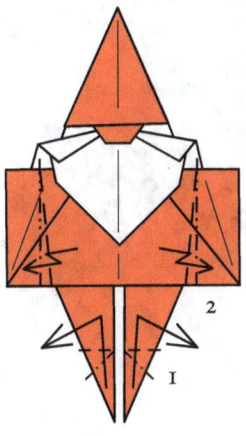

1. Make pleat folds.
2. Make pleat folds.

21

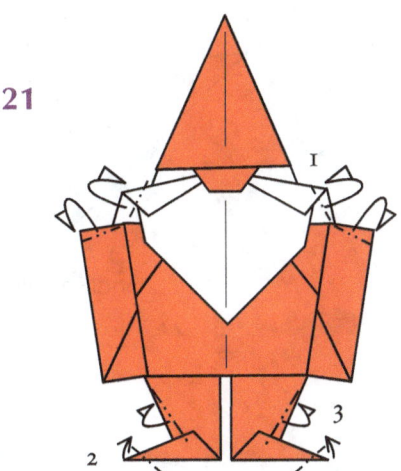

1. Fold behind.
2. Make reverse folds.
3. Fold behind.

22

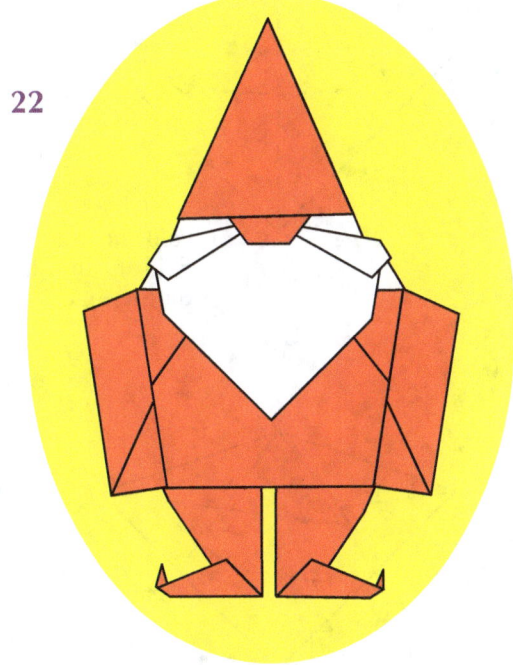

Grindle Cogflick

Willomert Tinklehoot

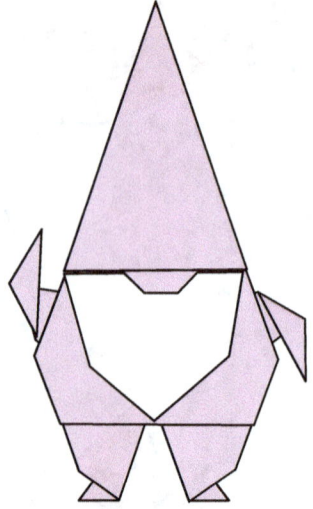

Willomert crafted a network of crystal orbs, each one carefully carved with tiny slots and secret channels. He tucked the orbs into tree hollows all throughout the forest, where they rest like sleeping stars. Whenever a gnome places a flower on one, the orbs glows a deep, delicious red—and out pops a warm slice of pizza topped with spicy bark chips. Gnomes know: Nothing beats an orb-baked pizza, hands down, toes up.

1

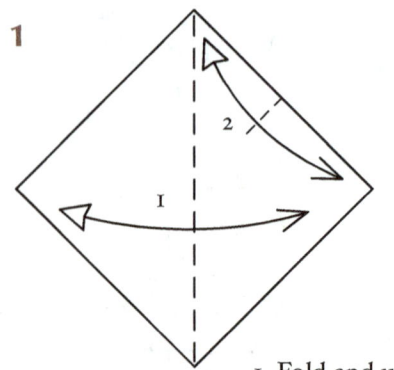

1. Fold and unfold.
2. Fold and unfold on the edge.

2

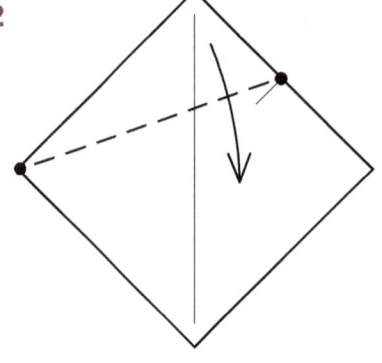

3

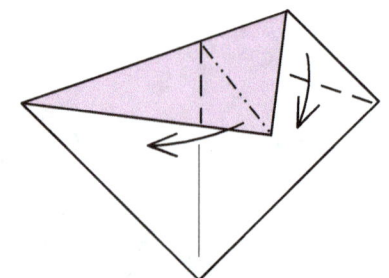

Squash-fold.

4

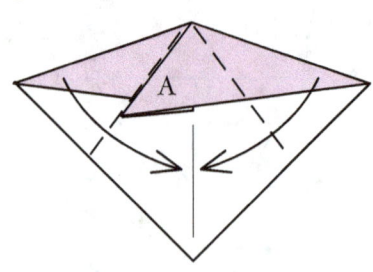

Keep flap A on top while folding to the center.

5

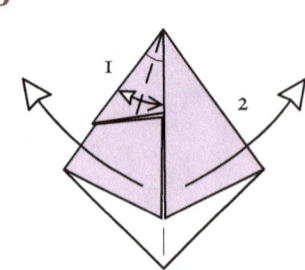

1. Fold and unfold.
2. Unfold.

6

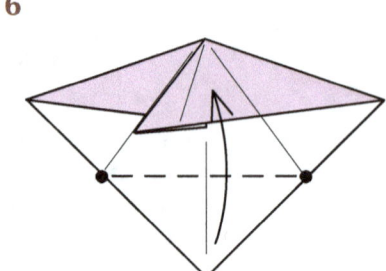

60 *Origami Gnomes of the Forest Wonderland*

7

8

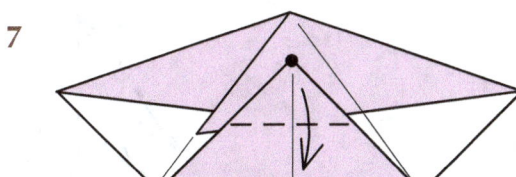
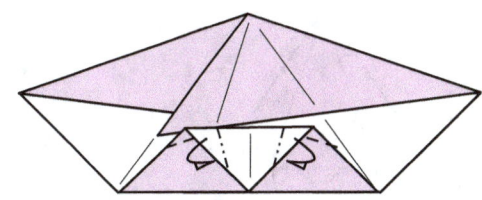

Fold inside.

9

10

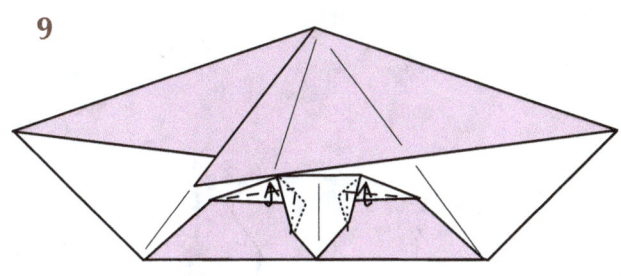
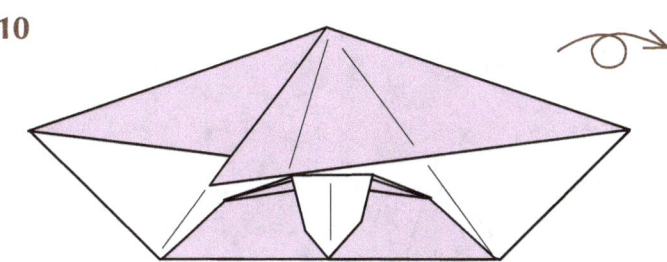

Make thin squash folds.

11

12

13

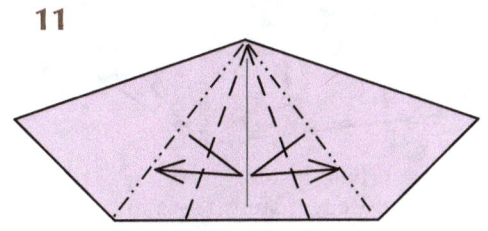
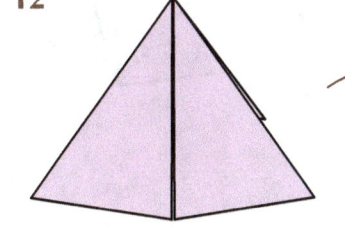
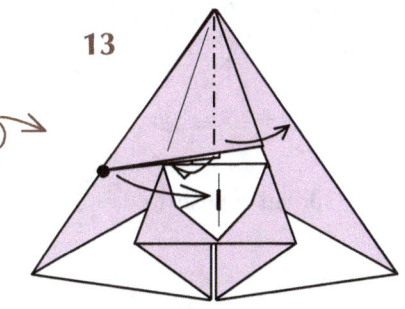

Pleat-fold to the center. Do not fold the hidden flap, shown as A in step 4.

Spread and squash fold.

14

15

16

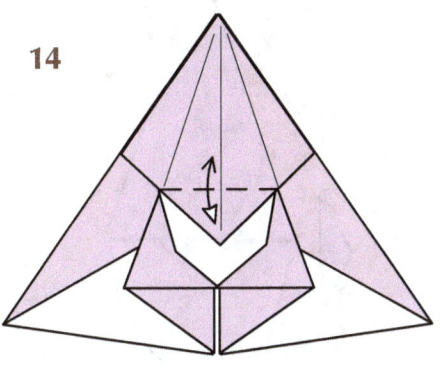
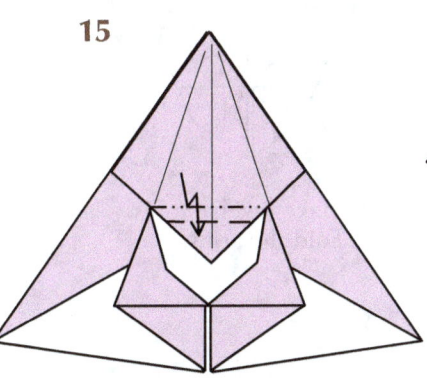
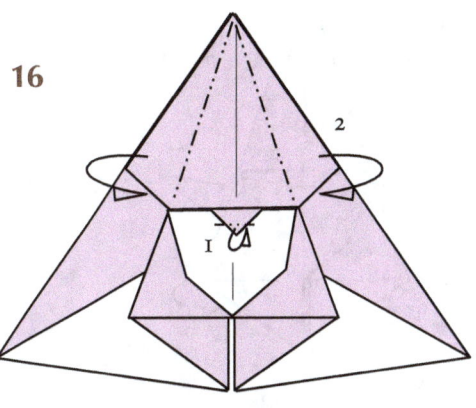

Fold and unfold.

Moutain-fold along the crease for this pleat fold.

1. Fold inside.
2. Fold inside.

Willomert Tinklehoot

17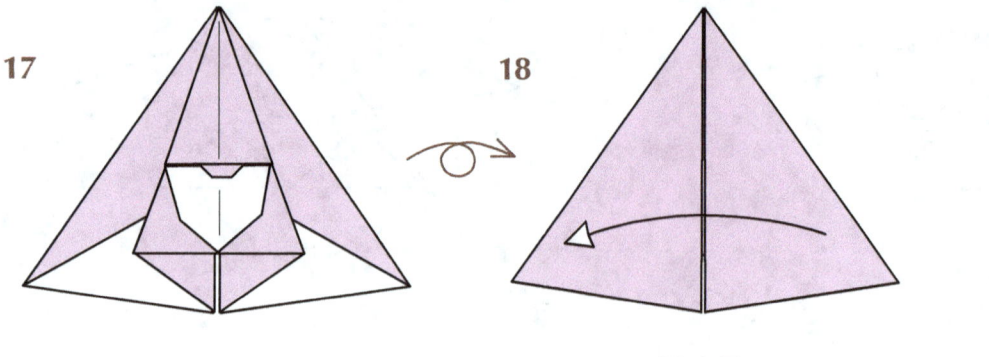

18 Unfold.

19 Rabbit-ear.

20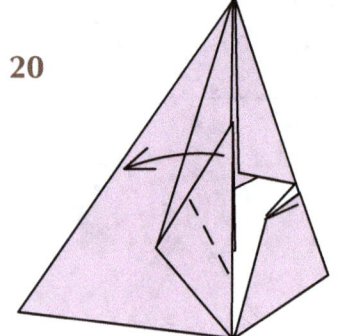
Spread-squash-fold.

21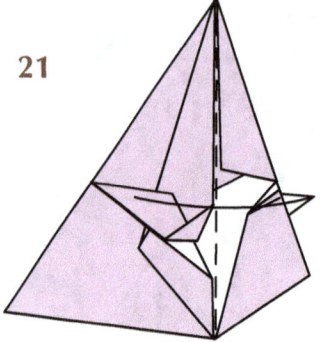

22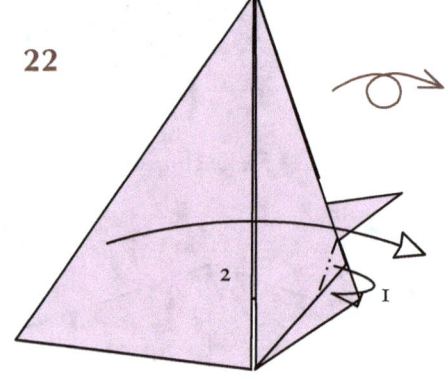
1. Fold inside.
2. Repeat steps 18–22 in the opposite direction.

23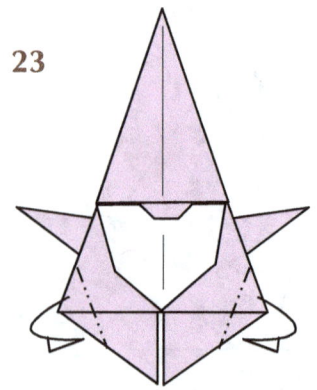
Fold inside.

24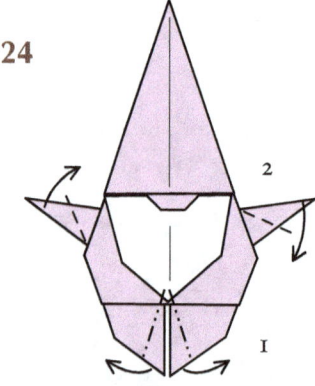
1. Make reverse folds.
2. Fold the arms.

25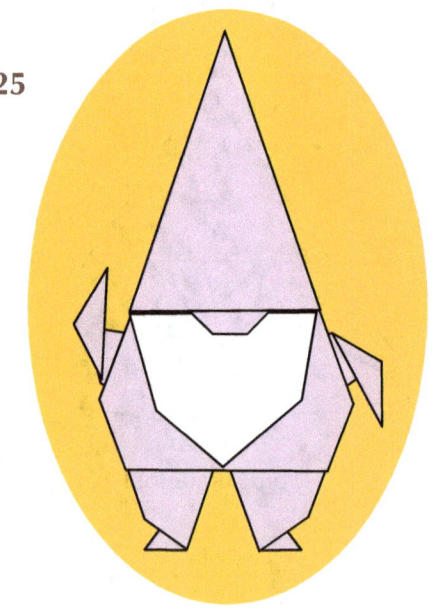

Willomert Tinklehoot

62   *Origami Gnomes of the Forest Wonderland*

Nibbleknock Crankletuft

Nibbleknock is famous for swapping the forest animals' snacks. Rabbits find blueberries in their carrot baskets, squirrels find carrots in the nut stashes, and birds find nuts stuffed into acorns. He always leaves a note: "*Try something new today.*"

1
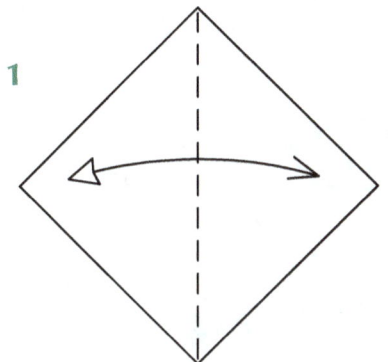
Fold and unfold.

2
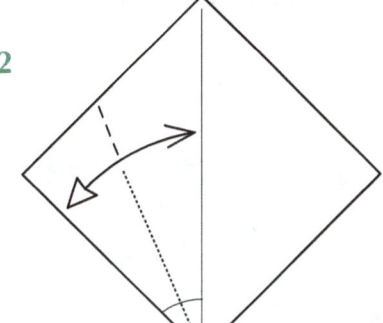
Fold and unfold on the edge.

3
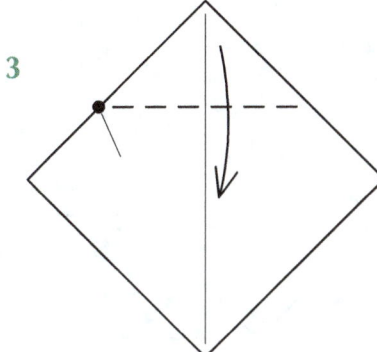
Fold down at the dot.

4
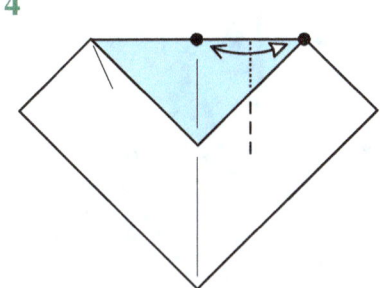
Fold and unfold.

5
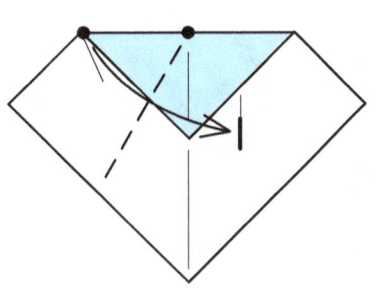
Bring the dot on the left to the crease.

6
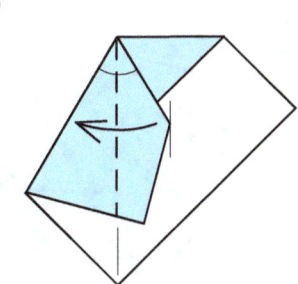

Nibbleknock Crankletuft   63

7

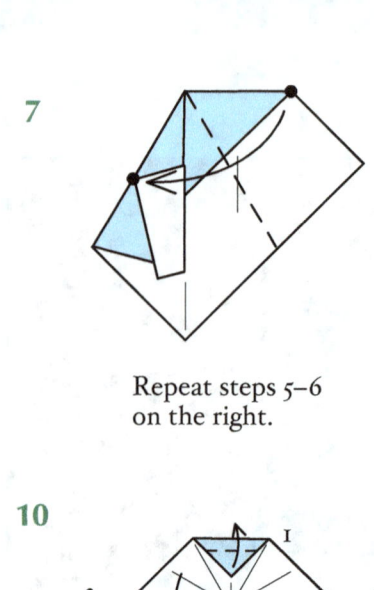

Repeat steps 5–6 on the right.

8

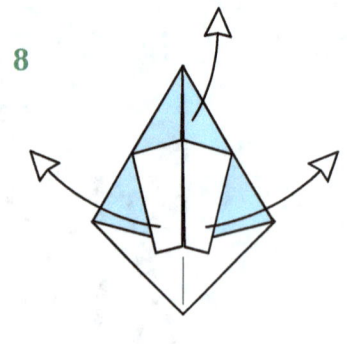

Unfold everything.

9

10

11

12

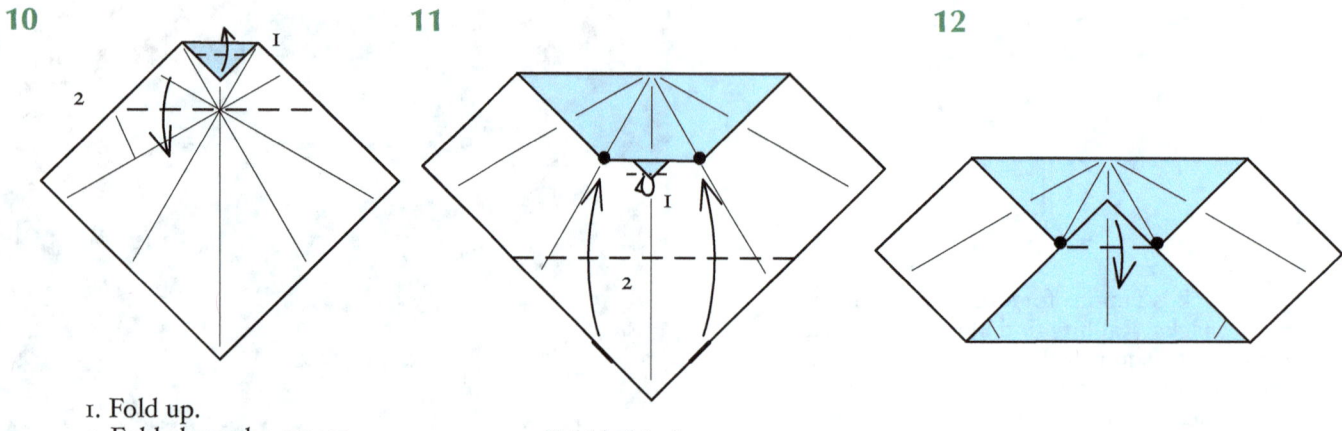

1. Fold up.
2. Fold along the crease.

1. Fold behind.
2. Fold up so the bold edges meet the dots.

13

14

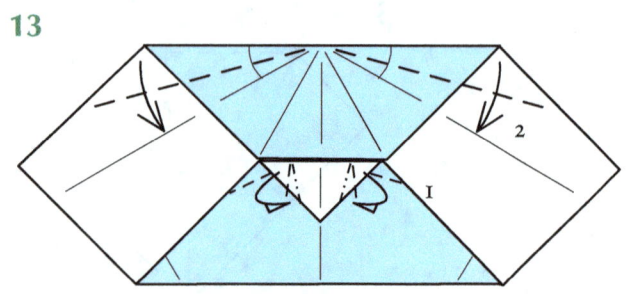

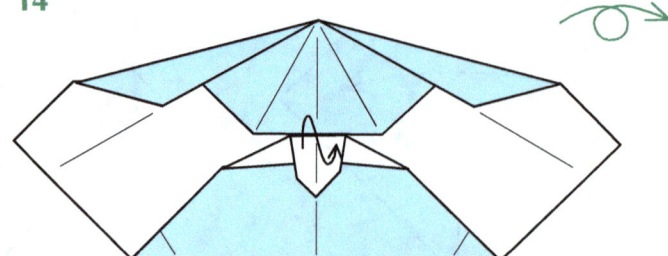

1. Fold inside.
2. Fold down.

Tuck inside.

15

16

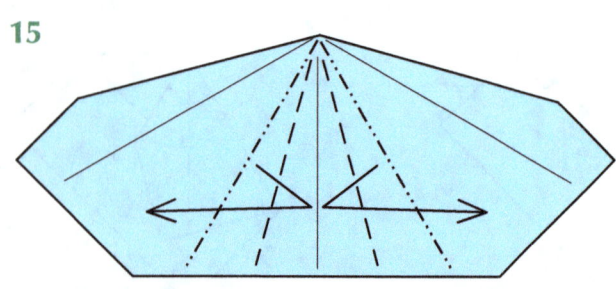

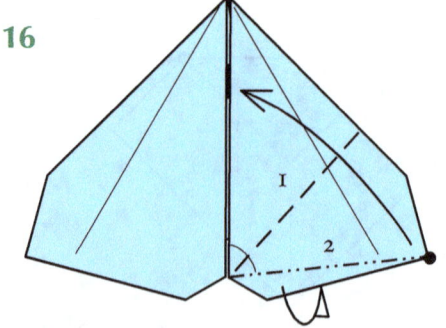

Mountain-fold along the creases for these pleat folds.

1. Bring the dot to the center line.
2. Fold behind.

64   *Origami Gnomes of the Forest Wonderland*

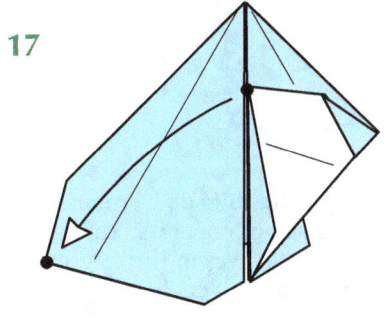

17

Unfold.

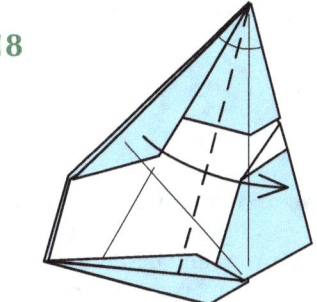

18

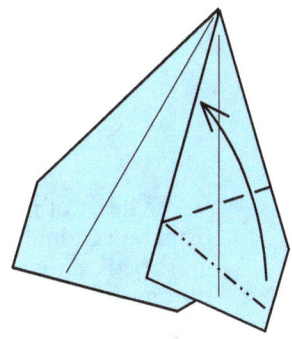

19

Valley-fold along the crease for this squash fold.

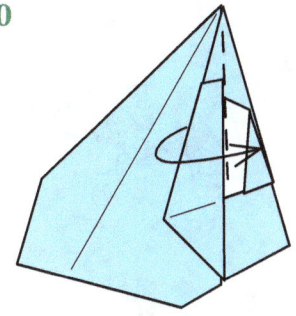

20

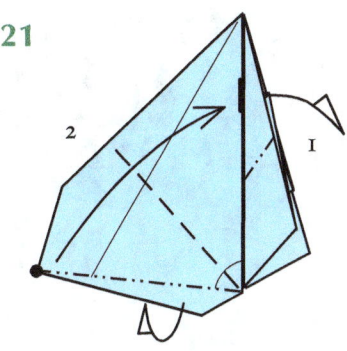

21

1. Mountain-fold the arm.
2. Repeat steps 16–21 on the left.

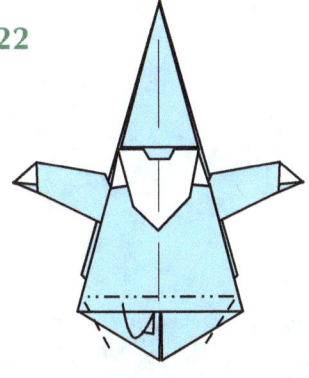

22

Fold inside.

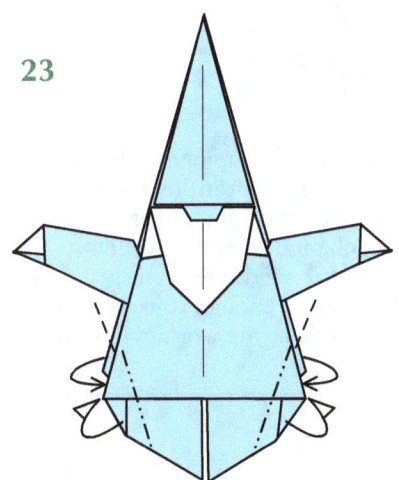

23

Fold inside, repeat behind.

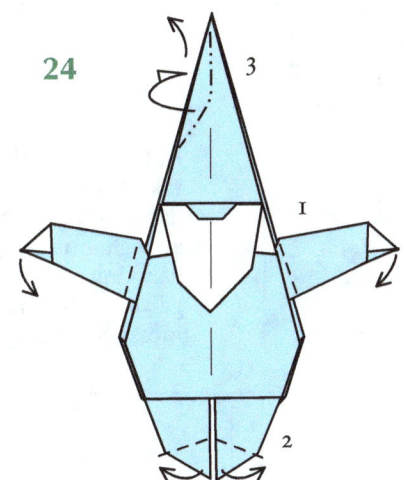

24

1. Fold the arms out.
2. Fold the feet out so the Gnome can stand.
3. Shape the hat.

25

Nibbleknock Crankletuft

Nibbleknock Crankletuft 65

Small Forest Animals

In the heart of the forest, gnomes live in harmony with a lively cast of forest animals. Rabbits deliver messages from one gnome to another while frogs sing cheerful tunes alongside them during twilight concerts. Turtles carry moss beds across the forest floor, and robins and cardinals serve as the gnomes' watchful eyes in the treetops, warning of incoming rain. Every creature, no matter how small, has a place and a purpose in this enchanted woodland.

Butterfly

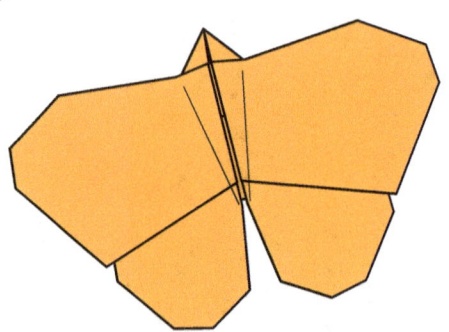

Butterflies land lightly on every moment. They always take the scenic route, drifting after flowers like daydreams with wings. And though they seem delicate, a single butterfly can change an entire meadow, carrying pollen that wakes seeds and quietly grows gardens. To any gnome wise enough to watch, their message is simple: rest often, the world will wait.

1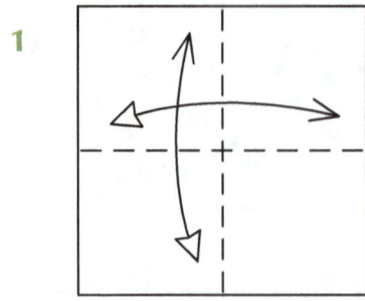
Fold and unfold.

2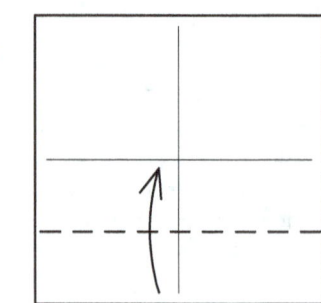
Fold to the center.

3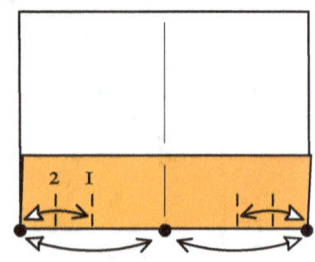
Fold and unfold in half, twice on the left and right.

66 *Origami Gnomes of the Forest Wonderland*

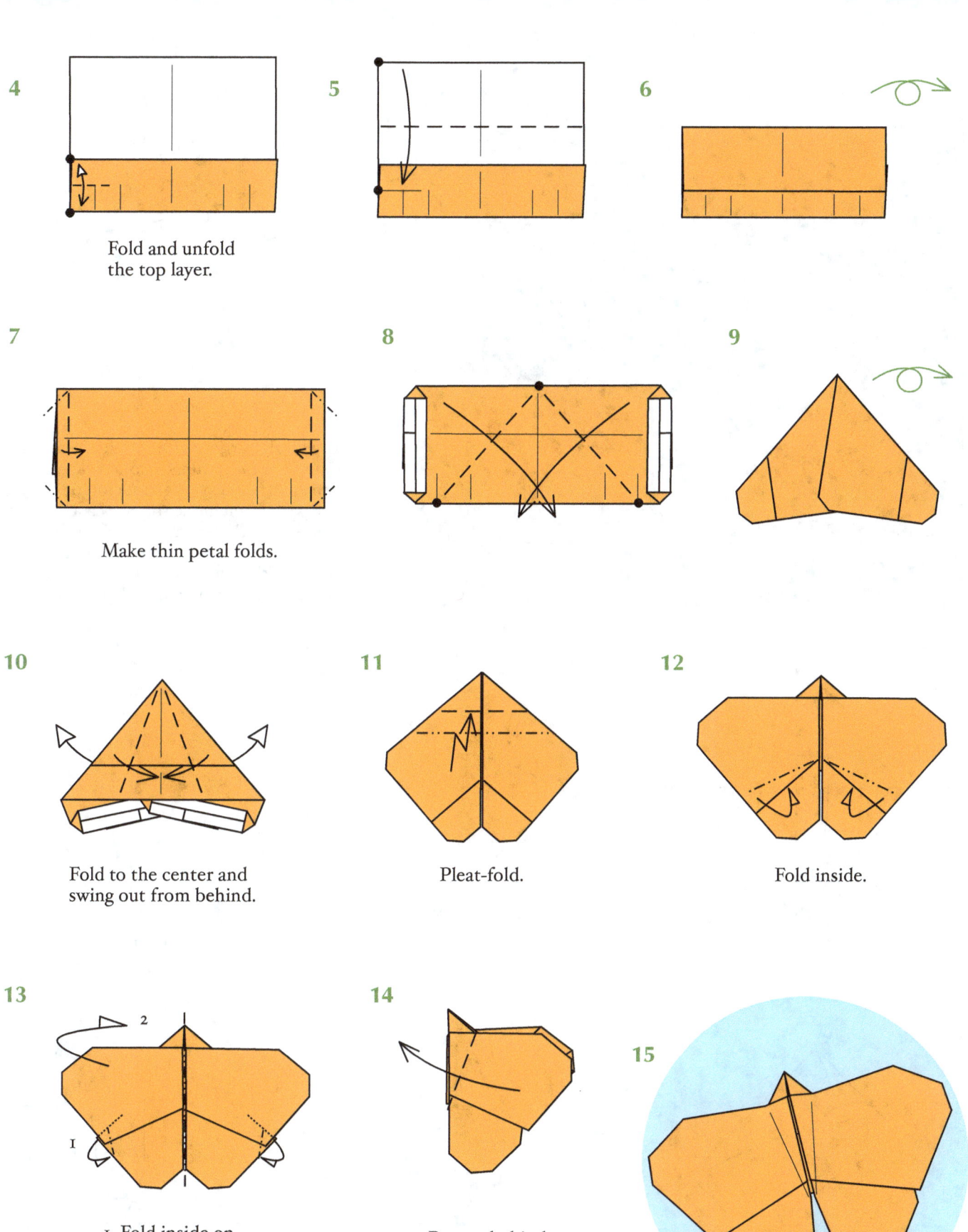

Butterfly

Dragonfly

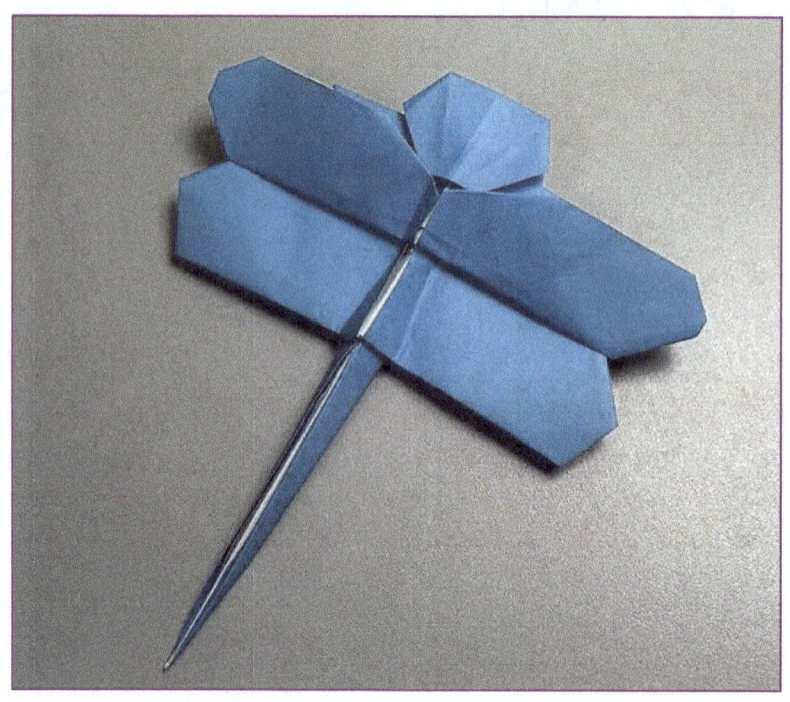

A dragonfly carries prism-bright eyes that seem to see everything—front, side, past, future, and whatever a gnome forgot on the windowsill. Even in the softest shadows they shimmer like tiny lanterns, zipping this way and that with the attention span of a spark. Their sparkle is for the gnomes watching from the reeds: glide more, flap less.

1

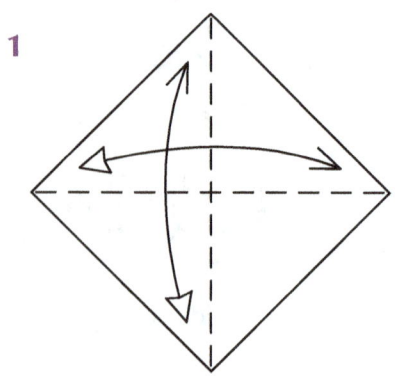

Fold and unfold.

2

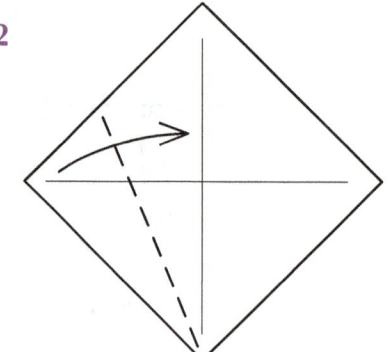

Fold to the center.

3

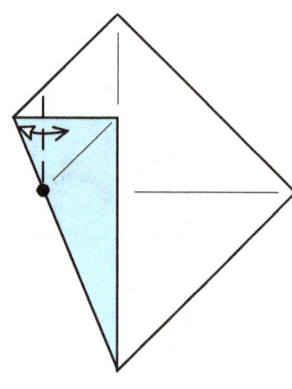

Fold and unfold.

4

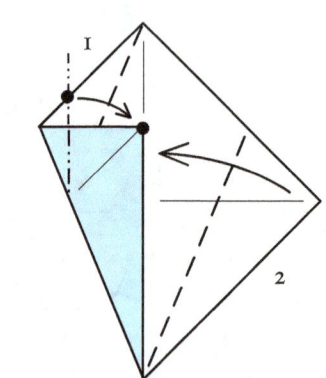

1. This is similar to a reverse fold.
2. Repeat steps 2–4 on the right.

5

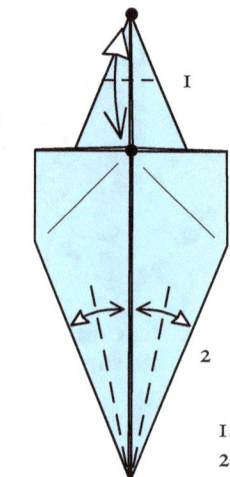

1. Fold and unfold.
2. Fold to the center and unfold.

6

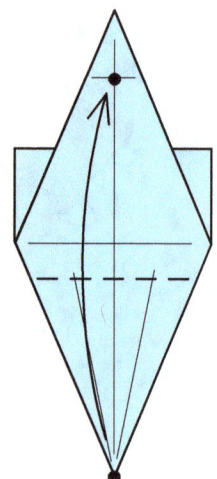

68 *Origami Gnomes of the Forest Wonderland*

7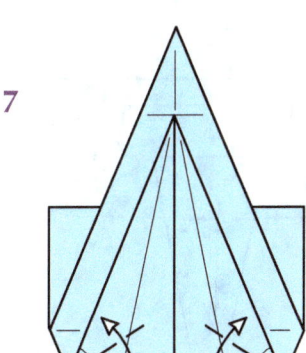
Fold and unfold.

8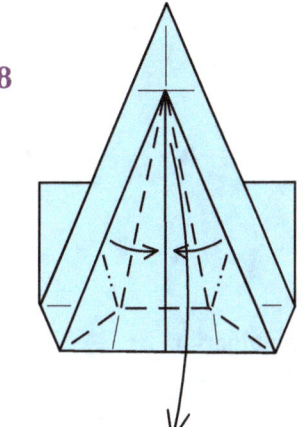
Fold along the creases.

9

10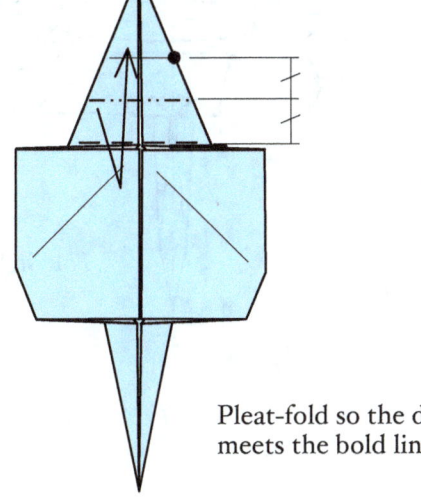
Pleat-fold so the dot meets the bold line.

11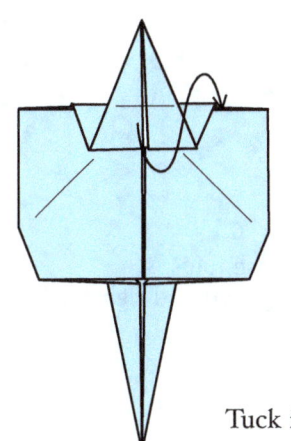
Tuck inside.

12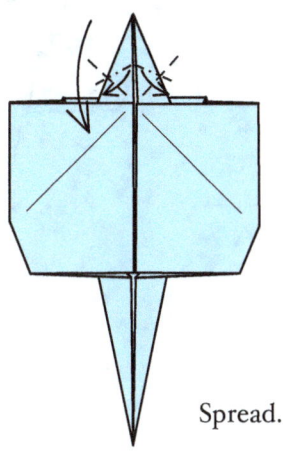
Spread.

13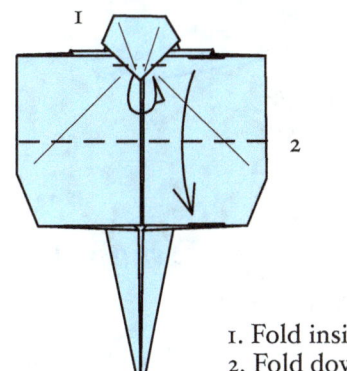
1. Fold inside.
2. Fold down.

14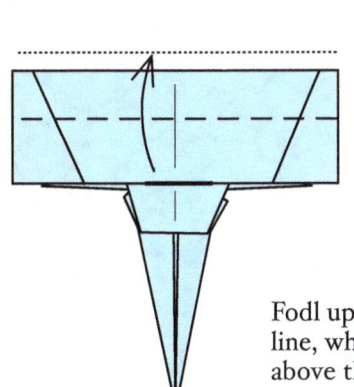
Fodl up to the dotted line, which is slightly above the top.

15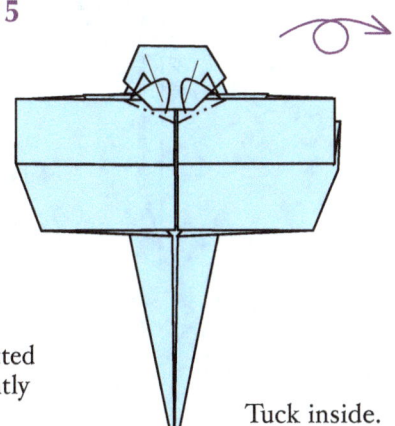
Tuck inside.

Dragonfly 69

16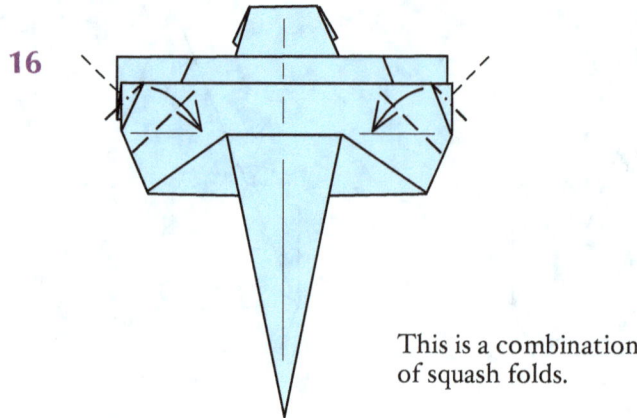

This is a combination of squash folds.

17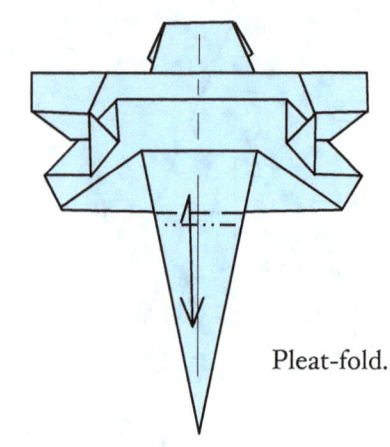

Pleat-fold.

18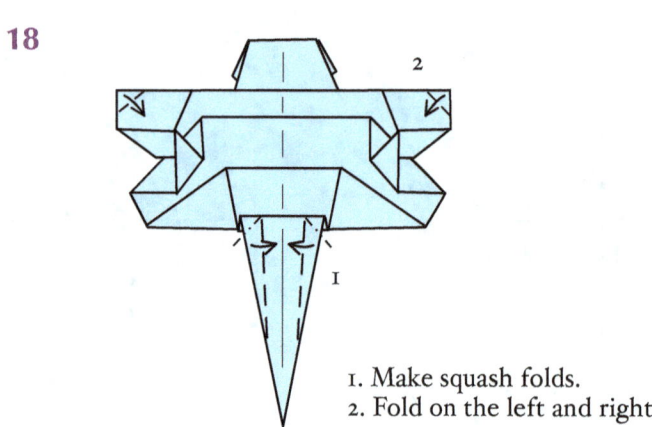

1. Make squash folds.
2. Fold on the left and right.

19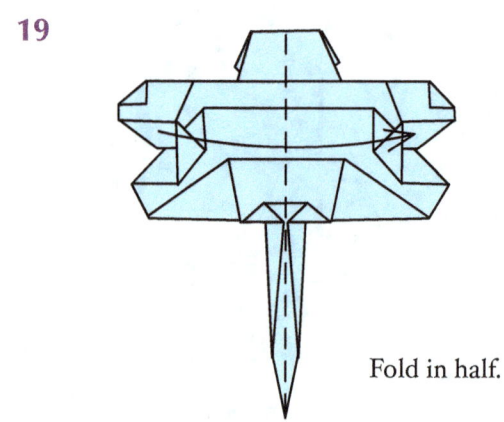

Fold in half.

20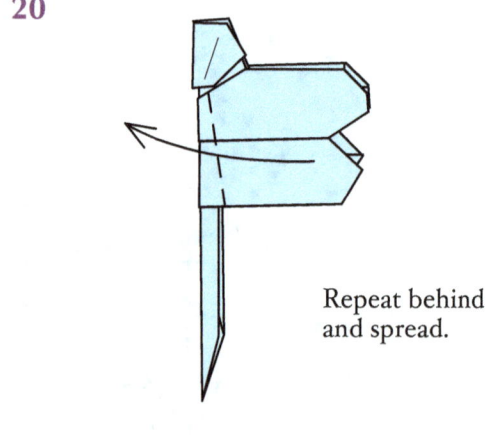

Repeat behind and spread.

21

Dragonfly

Spider

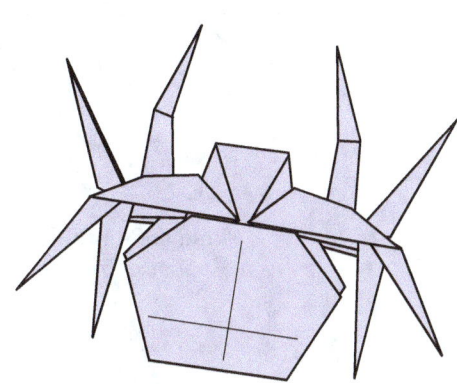

Spiders remind us that eight legs make steady work, though gnomes have tried and failed to construct extras. They handle disruptions calmly: webs get destroyed frequently from storms, boots, and wayward squirrels, yet spiders simply rebuild. A spider's web is art, engineering, and magic all in one.

1

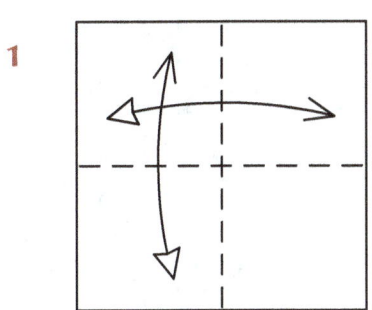

Fold and unfold.

2

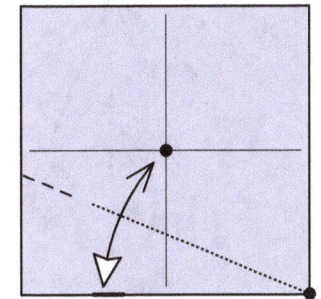

Bring the bottom edge to the center. Crease on the left.

3

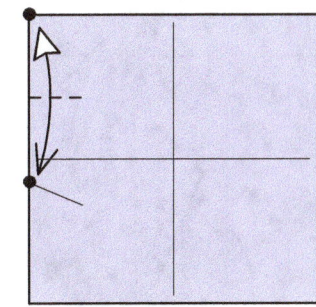

Fold and unfold on the left.

4

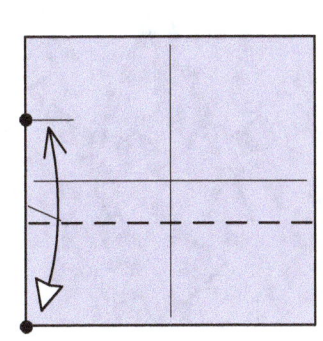

Fold and unfold.

5

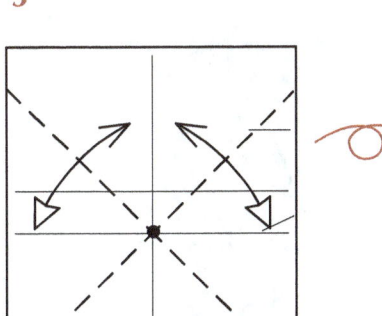

Fold and unfold. Rotate 180°.

6

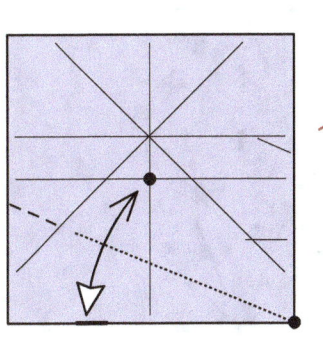

Repeat steps 2–5.

Spider 71

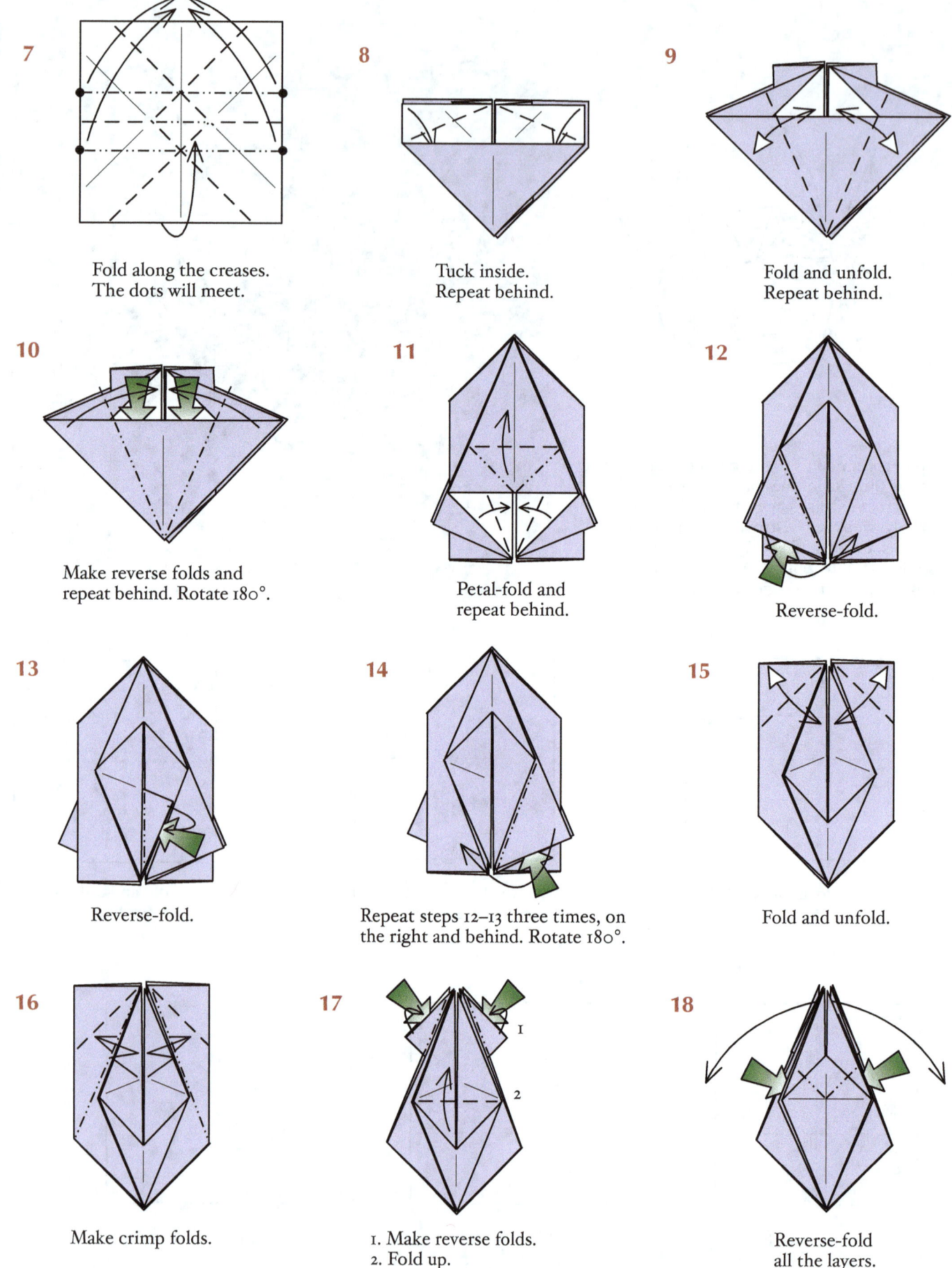

72 *Origami Gnomes of the Forest Wonderland*

19

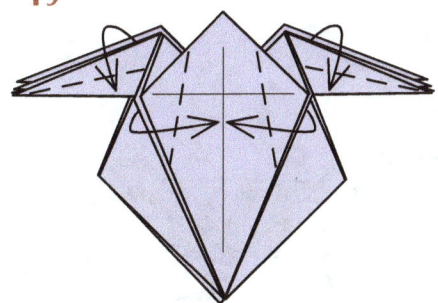

Fold several layers for these squash folds.

20

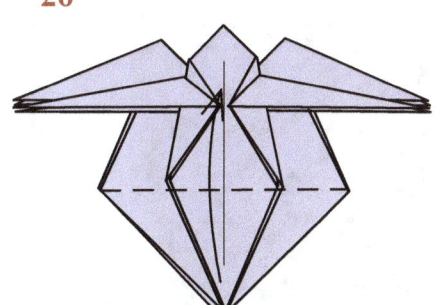

Fold the top flap up.

21

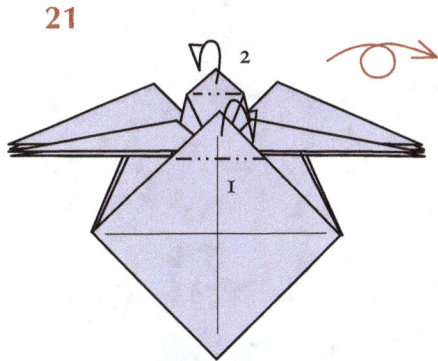

Fold behind at 1 and 2.

22

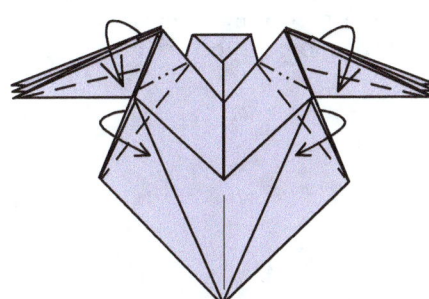

Fold several layers for these squash folds.

23

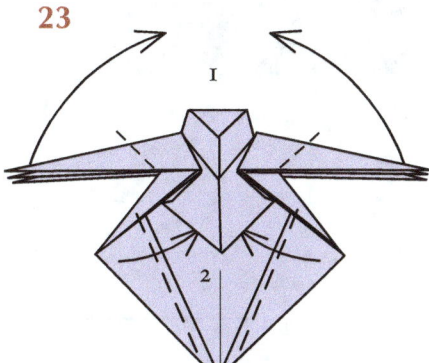

1. Outside-reverse-fold the top flaps.
2. Tuck inside.

24

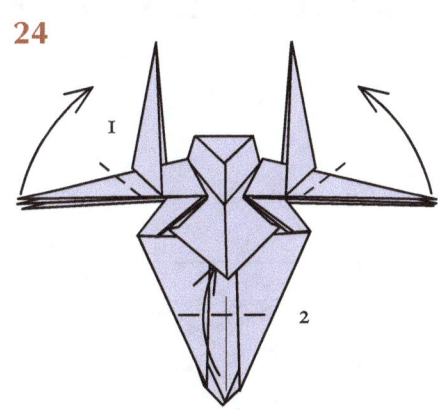

1. Outside-reverse-fold the top flaps.
2. Tuck inside.

25

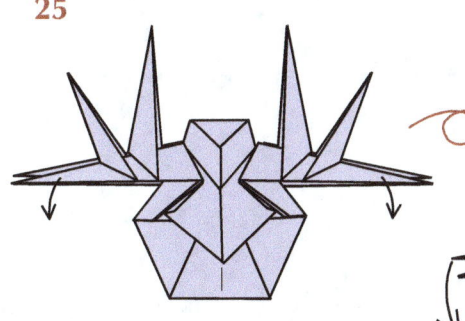

Separate the legs just a little bit.

26

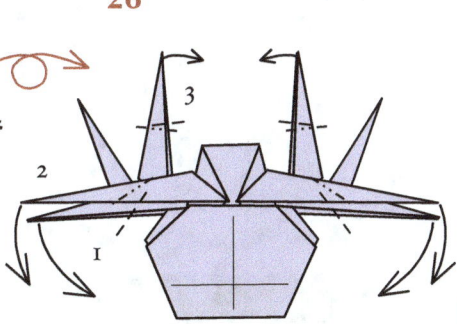

1. Outside-revrese-fold.
2. Inside-reverse-fold.
3. Crimp-fold.

27

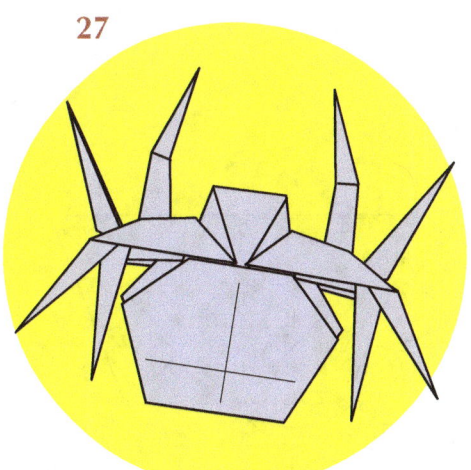

Spider

Spider

Grasshopper

Grasshoppers always find the greenest patch of grass, no matter how hidden. They are silent when danger is near and noisy when the day is safe. They chirp so loudly even the mushrooms complain. While they often misjudge a jump and land sideways or on a gnome's nose, they never apologize. Leap when the moment feels right.

1

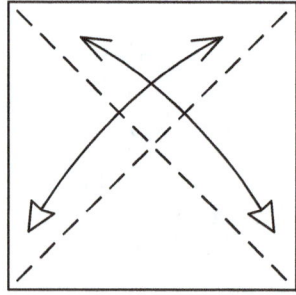

Fold and unfold.

2

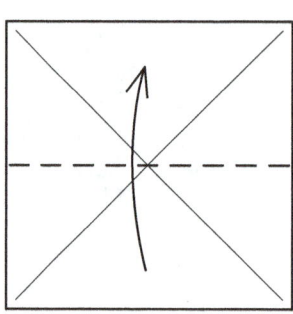

3

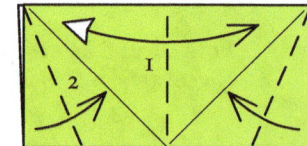

1. Fold and unfold.
2. Fold on the left and right.

4

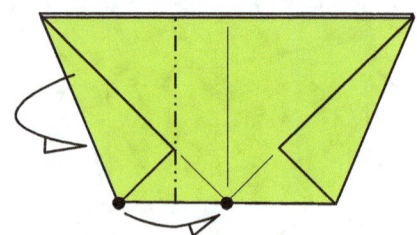

5

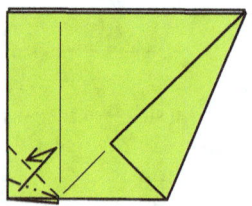

Pleat-fold all the layers.

6

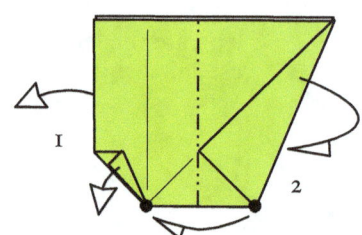

1. Unfold.
2. Repeat steps 4–6 on the right.

74 *Origami Gnomes of the Forest Wonderland*

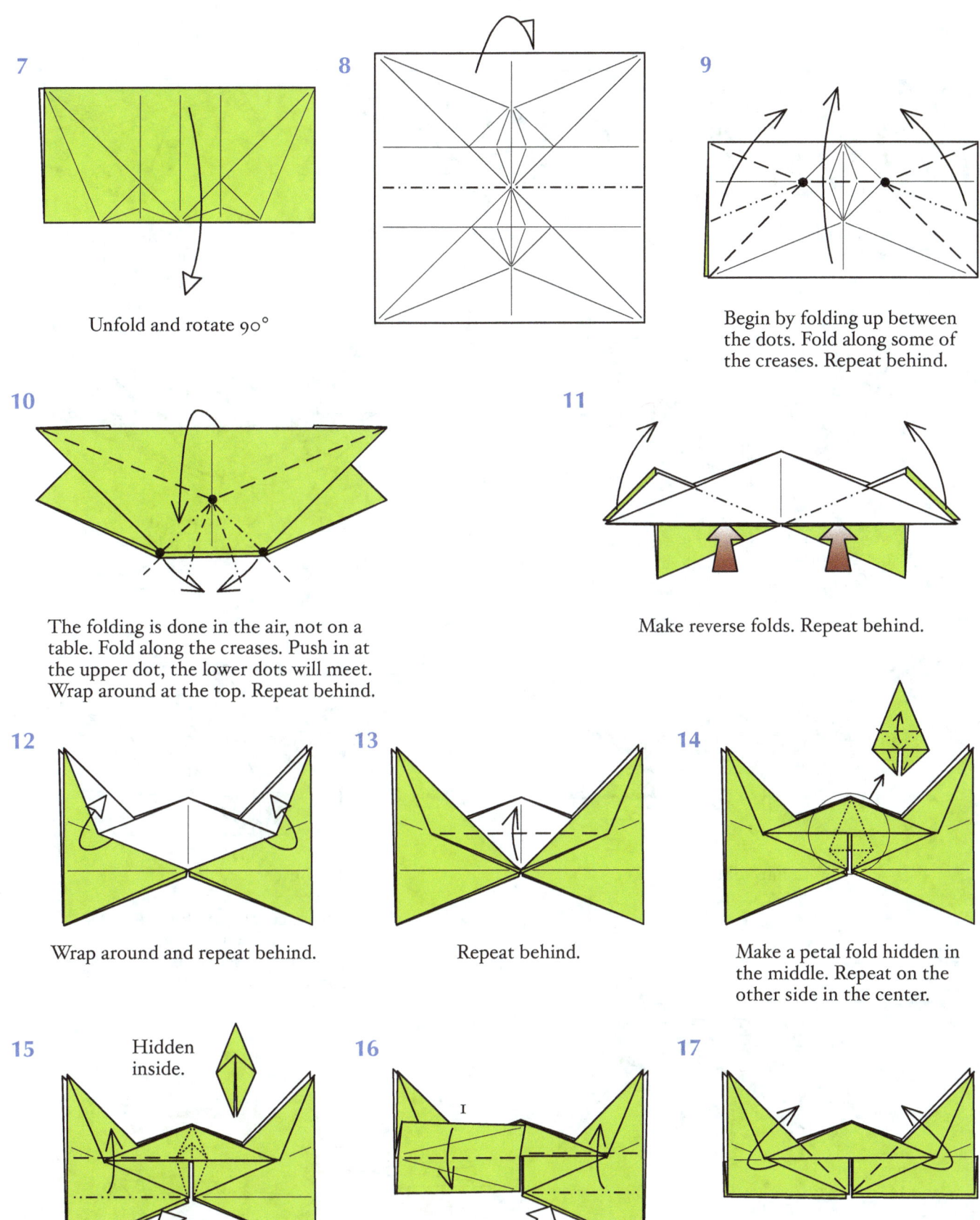

7 Unfold and rotate 90°

8

9 Begin by folding up between the dots. Fold along some of the creases. Repeat behind.

10 The folding is done in the air, not on a table. Fold along the creases. Push in at the upper dot, the lower dots will meet. Wrap around at the top. Repeat behind.

11 Make reverse folds. Repeat behind.

12 Wrap around and repeat behind.

13 Repeat behind.

14 Make a petal fold hidden in the middle. Repeat on the other side in the center.

15 Hidden inside. Spread-squash-fold but do not crease on the valley fold line.

16 This is 3D.
1. Fold down.
2. Repeat steps 15–16 on the right.

17 Repeat behind.

Grasshopper 75

18 Make squash folds. Repeat behind.

19 Fold inside and repeat behind.

20
1. Fold both layers.
2. Fold the top layer. Repeat behind.

21
1-3. Fold in order.
4. Fold the top layer in front and the next layer behind. Repeat behind.

22
1. Crimp-fold.
2. Crimp-fold.

23
1. Crimp-fold.
2. Make crimp folds.

24
1. Rabbit-ear.
2. Reverse-fold.
3. Push in at the top for this crimp fold. The legs at the bottom will separate.
Repeat behind.

25
1. Reverse-fold.
2. Crimp-fold.
3. Reverse-fold.
4. Thin and shape the legs.
Repeat behind.

26

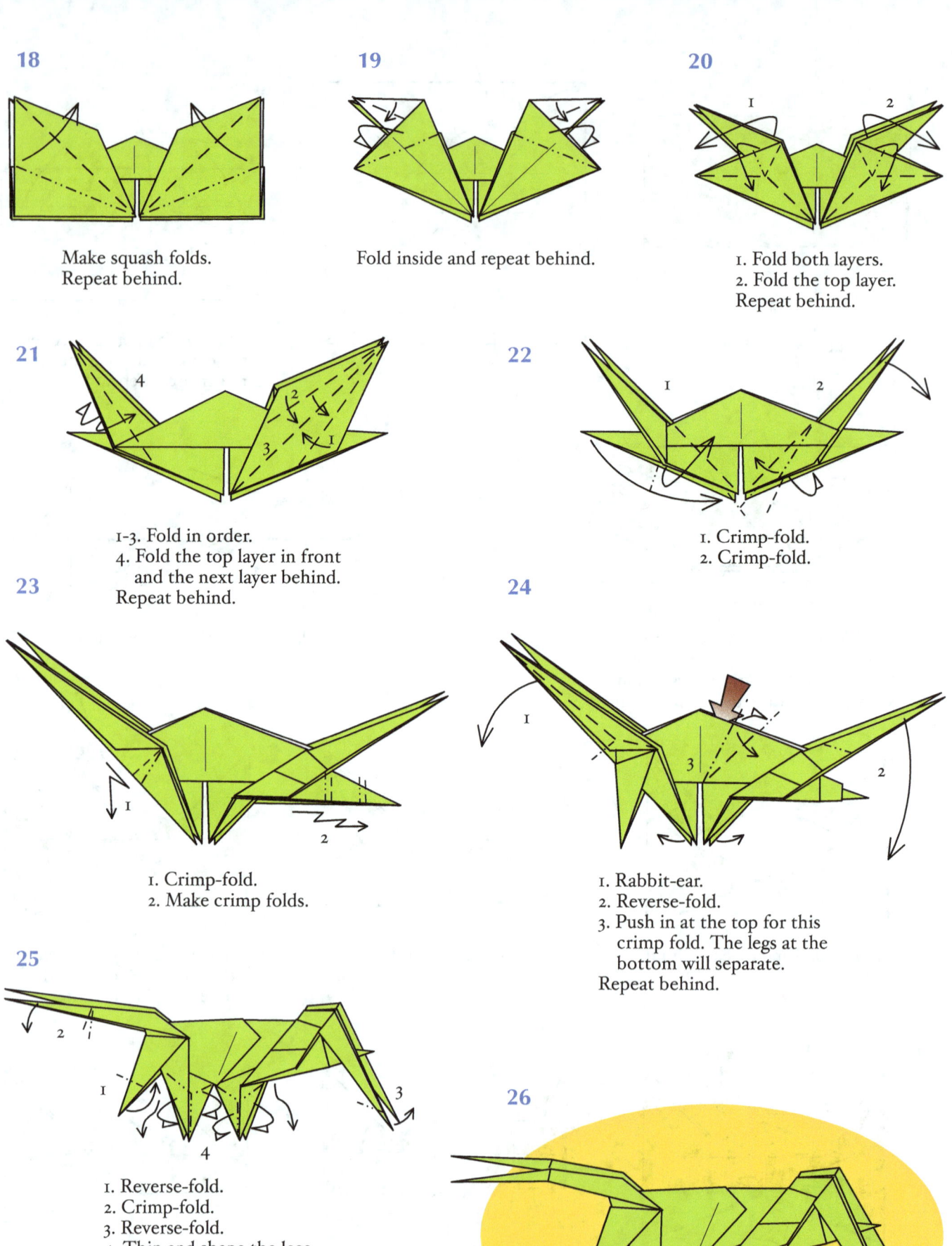

Grasshopper

76 *Origami Gnomes of the Forest Wonderland*

Snail

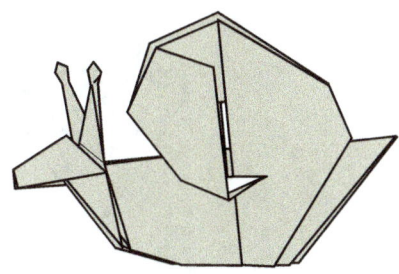

Snails are tiny nighttime explorers! During the day they hide in cool, damp places so they don't dry out. When the sun goes down, they slide out of their hiding spots and glide slowly across leaves, soil, and sidewalks looking for yummy plants to nibble. Their shiny slime trail helps them move smoothly and keeps their bodies from getting hurt.

1. Fold and unfold.

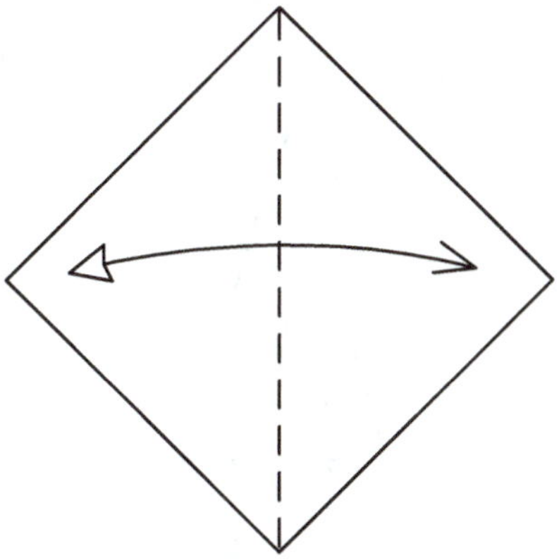

2. Fold and unfold.

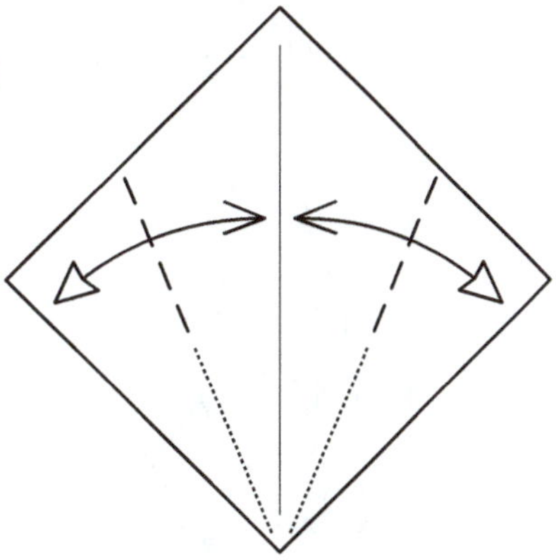

3. Bisect the angles.

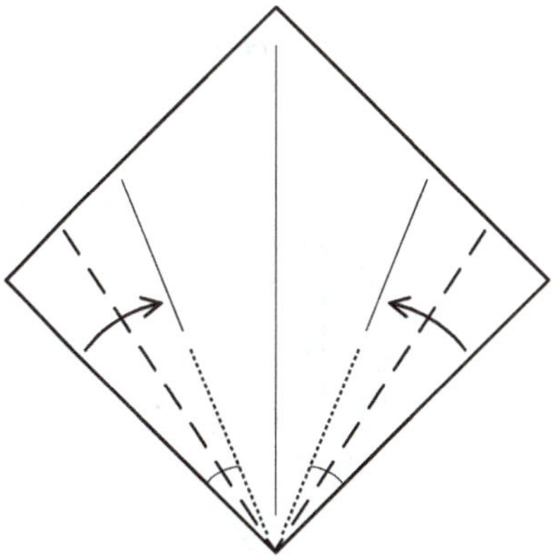

4. Fold and unfold.

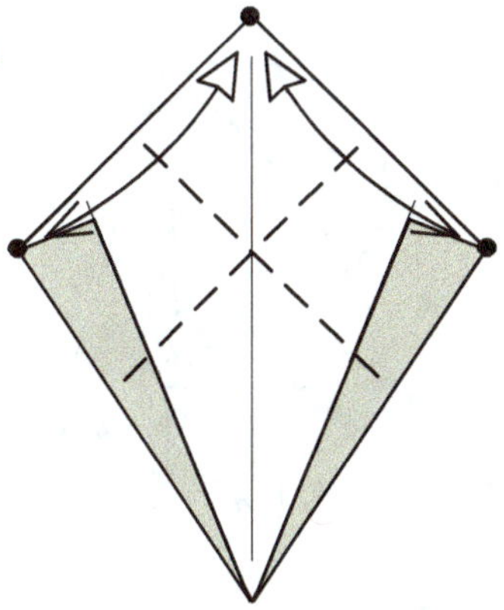

5.

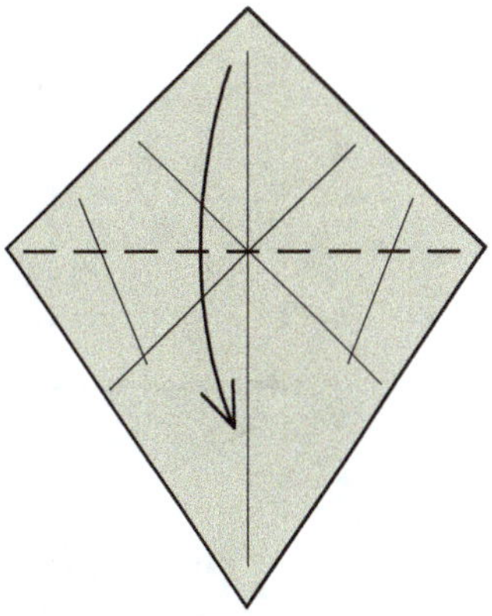

6. 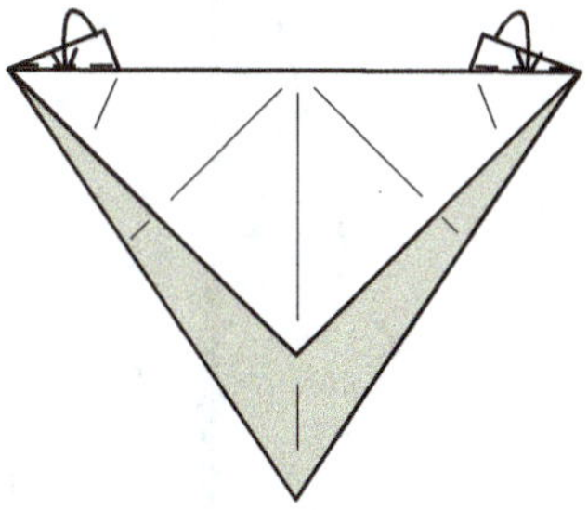 Tuck inside.

Snail 77

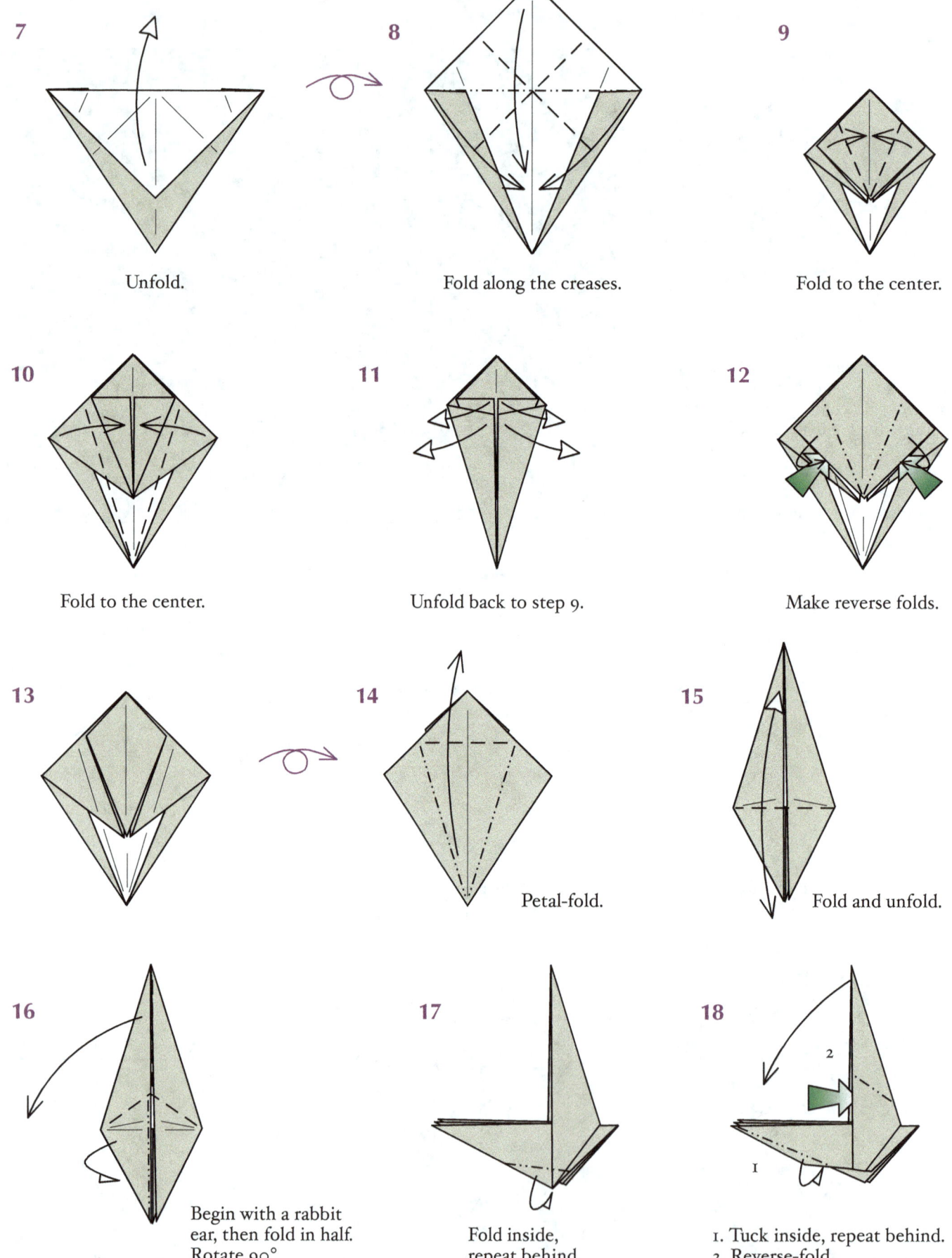

78 *Origami Gnomes of the Forest Wonderland*

19

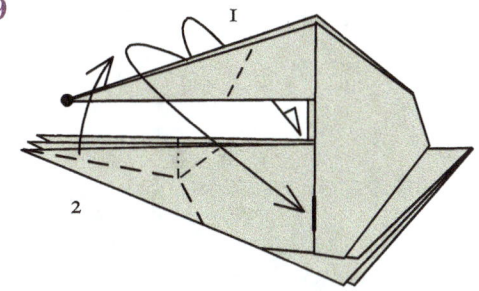

1. Outside-reverse-fold so the dot meets the bold line.
2. Rabbit-ear, repeat behind.

20

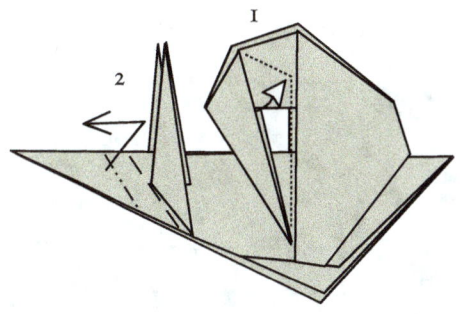

1. Pull out, repeat on the other side.
2. Make outside reverse folds.

21

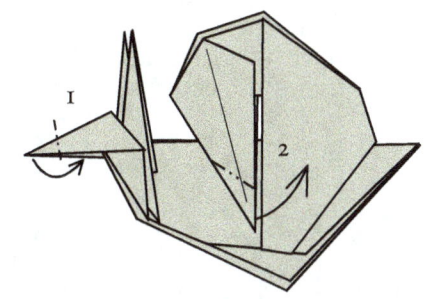

1. Reverse-fold.
2. Reverse-fold.

22

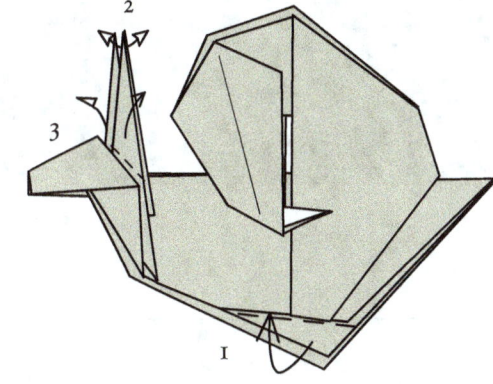

1. Tuck inside.
2. Spread to make a knob at the top.
3. Spread the antennae.
Repeat behind.

23

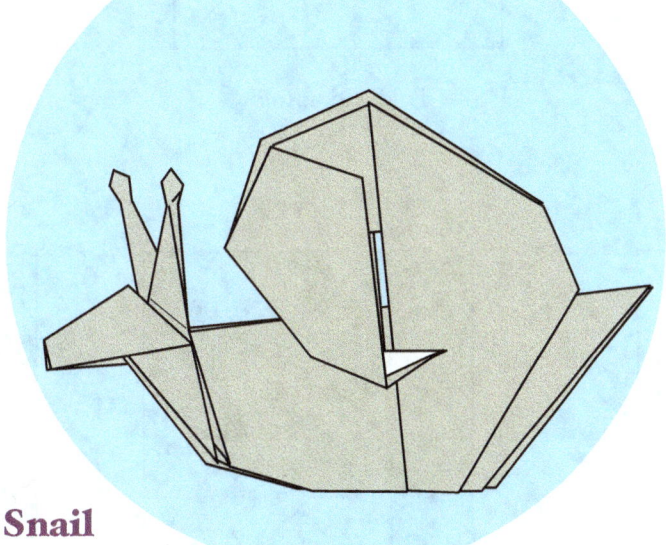

Snail

Frog

Frogs sing songs by the pond at night. Their secret is: they only croak when the time is right. Watch them jump, hop, and splash as we enjoy the quiet music of the forest.

1

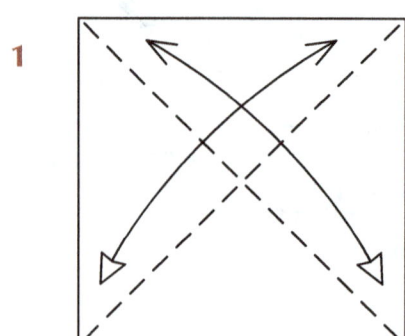

Fold and unfold.

2

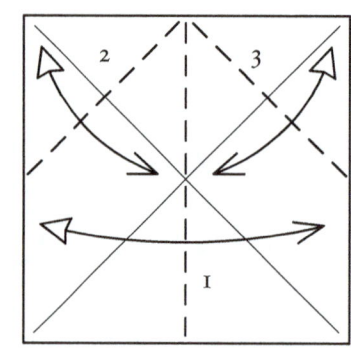

Fold and unfold at 1, 2, and 3.

3

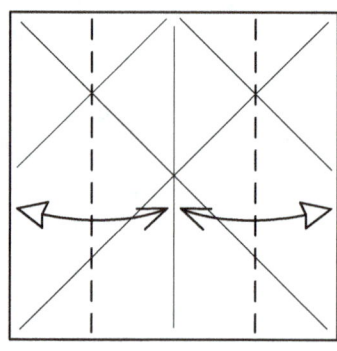

Fold to the center and unfold.

4

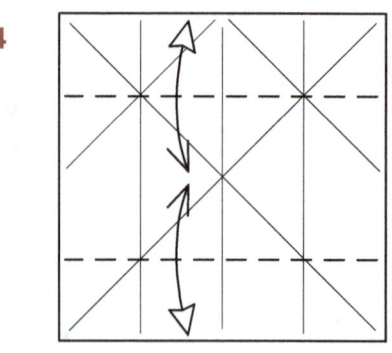

Fold and unfold.

5

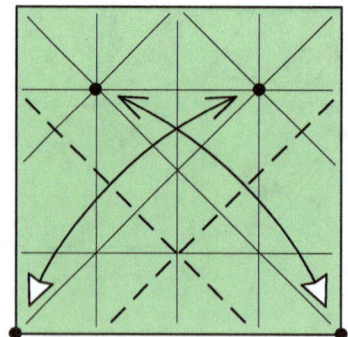

Fold and unfold.

6

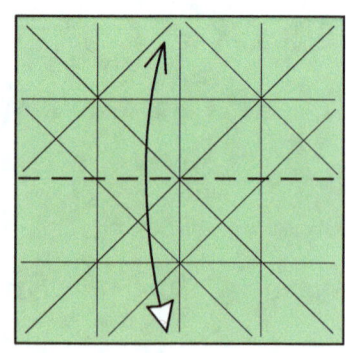

Fold and unfold.

80 *Origami Gnomes of the Forest Wonderland*

7
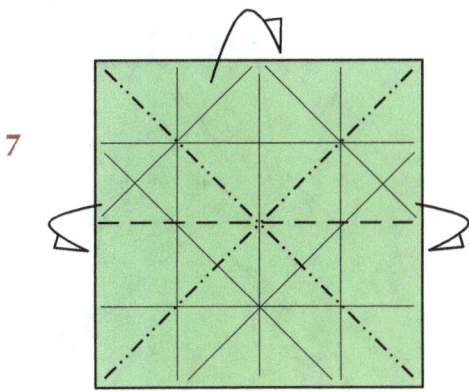
Fold along the creases.

8
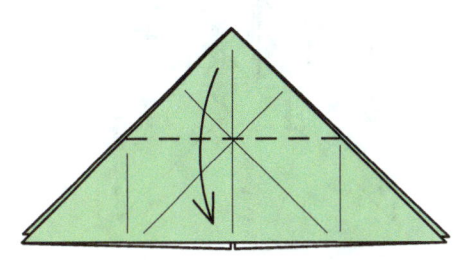
Fold along the crease.

9
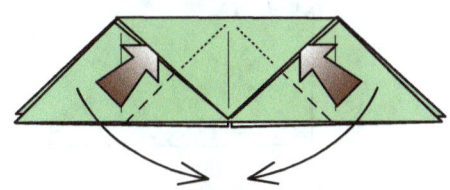
Valley-fold along the creases, including the hidden layers.

10
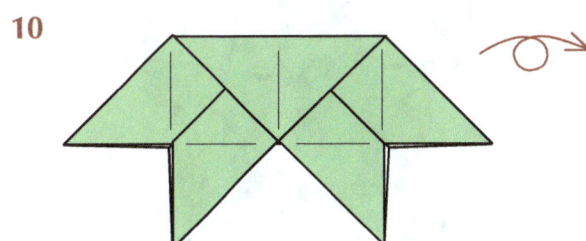

11
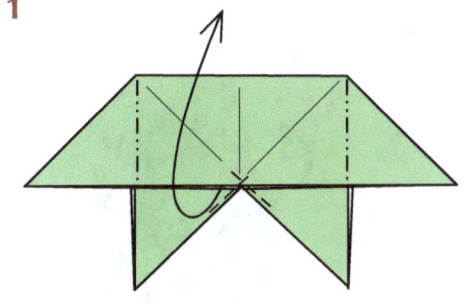
This is similar to a petal fold.

12
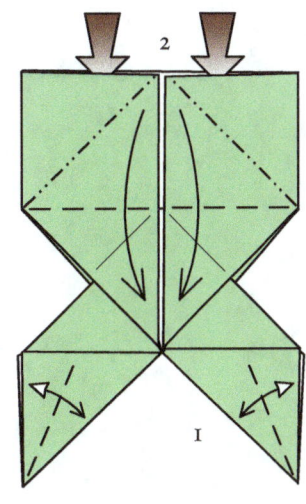
1. Fold and unfold.
2. Make squash folds.

13
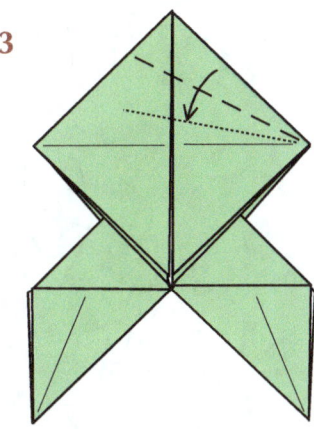
Fold down, slightly above the horizontal crease.

14
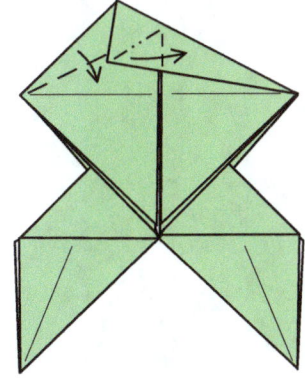
Squash-fold.

15
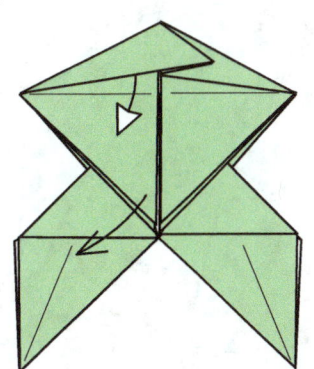
Unlock the paper.

16
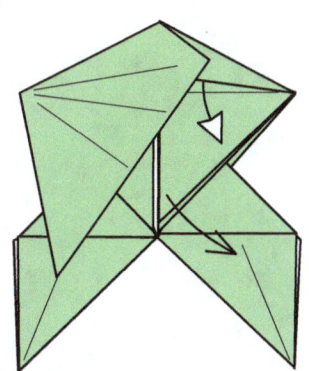
Unlock the paper.

Frog 81

17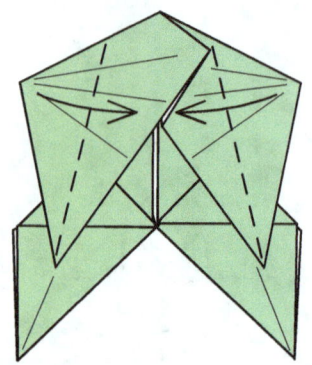

18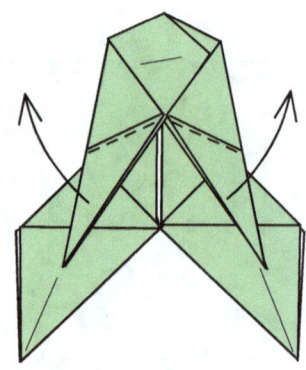

19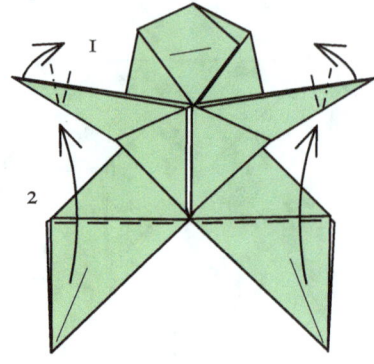

1. Make squash folds.
2. Fold up.

20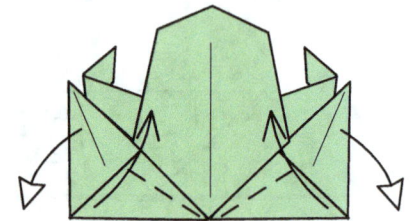

Fold up and swing out from behind.

21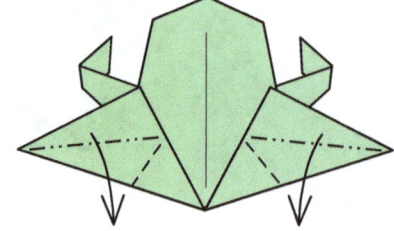

Moutain-fold along the creases for these squash folds.

22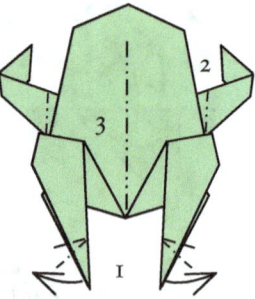

1. Make squash folds.
2. Bend the arms.
3. Bend in half so the Frog is sitting.

23

Frog

82 *Origami Gnomes of the Forest Wonderland*

Turtle

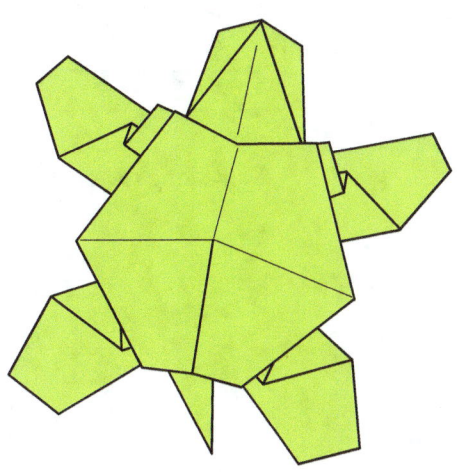

Turtles carry their homes on their backs as they take their time to enjoy the forest. Pause to notice the moss on the rocks, the sunlight on the leaves, and the tiny treasures hidden along the path.

1

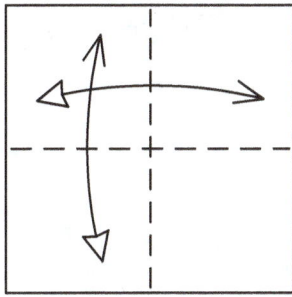

Fold and unfold.

2

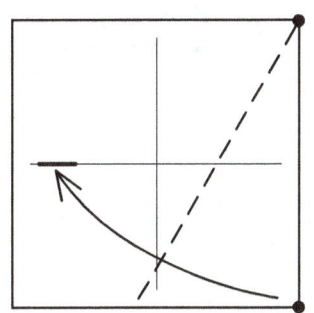

Bring the lower dot to the line.

3

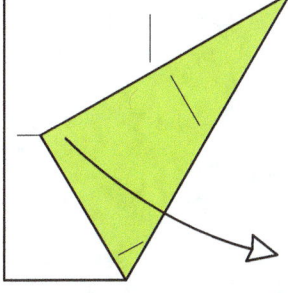

Unfold.

4

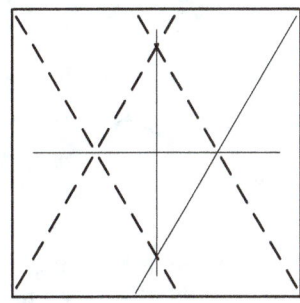

Fold and unfold three more times.

5

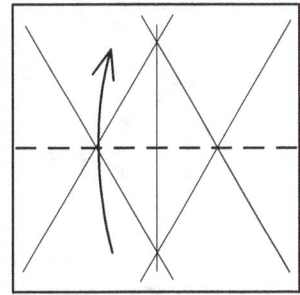

6

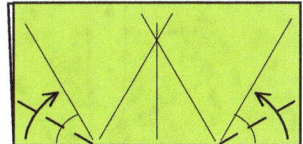

Turtle 83

7

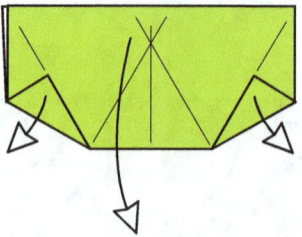

Unfold everything.

8

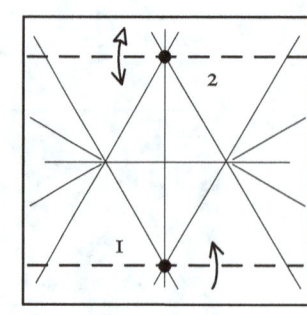

1. Fold up.
2. Fold and unfold.

9

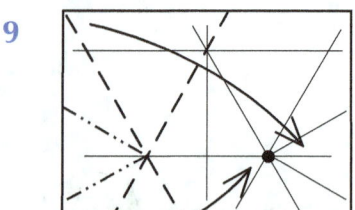

Fold along the creases.

10

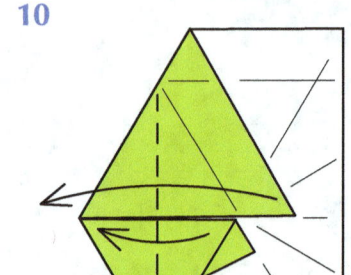

Fold along a hidden crease.

11

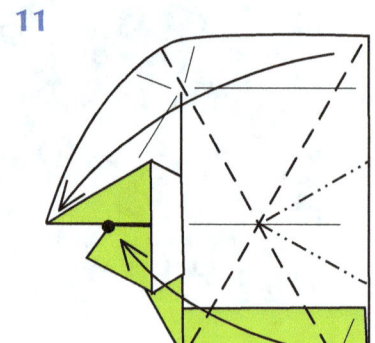

The top ot 3C.
Repeat steps 9–10 on the right and flatten.

12

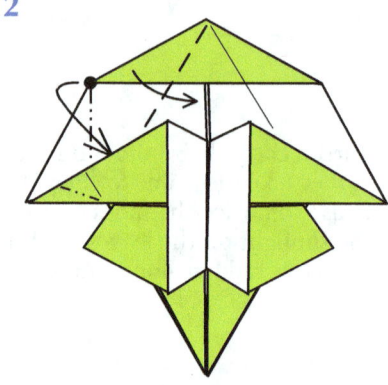

Tuck inside at the dot.

13

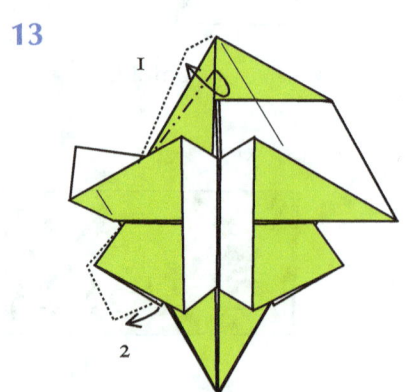

1. Slide out the top flap.
2. Slide out the hidden white paper.

14

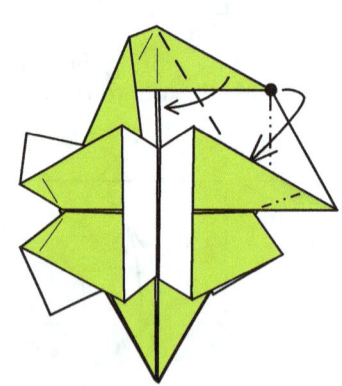

Repeat steps 12–113 on the right.

15

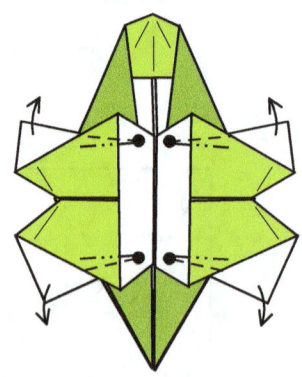

Pivot at the dots, folding on the dark paper which is hidden, to move the feet.

84 *Origami Gnomes of the Forest Wonderland*

16

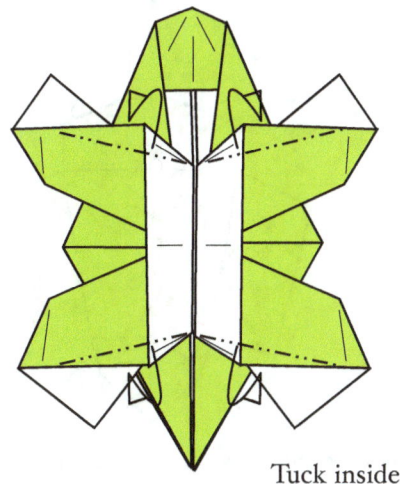

Tuck inside.

17

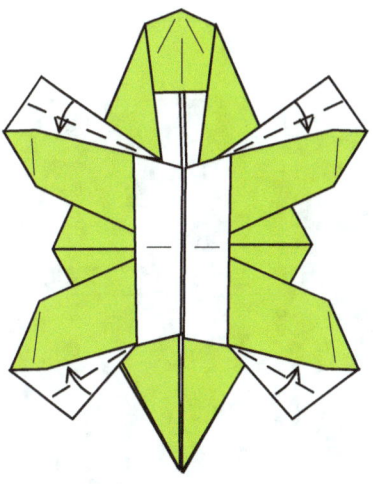

18

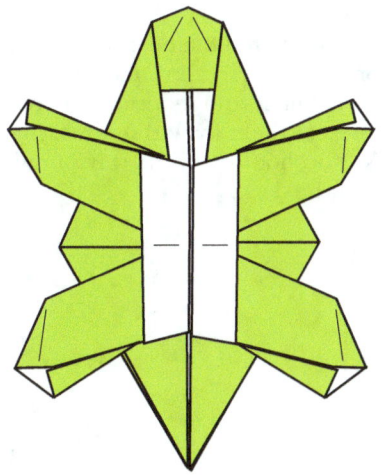

19

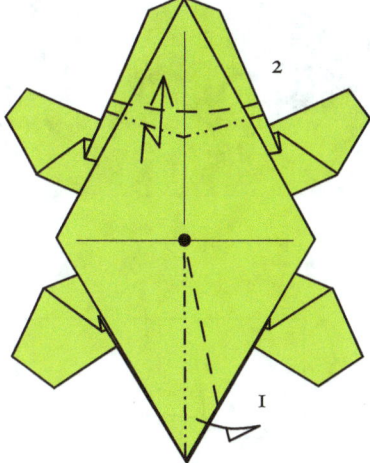

1. Puff out at the dot so the shell becomes 3D. Mountain-fold along the crease.
2. This is similar to a pleat fold.

20

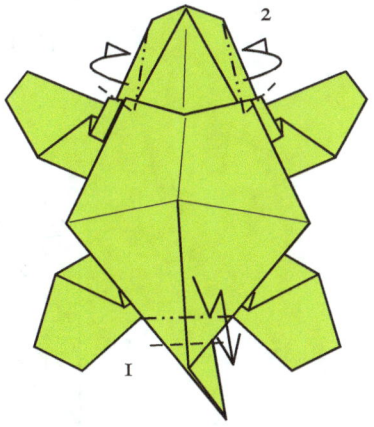

1. Pleat-fold.
2. Make thin squash folds.

21

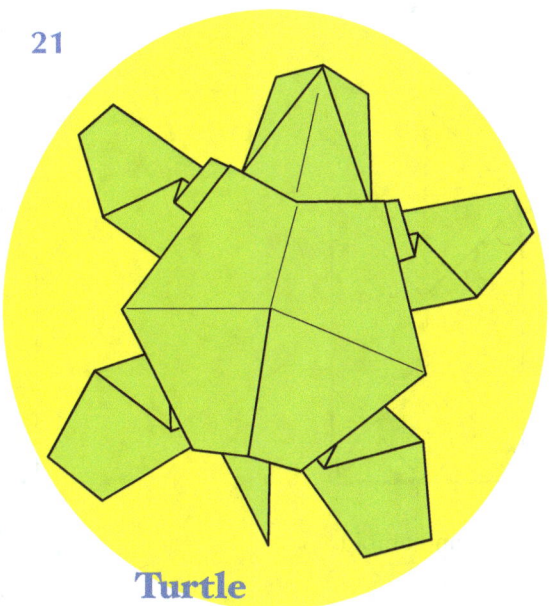

Turtle

Turtle 85

Owl

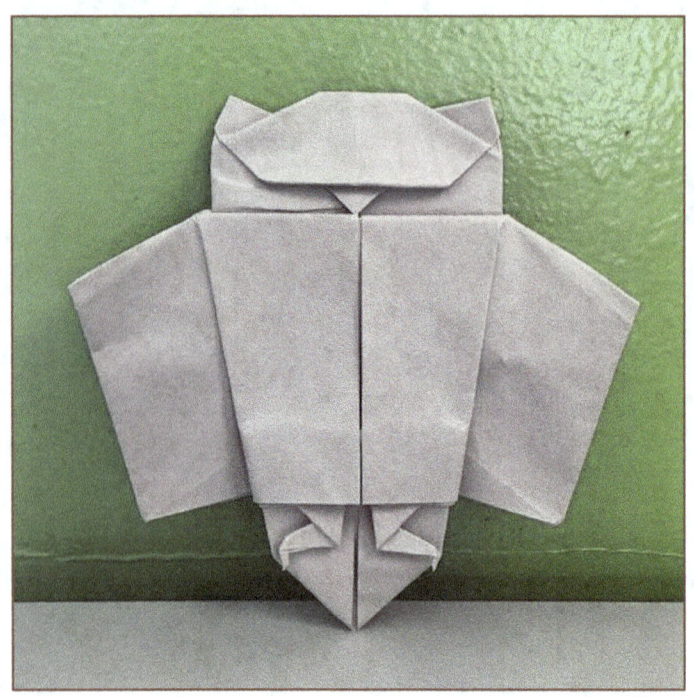

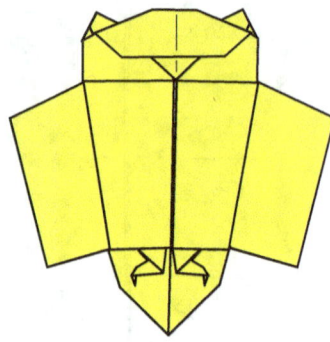

Owls are the super-silent flyers of the dark. All day long the sit very still in trees, looking like part of the bark, but when the sun goes down, they open their huge round eyes and swoop in the dark.

Owls have incredible hearing and excellent night vision, so they can spot mice, insects, and frogs even in almost total darkness. Their soft, special features let them fly without making a sound. An owl's "hoo-hoo" call is its way of talking to other owls in the dark.

1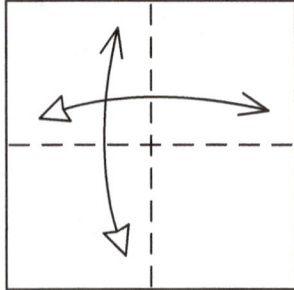
Fold and unfold.

2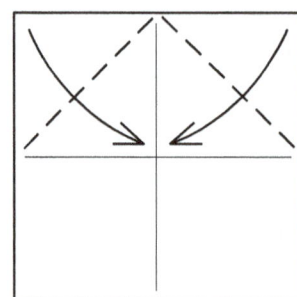

3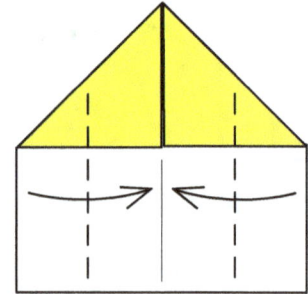
Fold to the center.

4
Fold and unfold.

5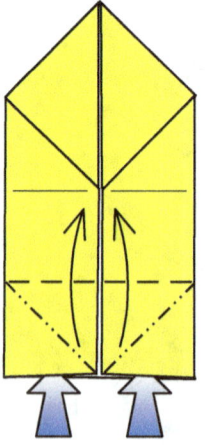
Make squash folds.

6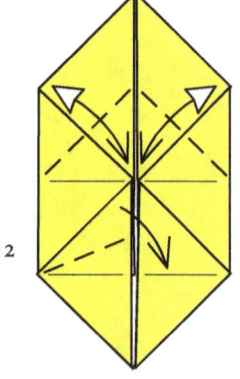
1. Fold and unfold.
2. Fold on the left.

86 *Origami Gnomes of the Forest Wonderland*

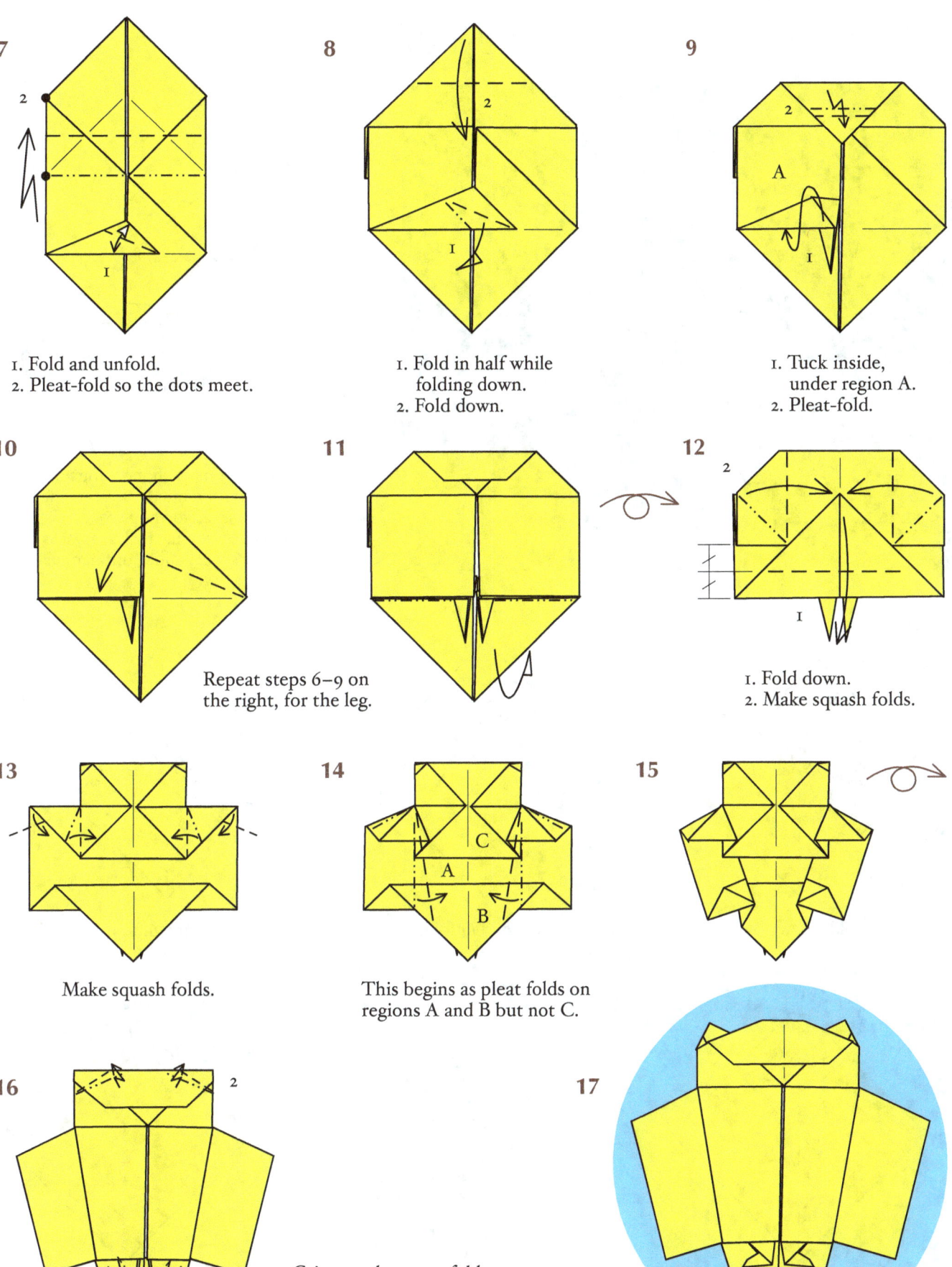

Robin

The robin greets each morning with a cheerful song, a reminder to start the day in a happy way as you hop around. When a robin is pecking in the leaves, it is looking for joy in simple, ordinary places.

1. Fold and unfold.

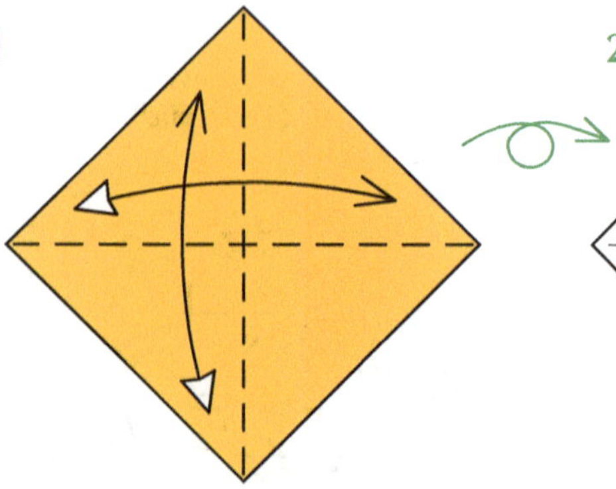

2. Fold and unfold.

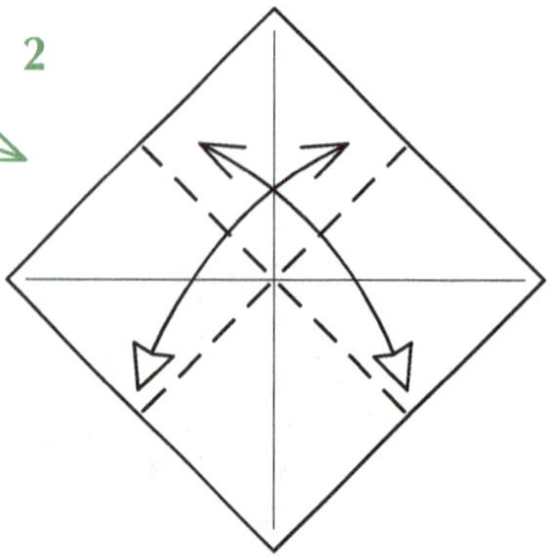

3. Fold and unfold.

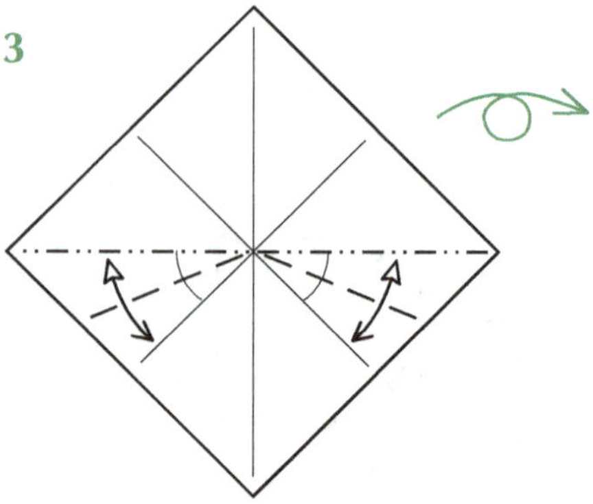

4. Bring the upper dot to the line.

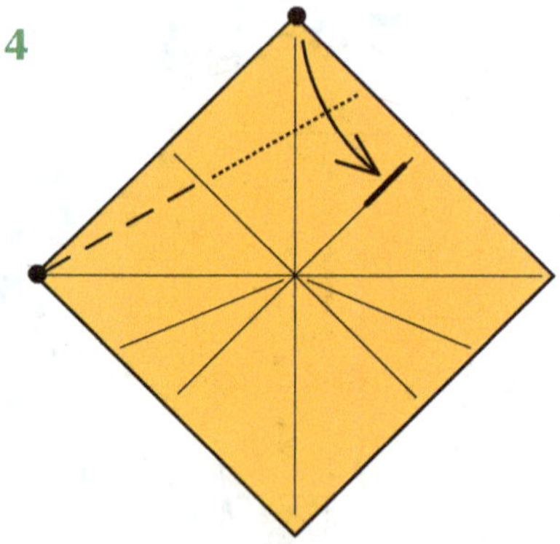

5. Unfold.

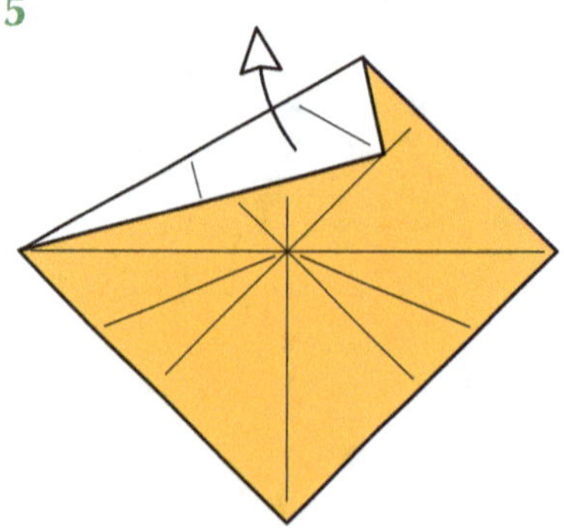

6. Repeat steps 4–5 on the right.

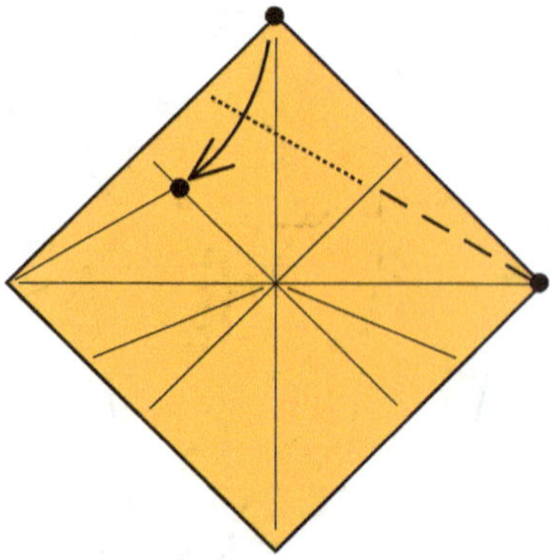

88 *Origami Gnomes of the Forest Wonderland*

7

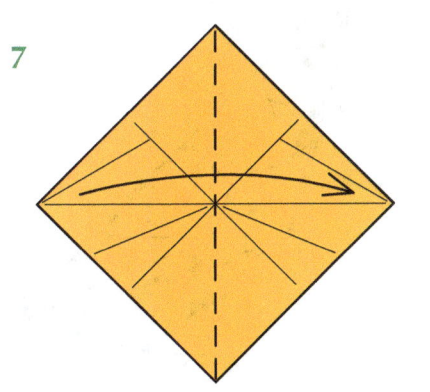

8

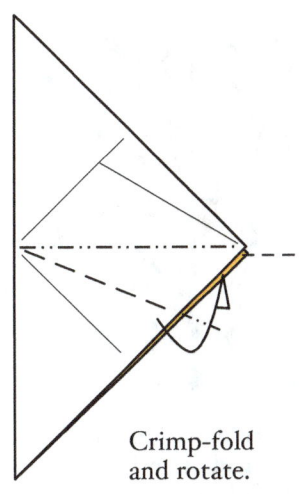

Crimp-fold and rotate.

9

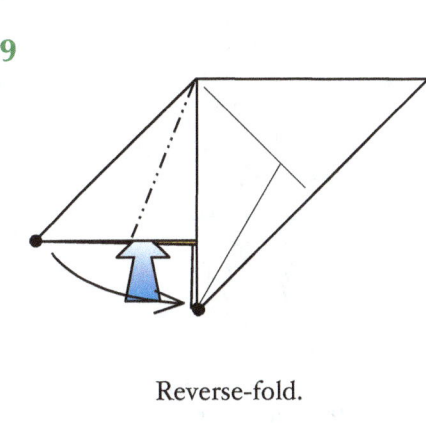

Reverse-fold.

10

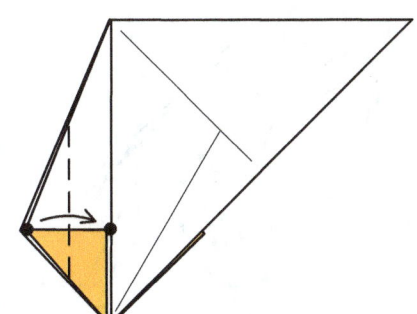

Repeat behind.

11

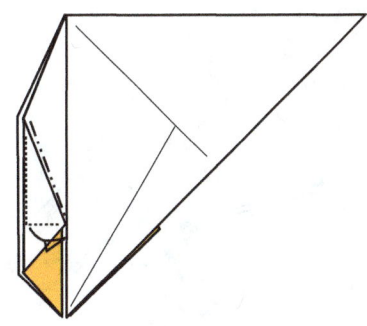

Fold the hidden layer inside. Repeat behind.

12

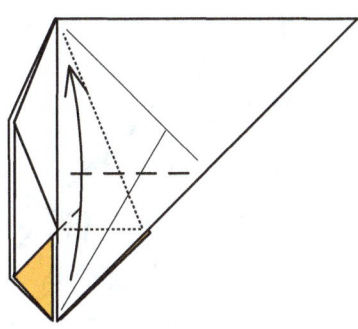

Squash-fold and repeat behind.

13

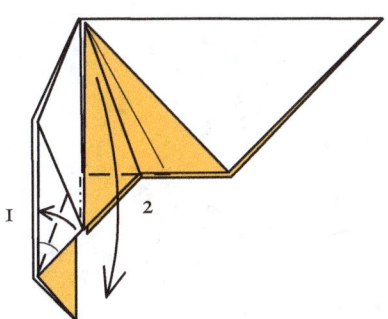

1. Reverse-fold.
2. Fold down.
Repeat behind.

14

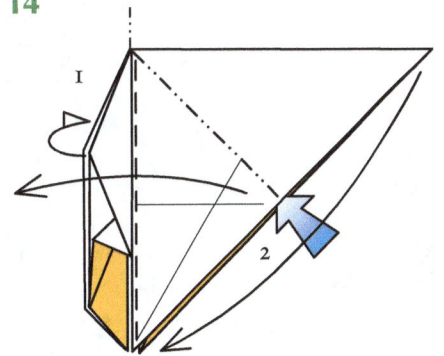

1. Fold behind.
2. Squash-fold.

15

Petal-fold. Fold along the hidden creases.

Robin 89

16

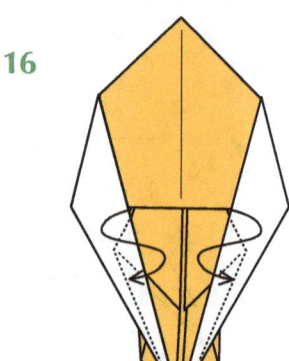

Bring the flaps in front of the white paper.

17

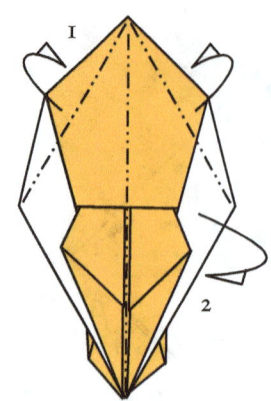

1. Fold behind on the left and right.
2. Fold in half. Rotate.

18

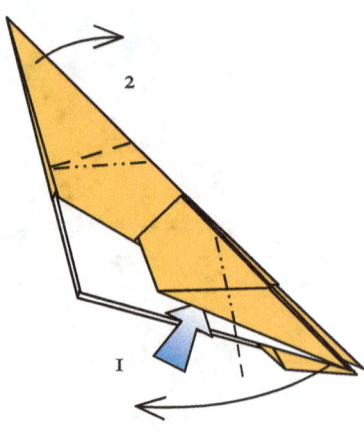

1. Reverse-fold, repeat behind.
2. Crimp-fold.

19

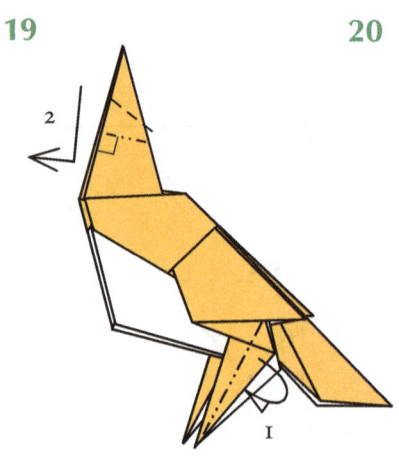

1. Fold inside, repeat behind.
2. Crimp-fold.

20

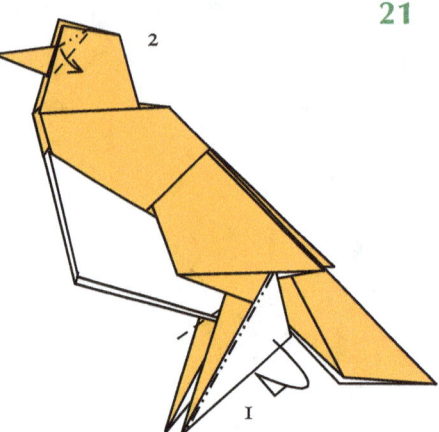

1. Reverse-fold.
2. Squash-fold. Repeat behind.

21

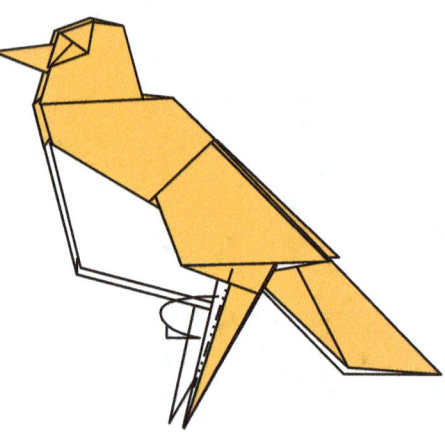

Reverse-fold, repeat behind.

22

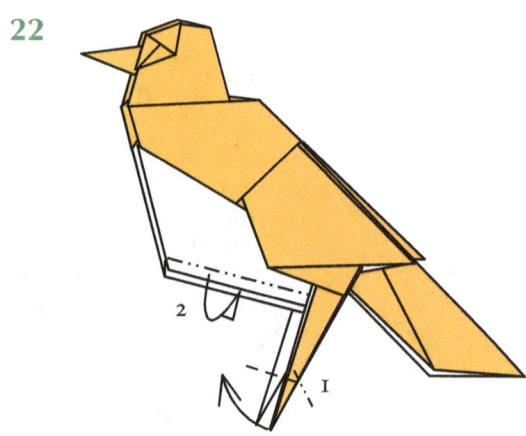

1. Crimp-fold.
2. Fold inside. Repeat behind.

23

Robin

90   *Origami Gnomes of the Forest Wonderland*

Cardinal

The cardinal flashes bright red through the trees like a little lantern. It whispers to stand out, be brave, and bring color to a quiet day.

1

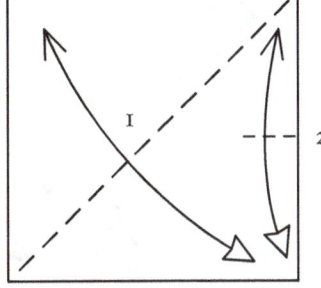

1. Fold and unfold.
2. Fold and unfold on the right.

2

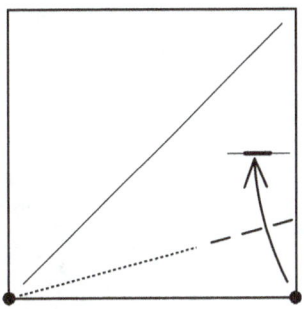

Bring the corner to the line.

3

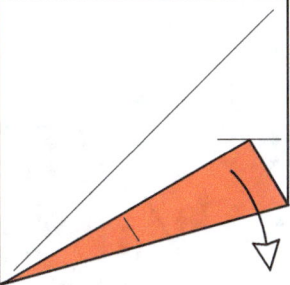

Unfold.

4

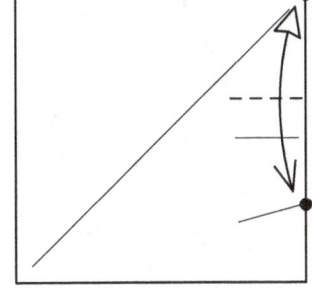

Fold and unfold.

5

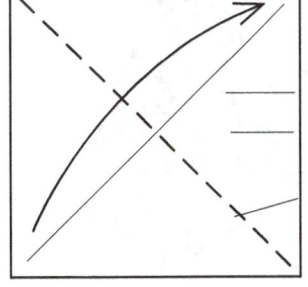

Rotate.

6

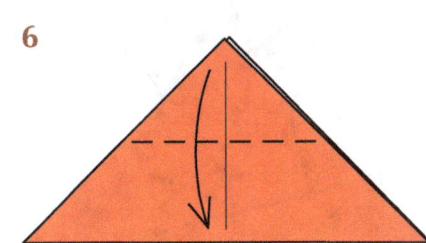

Fold the top layer.

Cardinal 91

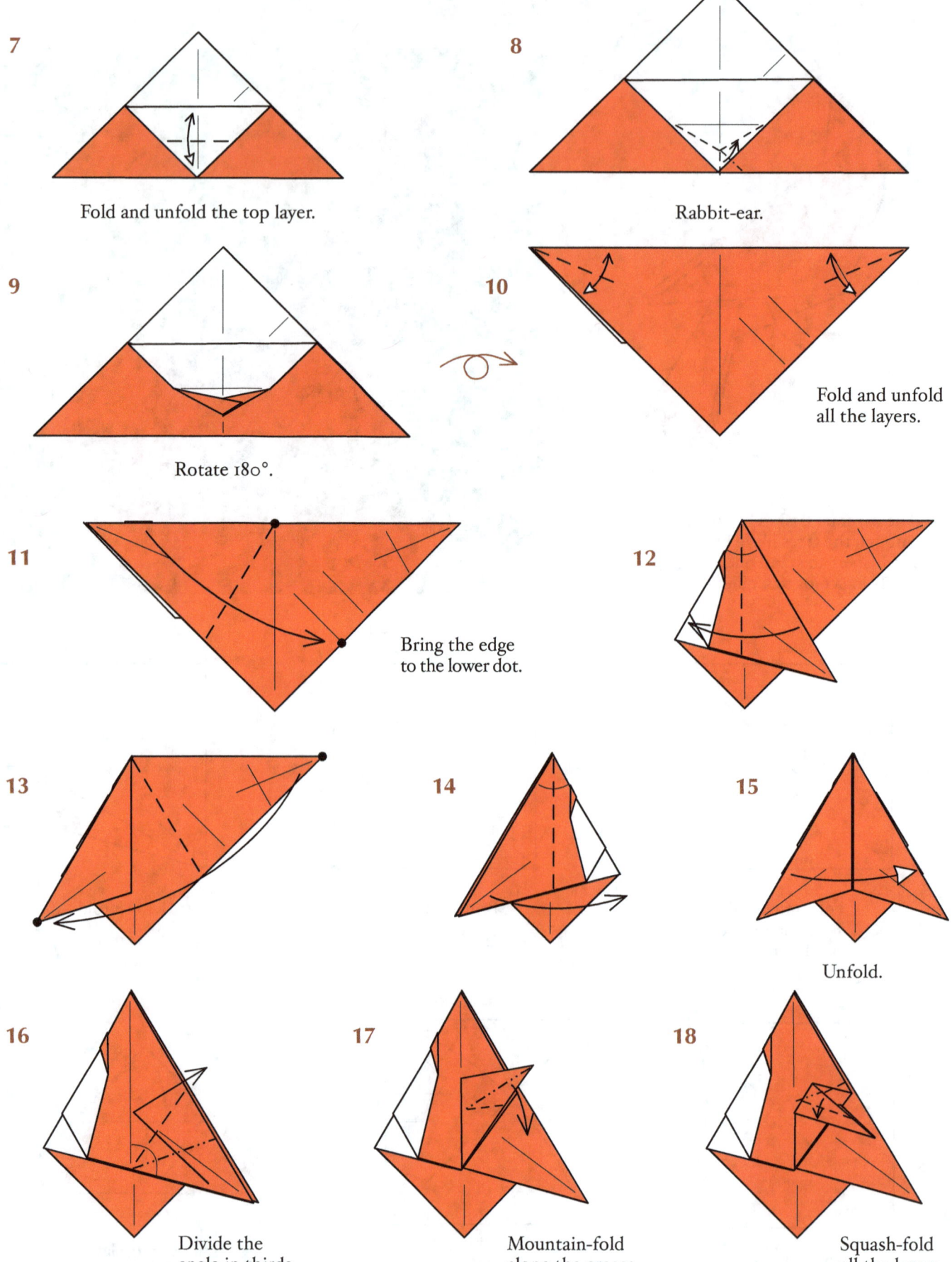

92 *Origami Gnomes of the Forest Wonderland*

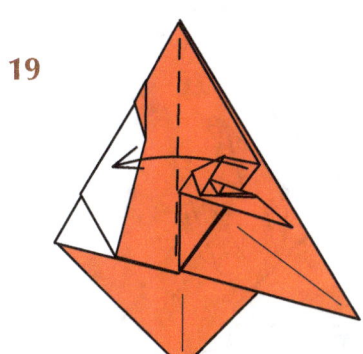

19

20

Repeat steps 15–19 on the right.

21

Fold in half and rotate.

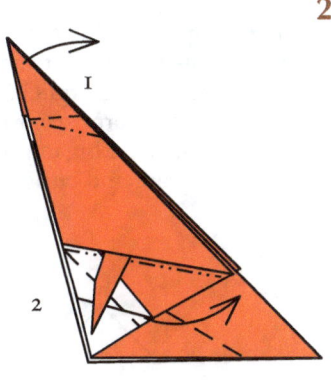

22

1. Crimp-fold.
2. Reverse-fold, repeat behind.

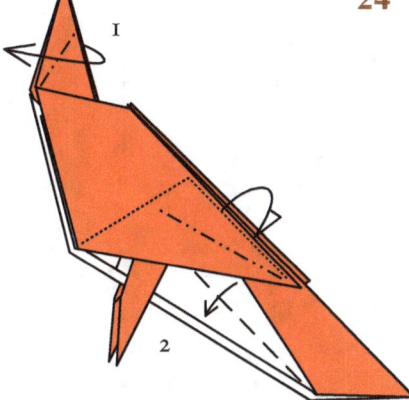

23

1. Pull out the top layers.
2. Reverse-fold.
Repeat behind.

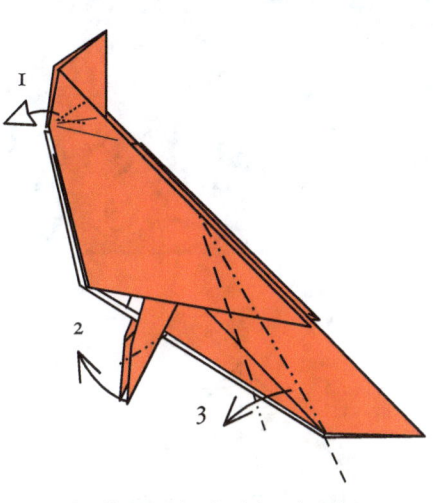

24

1. Pull out the hidden beak.
2. Reverse-fold, repeat behind.
3. Crimp-fold.

25

1. Fold along the creases with soft folds. Repeat behind.
2. Reverse-fold.

26

Cardinal

Cardinal 93

Rabbit

Rabbits dart, hop, and hide among the leaves, showing us to stay alert and explore playfully. They are quick, clever, and always ready for a surprise adventure. Even small feet can leave big impressions if you move with care and curiosity.

1

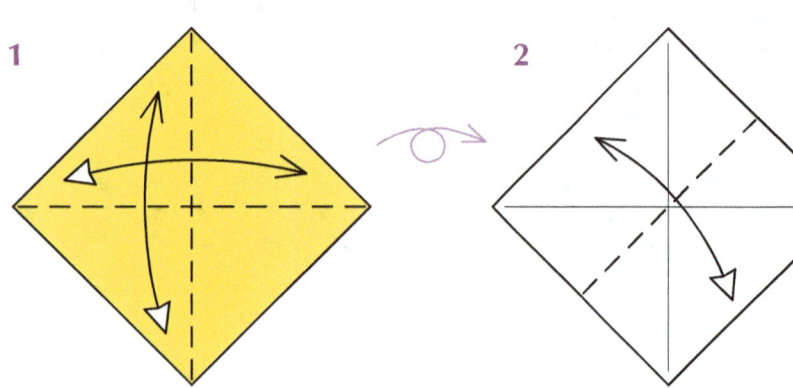

Fold and unfold.

2

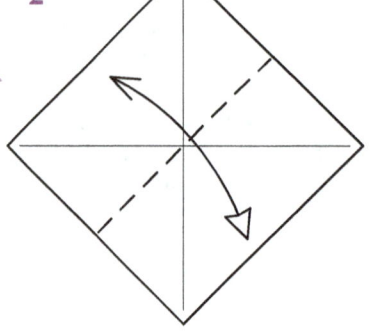

Fold and unfold.

3

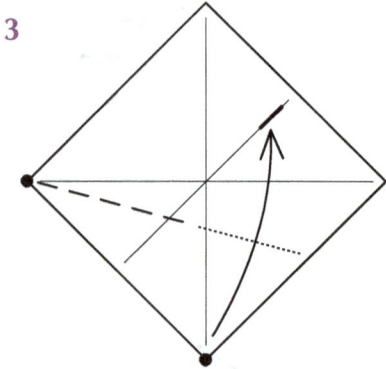

Bring the corner to the line.

4

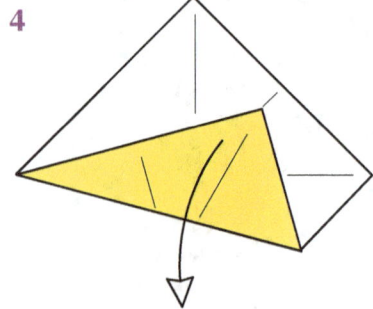

Unfold and rotate 180°.

5

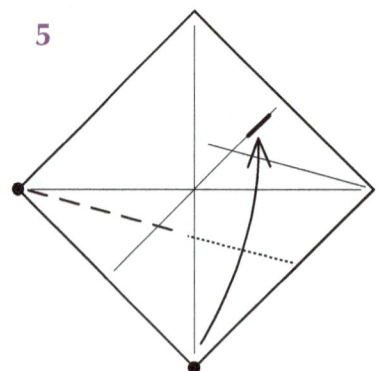

Repeat steps 3–4.

6

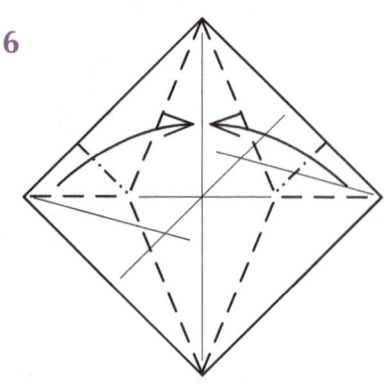

Make rabbit ears.

94   *Origami Gnomes of the Forest Wonderland*

7

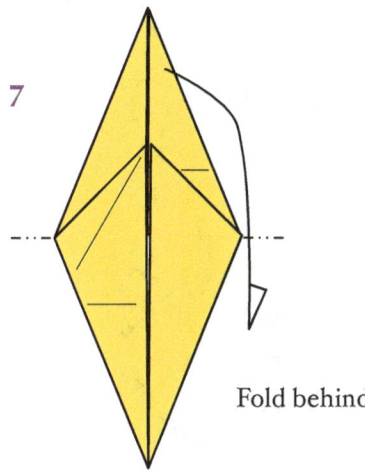

Fold behind.

8

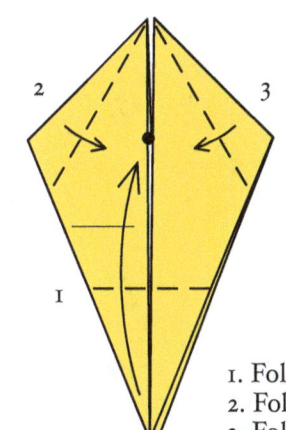

1. Fold the top flap.
2. Fold along the crease.
3. Fold along the hidden crease on the back.

9

1. Fold down.
2. Fold up from behind.

10

1. Fold inside.
2. Unfold.

11

1. Fold inside along the creases.
2. Fold the flap on the left.

12

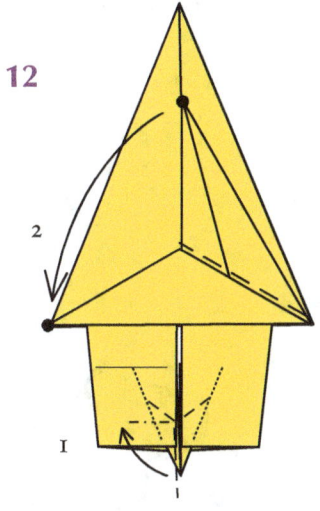

1. Rabbit-ear so the flap goes to the top.
2. Fold the flap on the right.

13

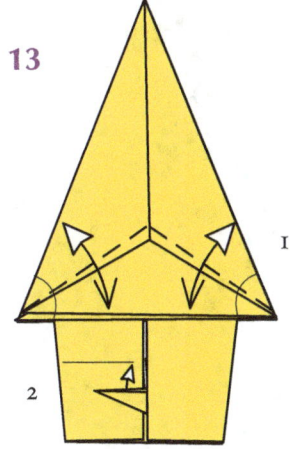

1. Fold and unfold.
2. Pull out on both sides.

14

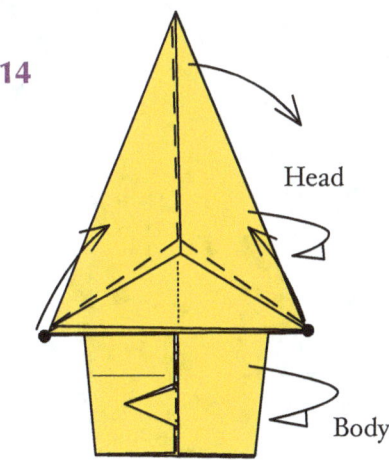

Fold the head and body in half while lifting the ears up, shown at the dots. Rotate.

15

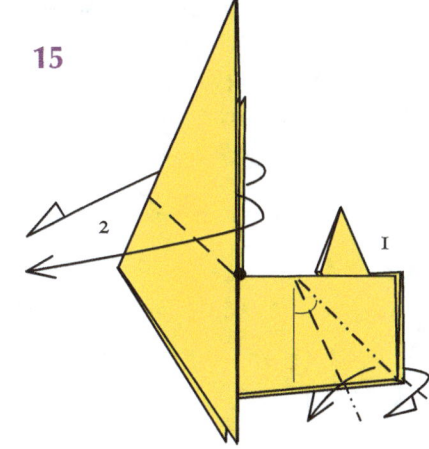

1. Crimp-fold.
2. Outside-reverse-fold.

Rabbit 95

16

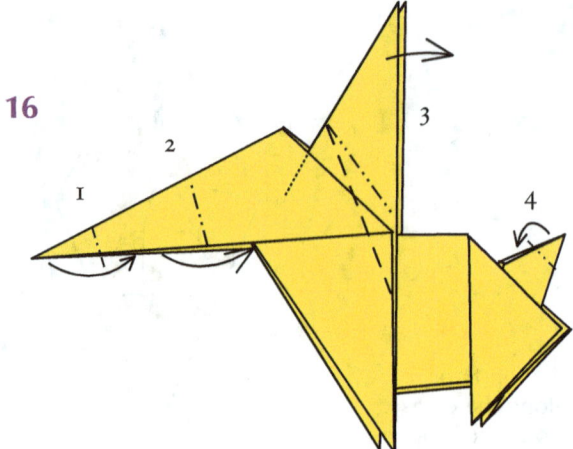

1. Reverse-fold.
2. Reverse-fold.
3. Pleat-fold, repeat behind.
4. Reverse-fold.

17

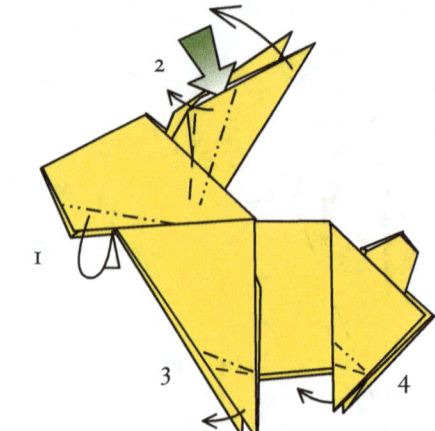

1. Fold inside.
2. Squash-fold.
3. Crimp-fold.
4. Crimp-fold.
Repeat behind.

18

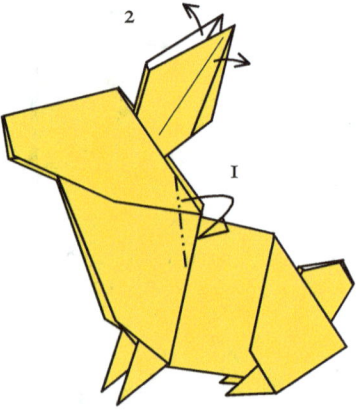

1. Fold inside, repeat behind.
2. Spread the ears.

19

Rabbit

96 *Origami Gnomes of the Forest Wonderland*

Squirrel

Squirrels gather nuts and prepare for the seasons ahead, teaching us to plan, save, and enjoy things along the way. They leap from branch to branch with courage and curiosity.

1

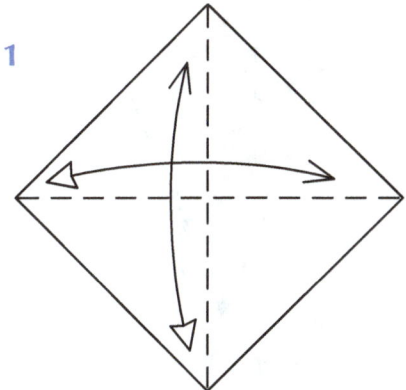

Fold and unfold.

2

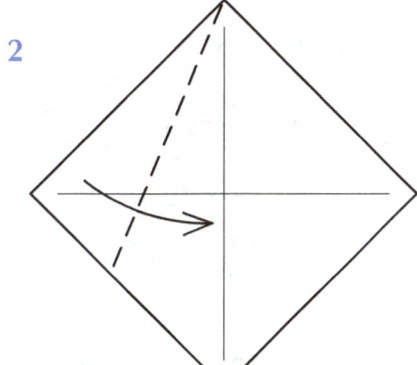

Fold to the center.

3

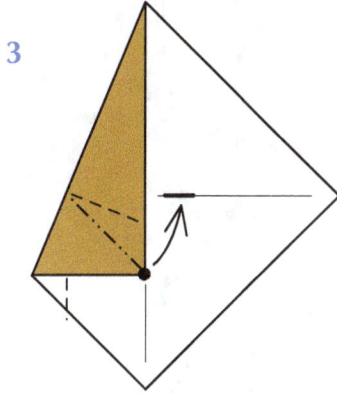

Squash-fold so the dot meets the line.

4

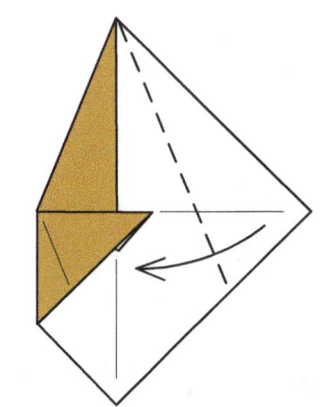

Repeat steps 2–3 on the right.

5

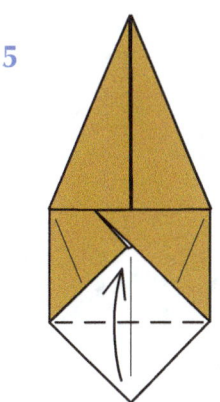

6

Fold to the center.

Squirrel 97

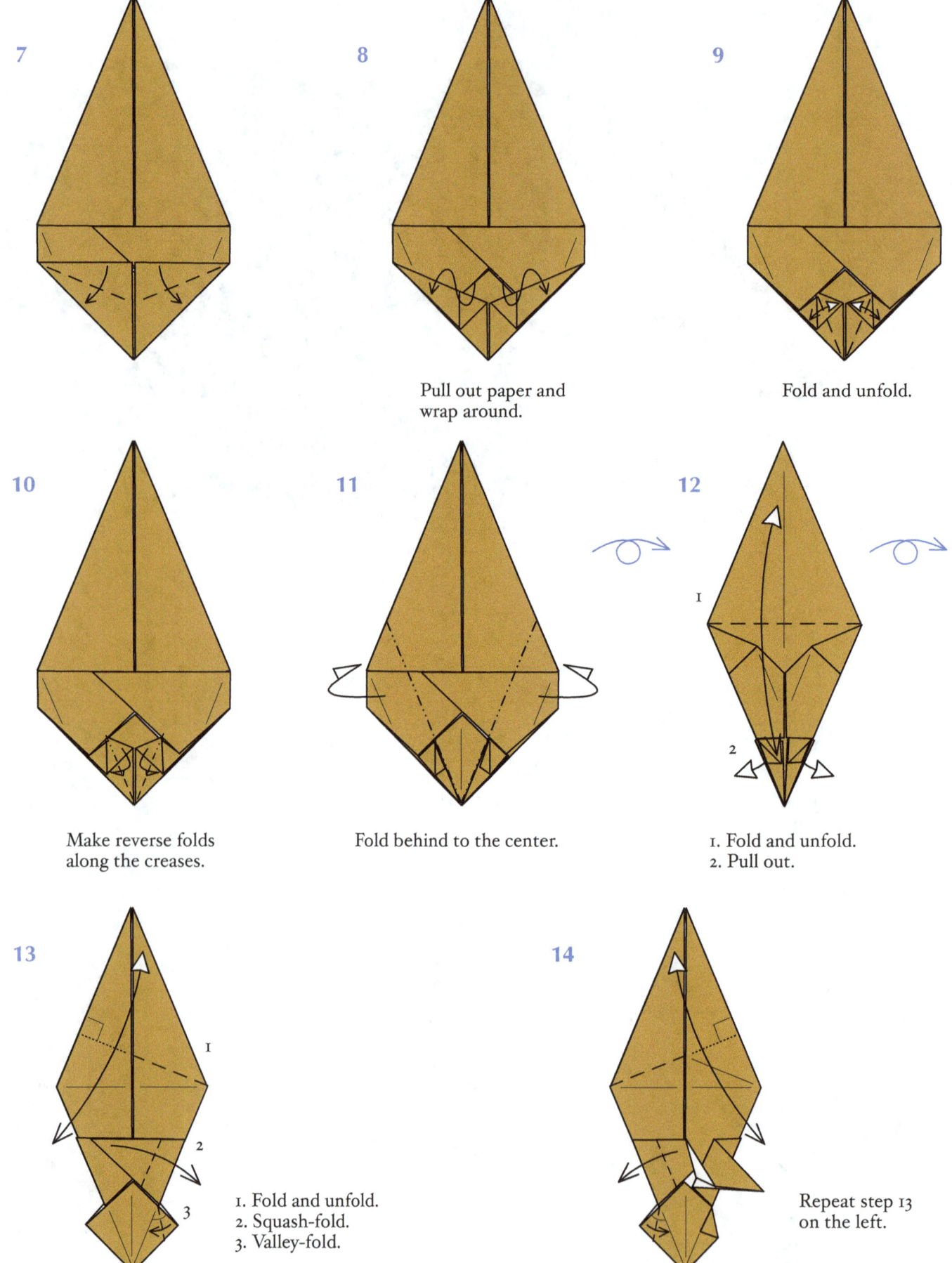

98　*Origami Gnomes of the Forest Wonderland*

15

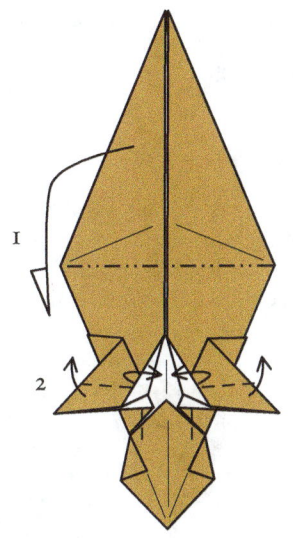

1. Fold behind.
2. Fold up with small squash folds.

16

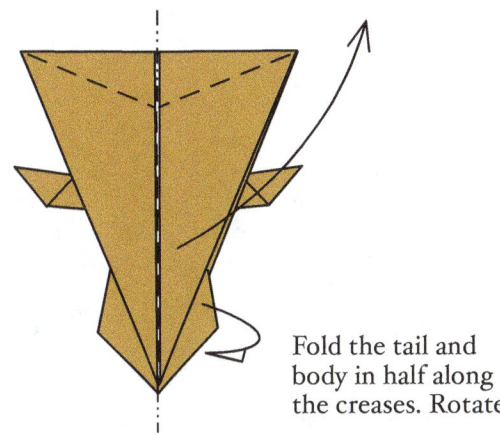

Fold the tail and body in half along the creases. Rotate.

17

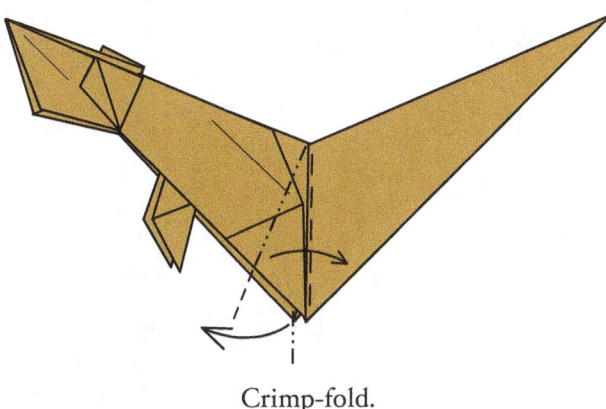

Crimp-fold.

18

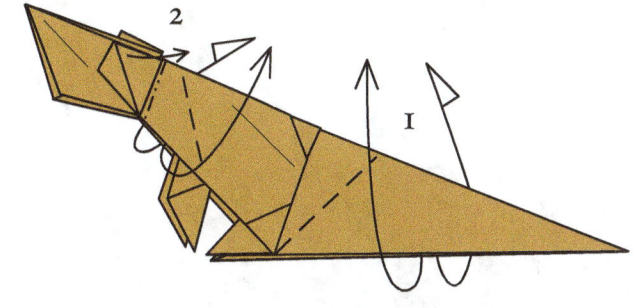

1. Outside-reverse-fold.
2. Crimp-fold at the ears.

19

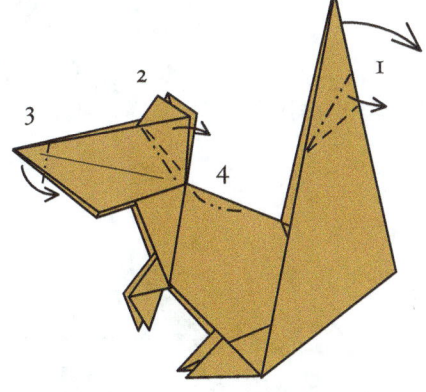

1. Outside-reverse-fold and spread.
2. Pleat-fold, repeat behind.
3. Reverse-fold.
4. Shape the back.

20

Squirrel

Squirrel 99

Deep in the Forest

Deep in the forest live gnomes who play tricks, tinker with clever devices, and conjure enchantments—all while caring for the woodland around them. Their mischief keeps the forest lively: animals grow accustomed to their playful surprises, even the oldest trees seems to notice the gnome's antics. They build miniature bridges and ladders for squirrels and rabbits, waterwheels and tiny mills to tend to ponds, and glowing lanterns to guide nocturnal animals.

Jorlip Snickfern

Jorlip paints smiley faces on stones using berry juice. As hikers pass by, the stones bounce around them, making squeaky sounds.

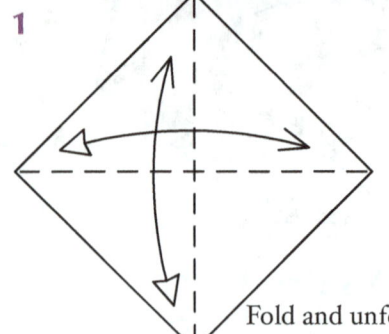

1

Fold and unfold.

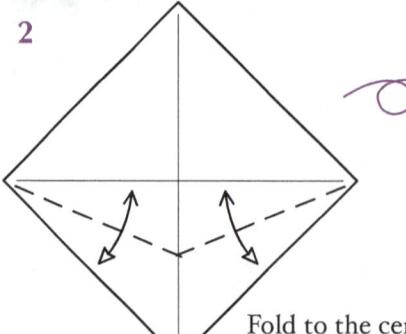

2

Fold to the center and unfold.

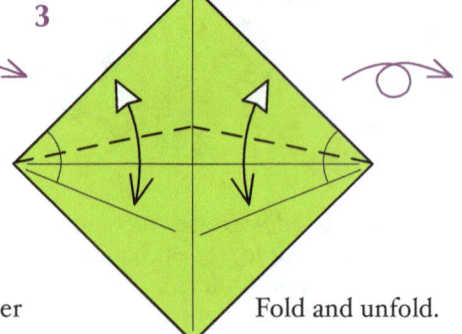

3

Fold and unfold.

100 *Origami Gnomes of the Forest Wonderland*

4

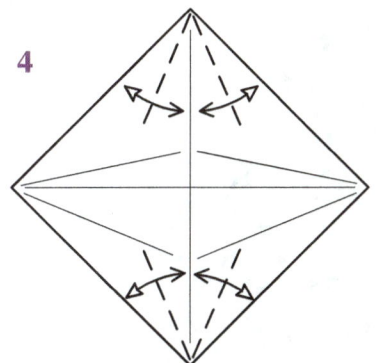

Fold to the center and unfold.

5

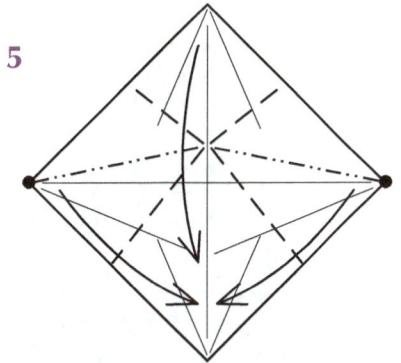

Mountain-fold along the creases and bring the dots to the vertical line in the center.

6

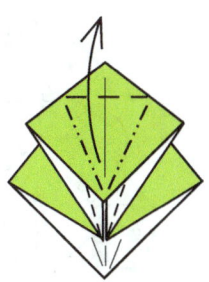

Petal-fold.

7

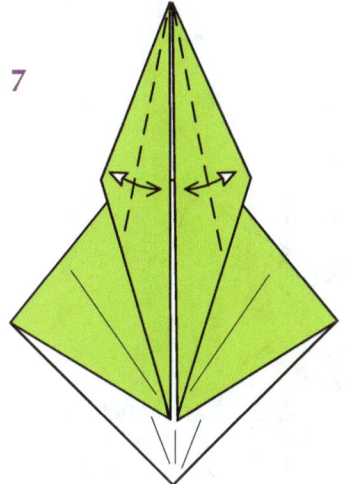

Fold to the center and unfold.

8

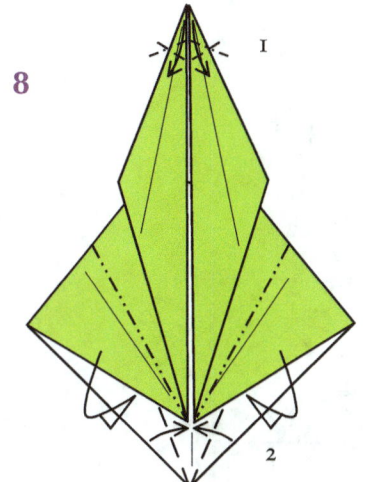

1. Spread.
2. Make reverse folds.

9

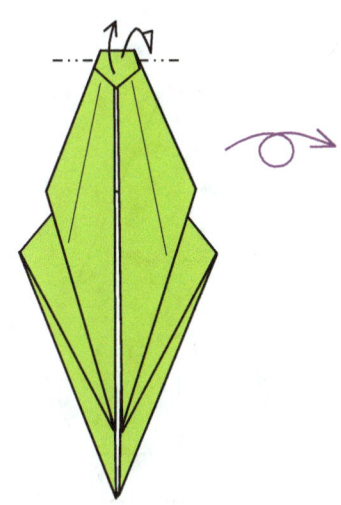

Fold behind and swing up from in front.

10

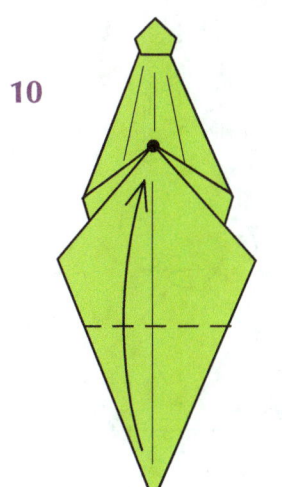

11

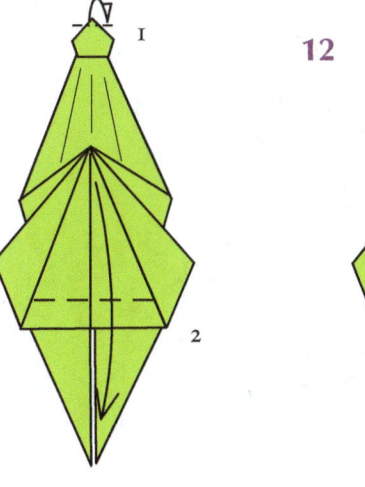

1. Fold behind.
2. Fold down near the bottom.

12

1. Fold and unfold.
2. Pull out to the dotted vertical lines.

13

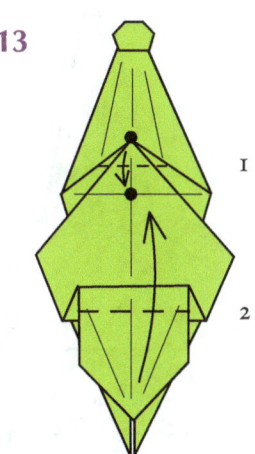

1. Fold down.
2. Fold up.

Jorlip Snickfern 101

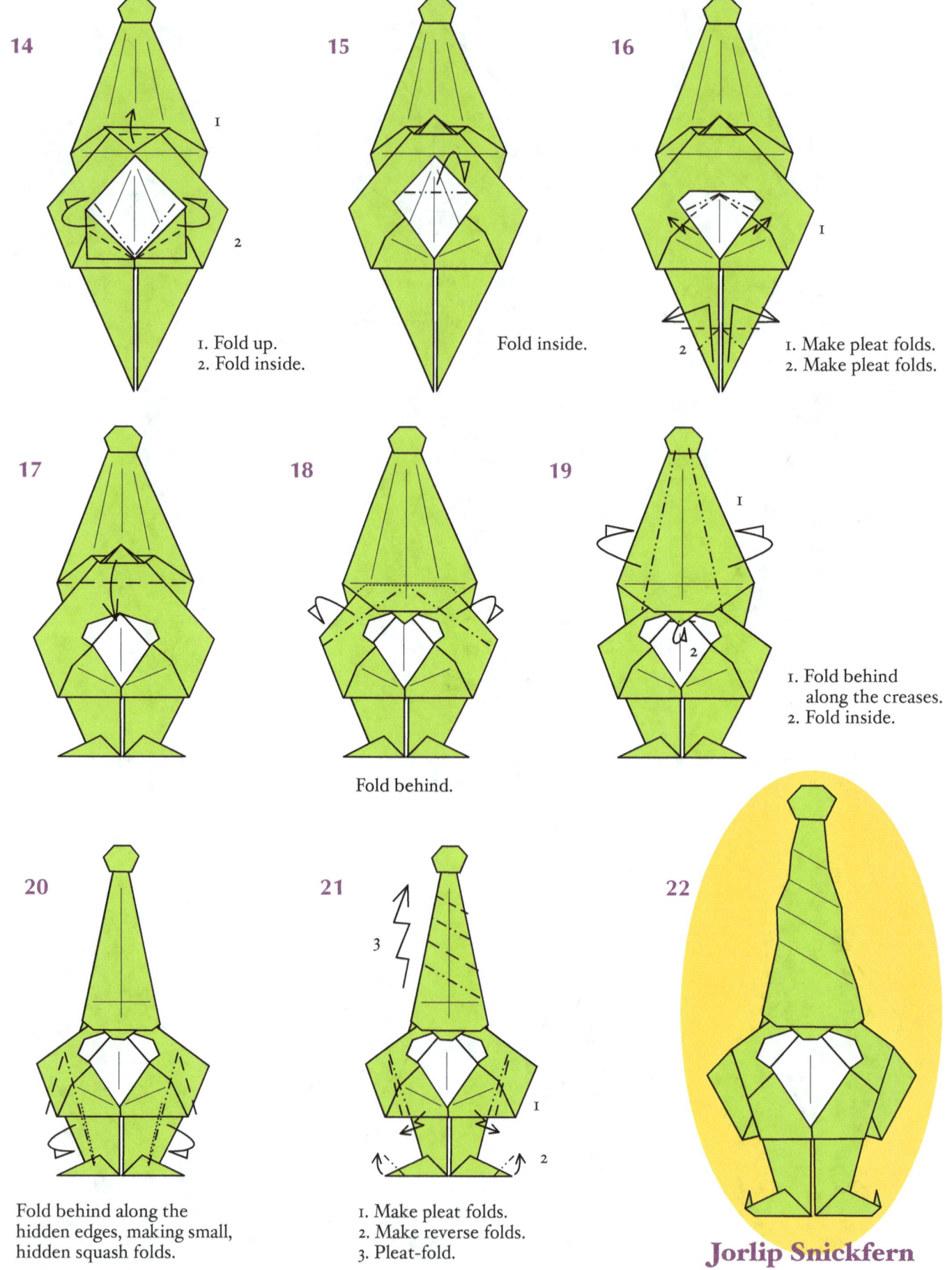

14
1. Fold up.
2. Fold inside.

15
Fold inside.

16
1. Make pleat folds.
2. Make pleat folds.

17

18
Fold behind.

19
1. Fold behind along the creases.
2. Fold inside.

20
Fold behind along the hidden edges, making small, hidden squash folds.

21
1. Make pleat folds.
2. Make reverse folds.
3. Pleat-fold.

22
Jorlip Snickfern

102   *Origami Gnomes of the Forest Wonderland*

Tipple Twiddlecap

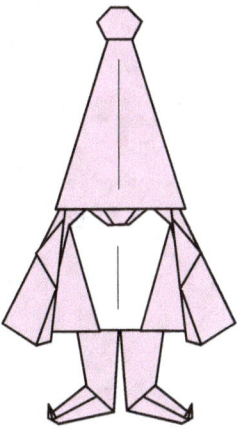

Tipple has a talent for accelerating plant growth, but only in the most inconvenient way. He can make a tiny sprout burst into a giant beanstalk overnight, or make someone's prized garden grow entirely upside down. He fashions meticulously shaped hedges to sprout enormous, comical mustaches and beards of white lilies. As Tipple says: "A tidy garden is a boring one, let things grow wild now and then, you might discover something wonderful."

1

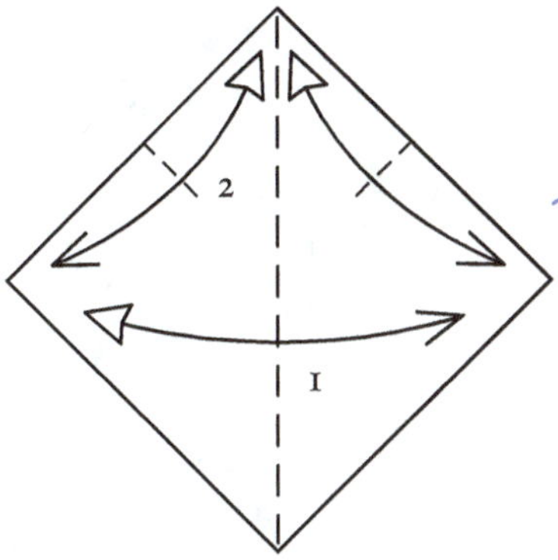

1. Fold and unfold.
2. Fold and unfold on the edges.

2

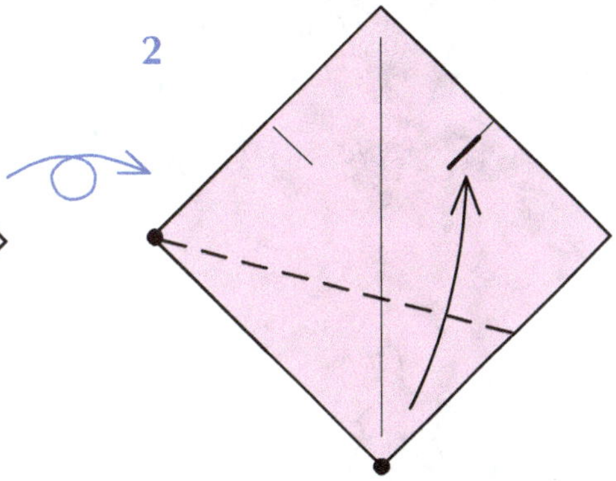

Bring the lower dot to the bold line.

3

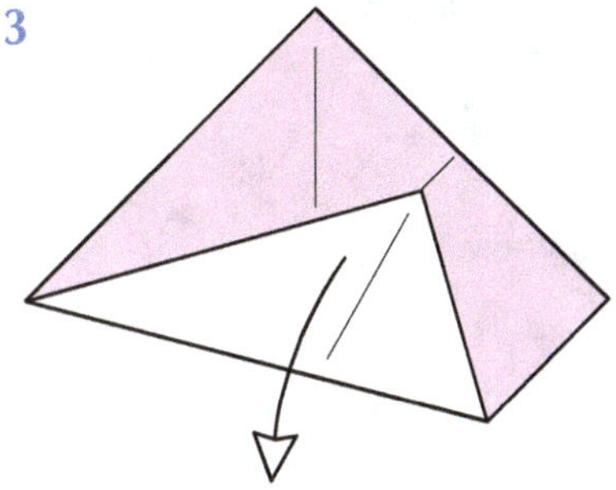

Unfold.

4

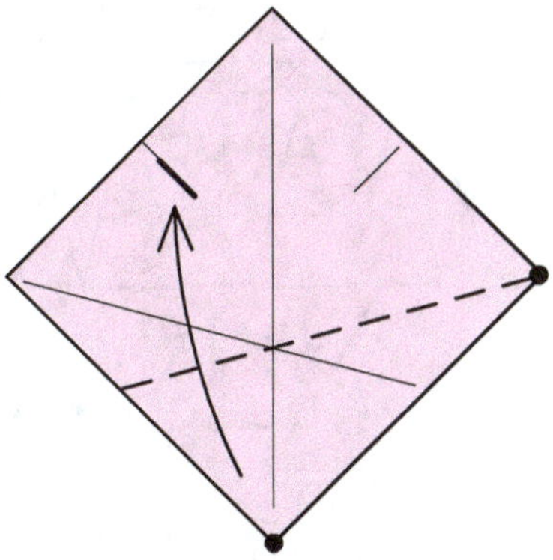

Repeat steps 2–3 in the opposite direction. Rotate 180°.

5

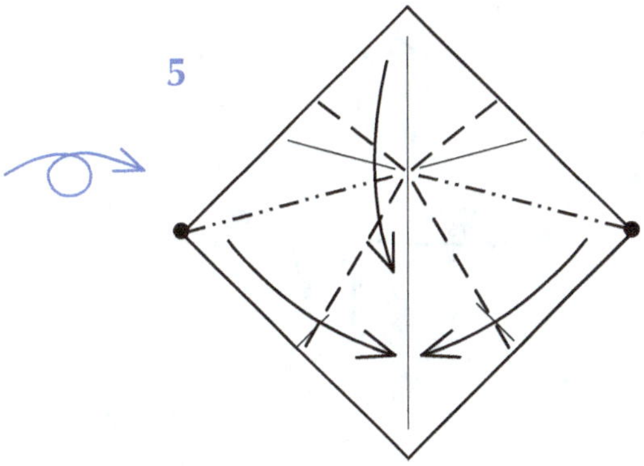

Bring the dots to the center line.

6

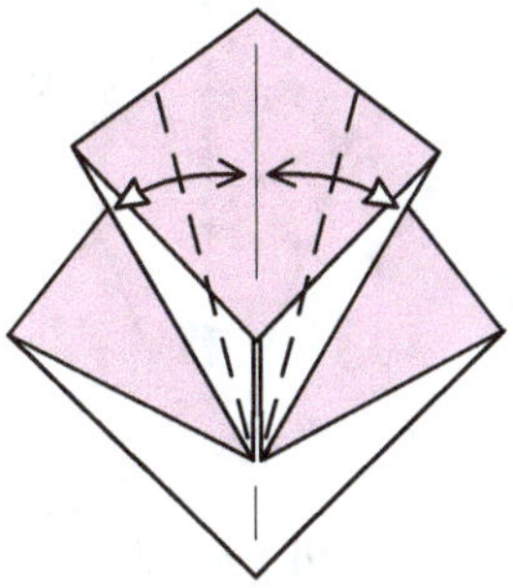

Fold to the center and unfold.

Tipple Twiddlecap 103

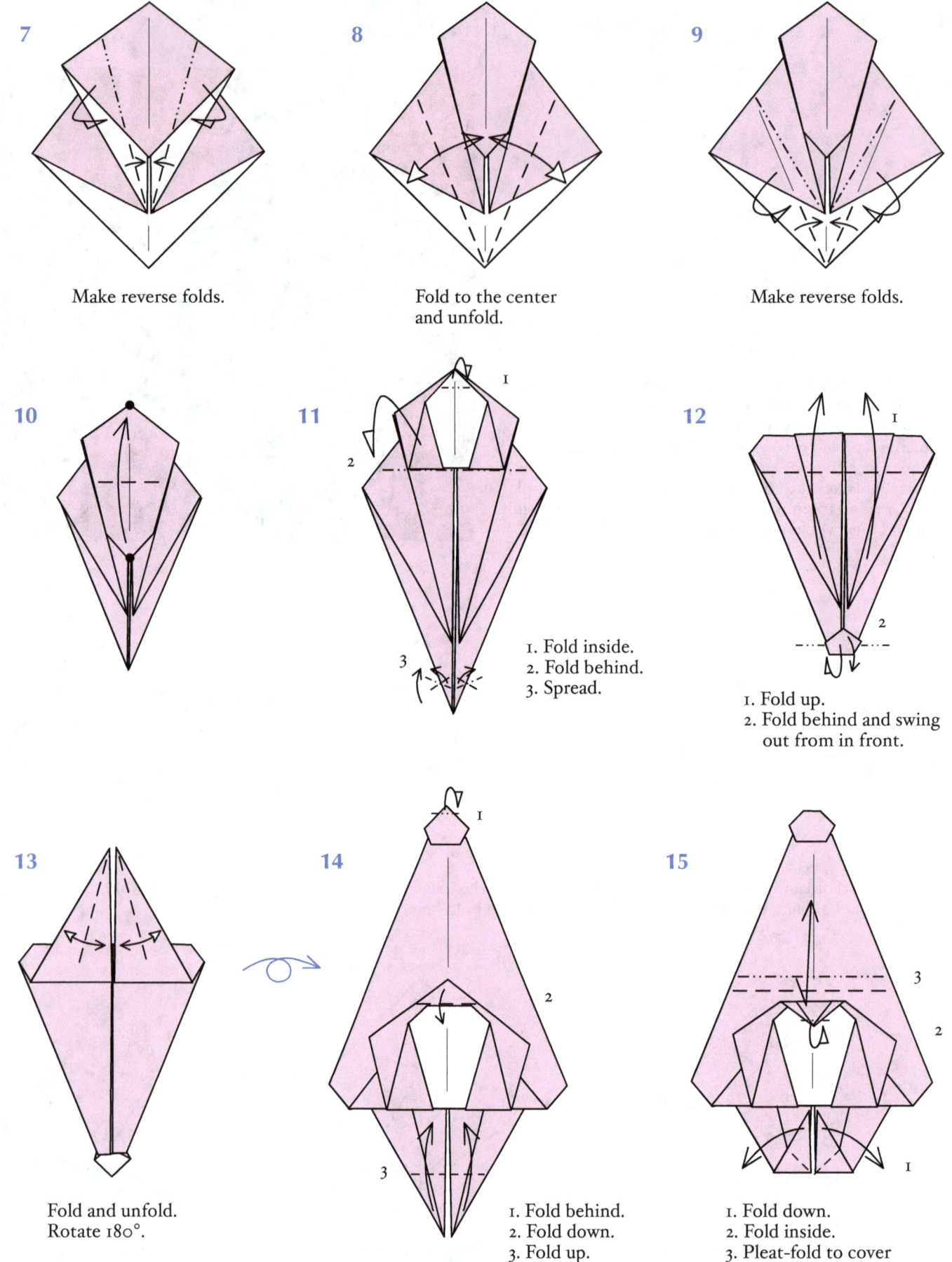

104 *Origami Gnomes of the Forest Wonderland*

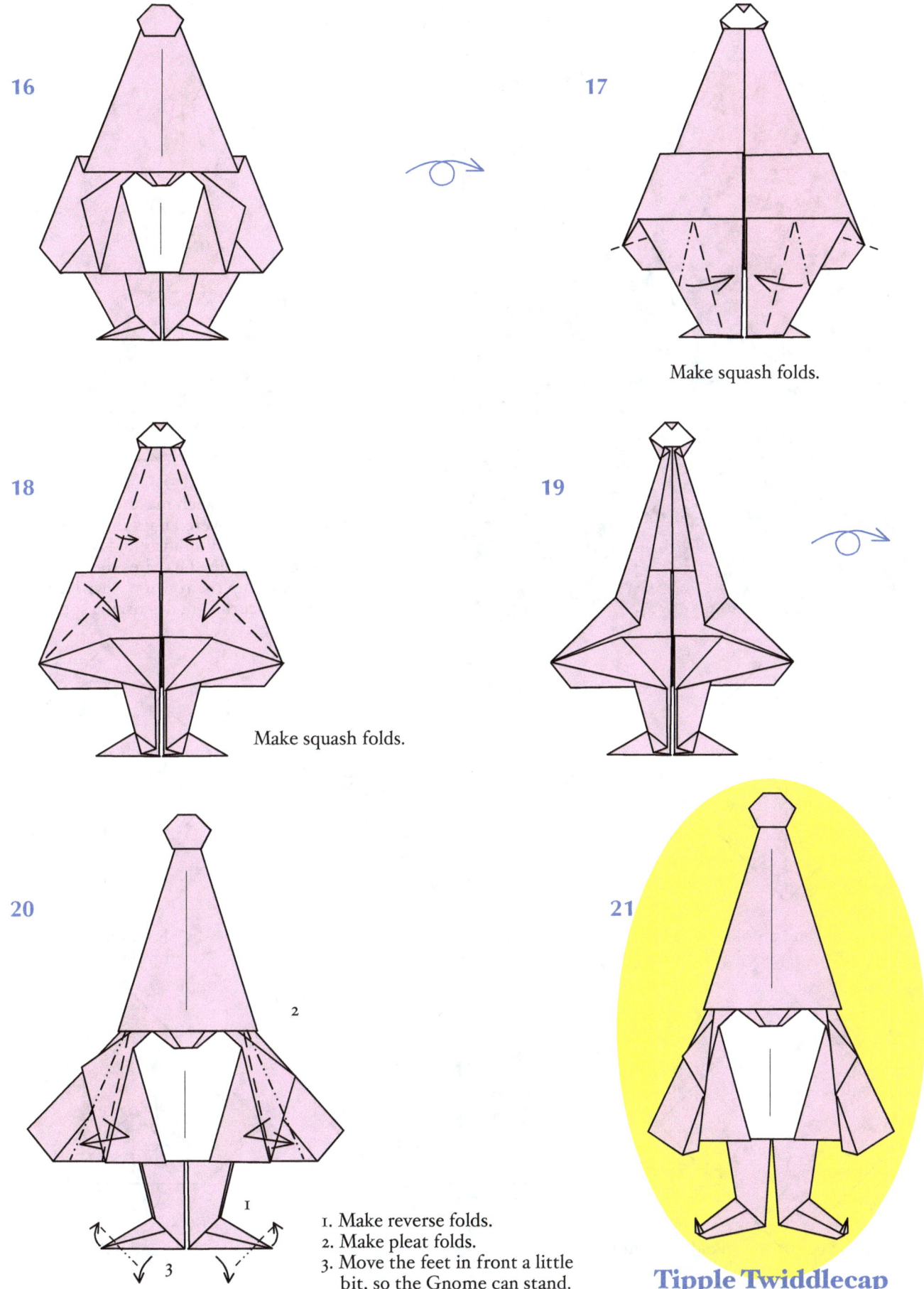

16

17 Make squash folds.

18 Make squash folds.

19

20
1. Make reverse folds.
2. Make pleat folds.
3. Move the feet in front a little bit, so the Gnome can stand.

21 **Tipple Twiddlecap**

Tipple Twiddlecap 105

Cloverleaf Sparklebranch

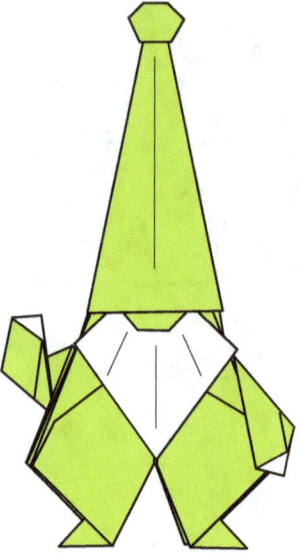

Cloverleaf Sparklebranch makes snacks of dried berries and moss-covered nuts and hides them under roots so hungry animals find treats on cold nights. Every morning he scares the darkness away and wakes up the roosters, inviting them to sing their cheerful good-morning song.

1

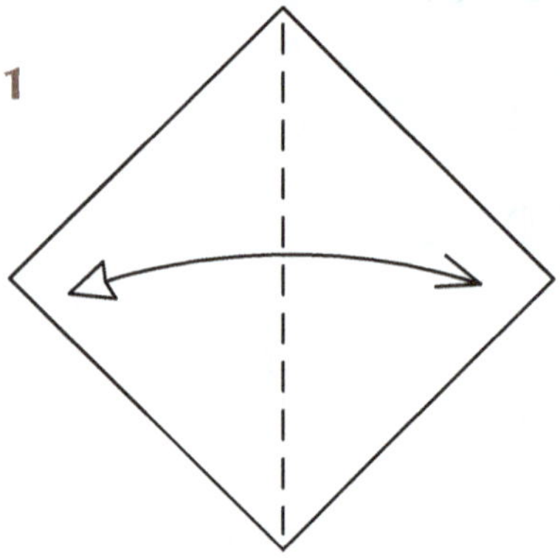

Fold and unfold.

2

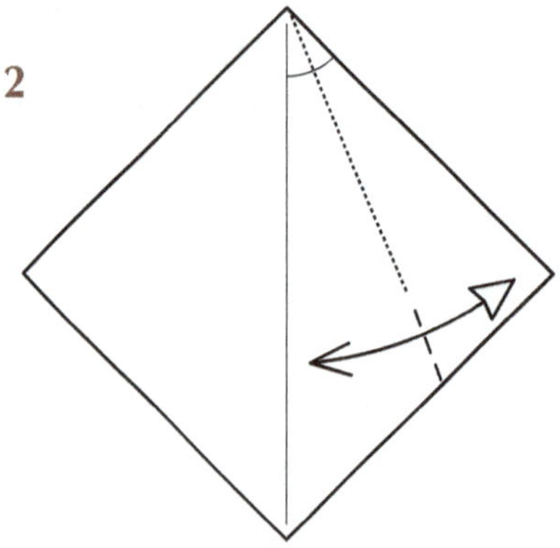

Fold and unfold on the edge.

3

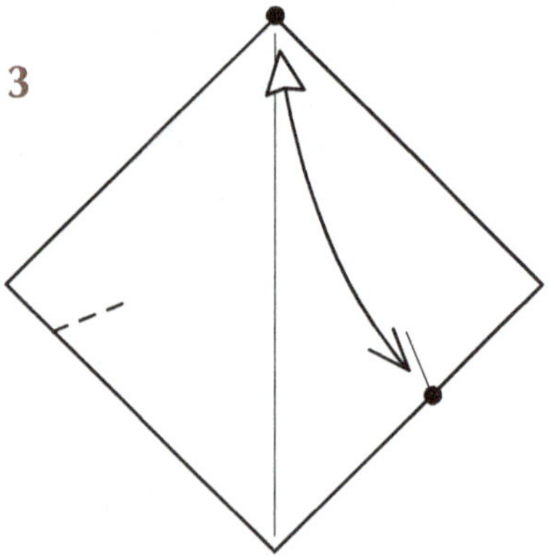

Fold and unfold on the edge.

4

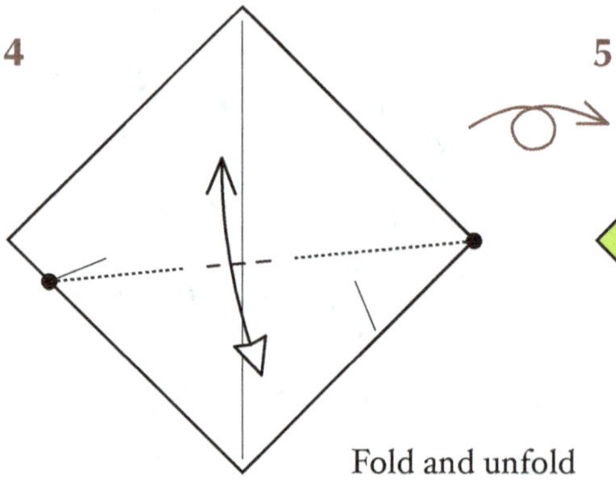

Fold and unfold on the diagonal. Rotate 180°.

5

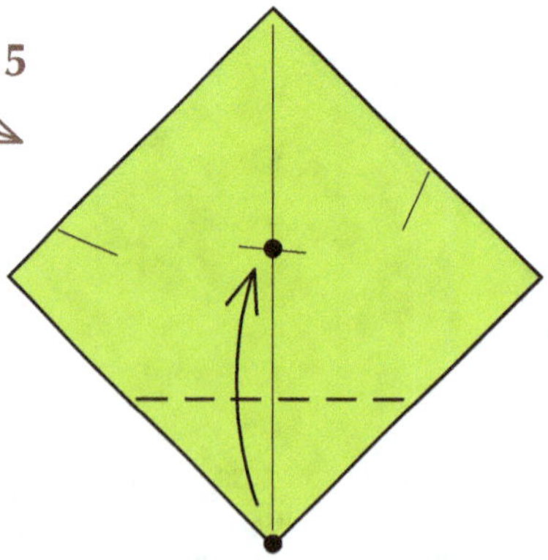

6

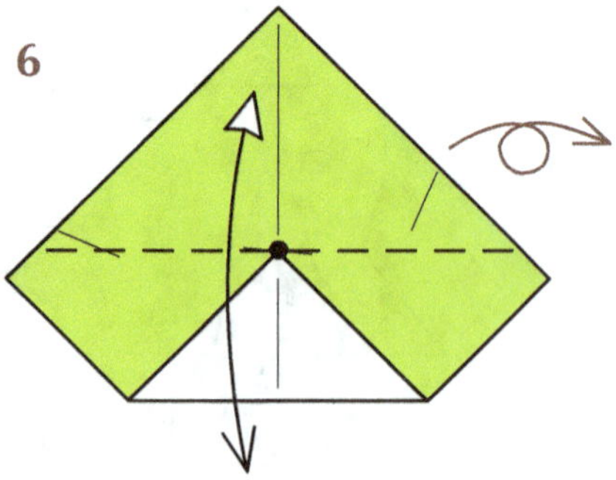

Fold and unfold.

106   *Origami Gnomes of the Forest Wonderland*

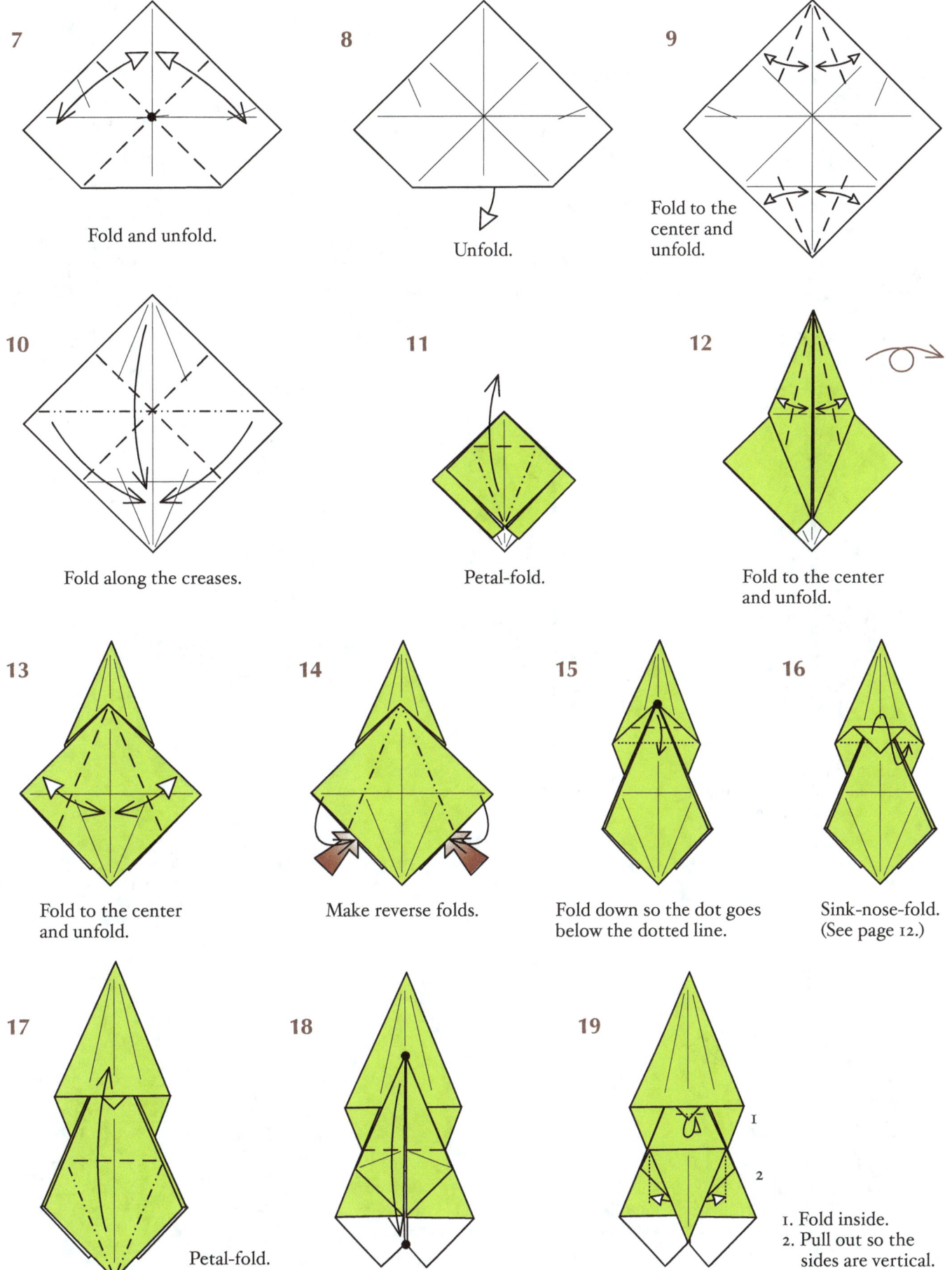

Cloverleaf Sparklebranch 107

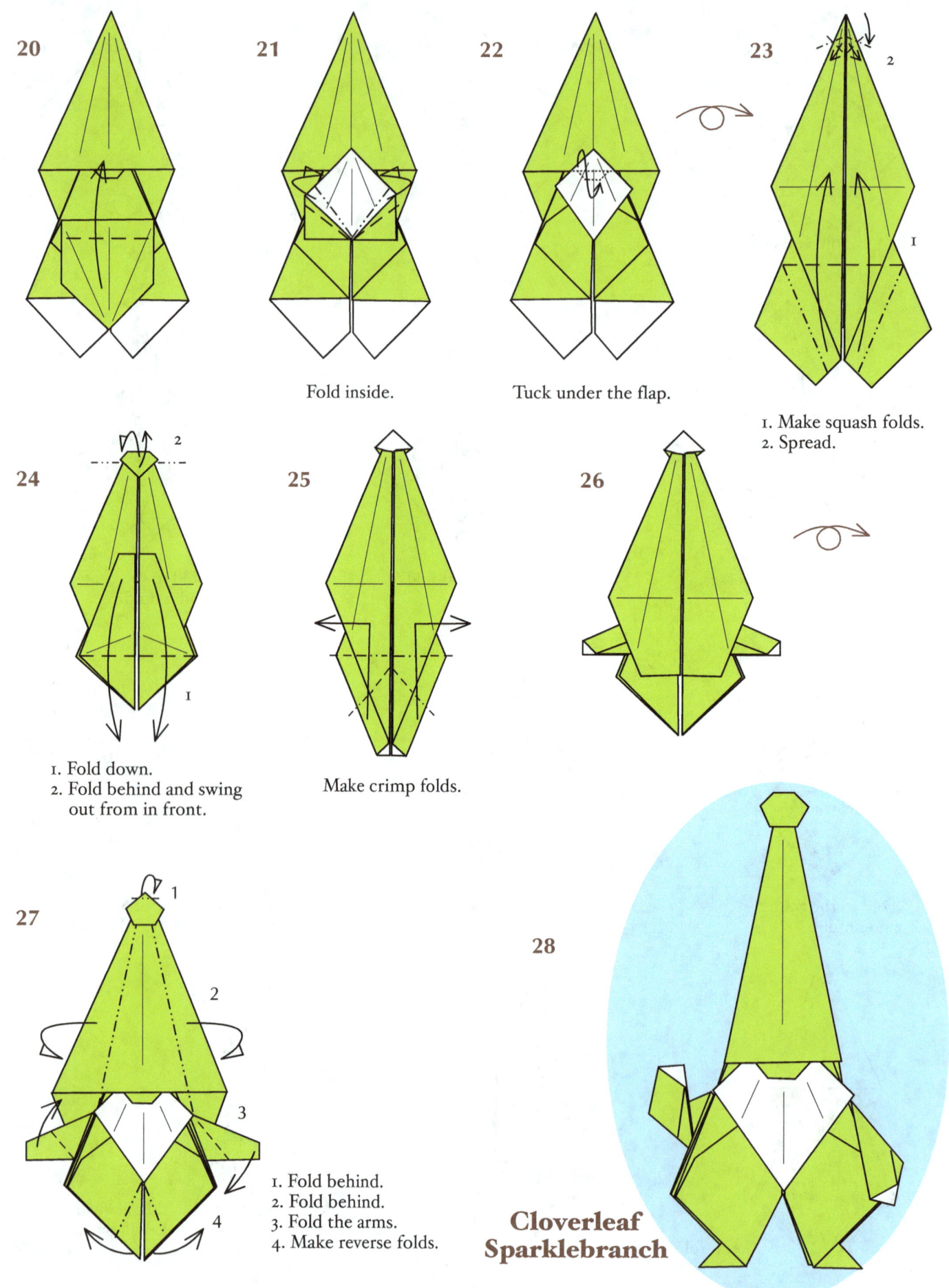

108 *Origami Gnomes of the Forest Wonderland*

Grimble Brackenblink

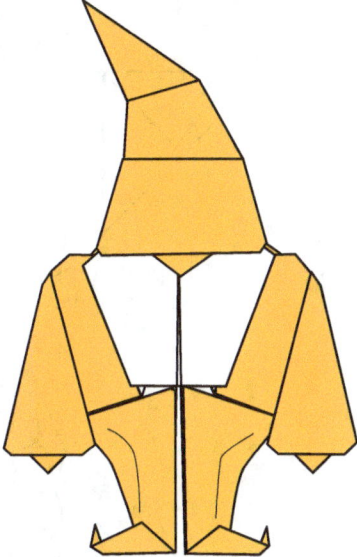

Grimble makes trees perform symphonies. He creates tiny holes in leaves, so they whistle in the wind. Using branch magic, branches pound each other creating percussive sounds. Birds chirp and animals howl, adding to the forest cacophony.

1
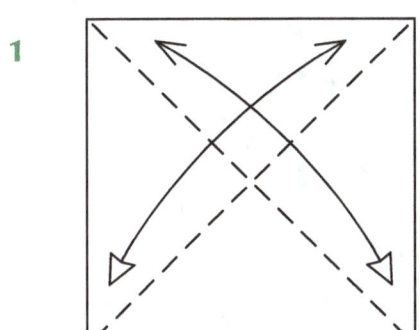
Fold and unfold.

2
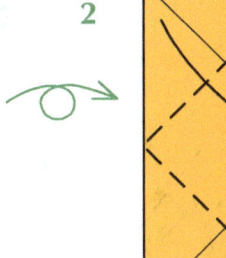
Fold to the center.

3
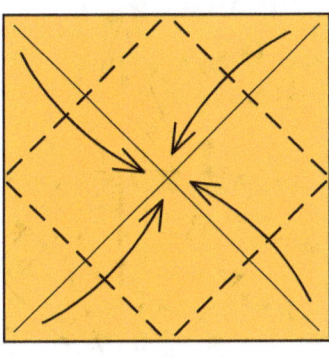
Fold to the center and unfold, creasing in the middle.

4
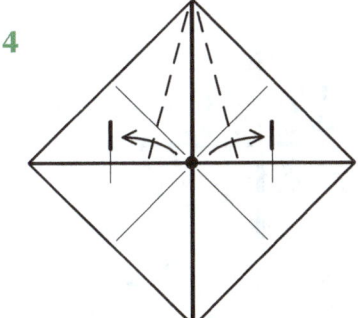
Fold the top layer on the left and right so the dot meets the lines.

5
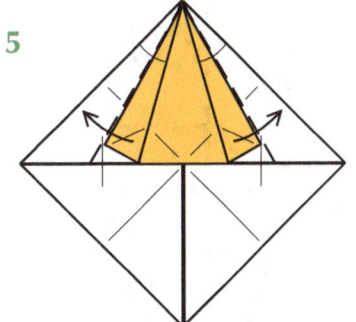

6
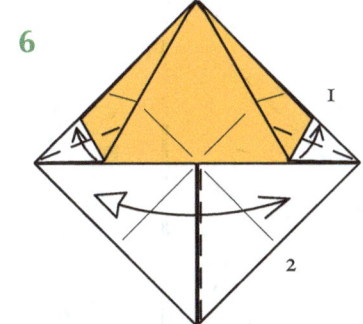
1. Fold up on the left and right.
2. Fold and unfold.

Grimble Brackenblink 109

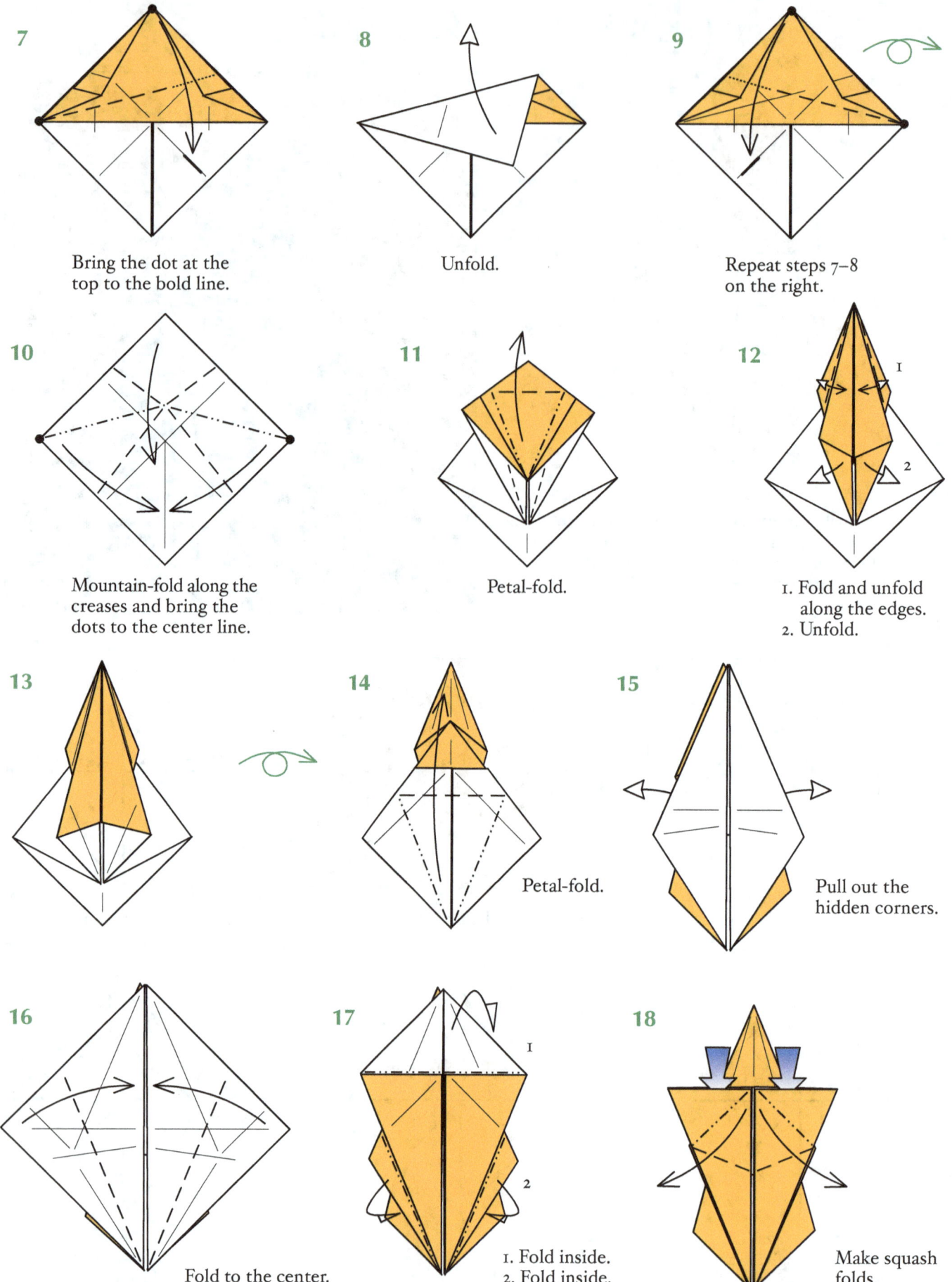

110 *Origami Gnomes of the Forest Wonderland*

19

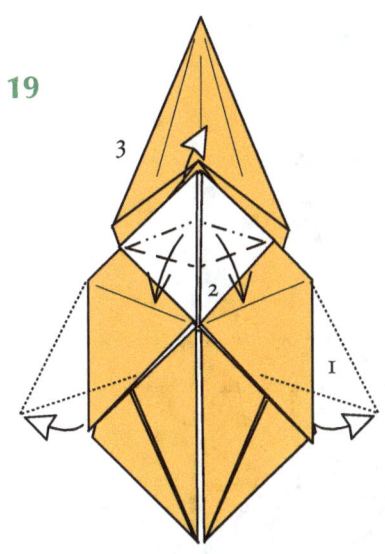

Do these fold together. Begin by
1. Pivoting the arms out and
2. spreading the white paper while folding down and
3. swinging out from inside.

20

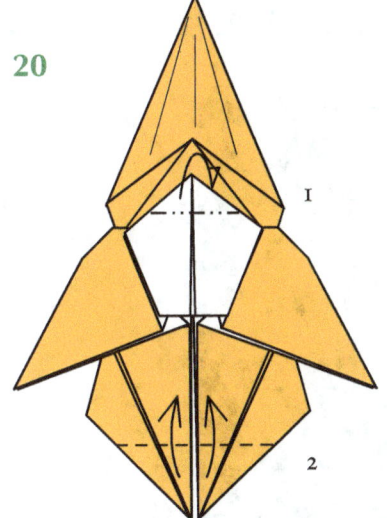

1. Fold inside.
2. Fold up.

21

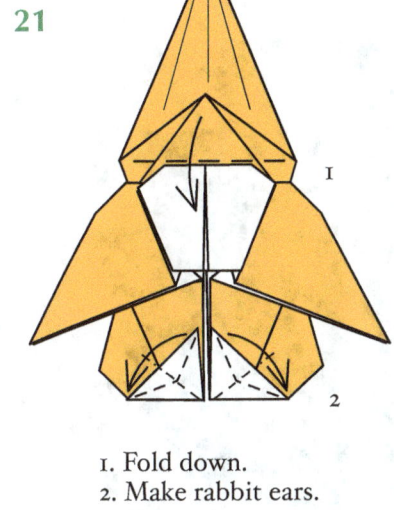

1. Fold down.
2. Make rabbit ears.

22

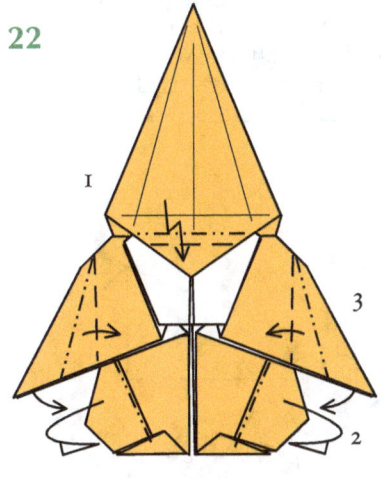

1. Pleat-fold.
2. Fold behind.
3. Make squash folds.

23

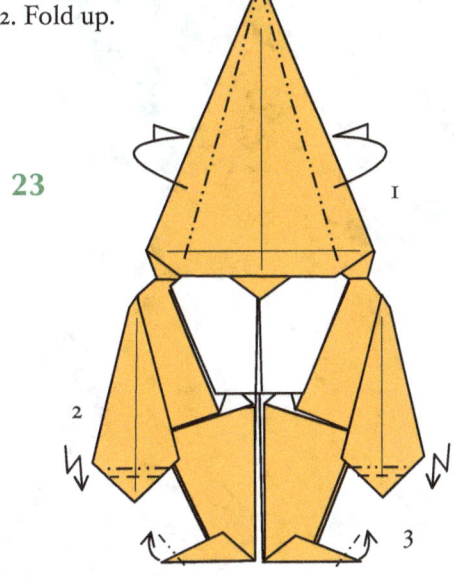

1. Fold along the creases and tuck inside.
2. Make pleat folds.
3. Make reverse folds.

24

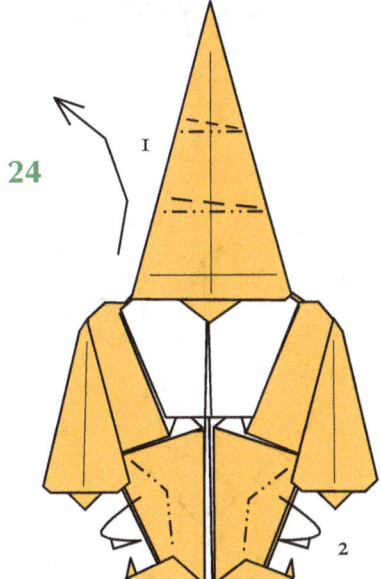

1. Pleat-fold.
2. Shape the legs.

25

Grimble Brackenblink

Grimble Brackenblink III

Bramblethorn Whistlewind

Bramblethorn Whistlewind teaches the frogs how to hop across his mushroom patch, creating different musical notes on each mushroom. He has composed symphonic music if the frogs hop on the right mushrooms at the right time. For the past 400 years, Bramblethorn Whistlewind has been trying, perhaps next year the frogs will create his beautiful forest music.

1

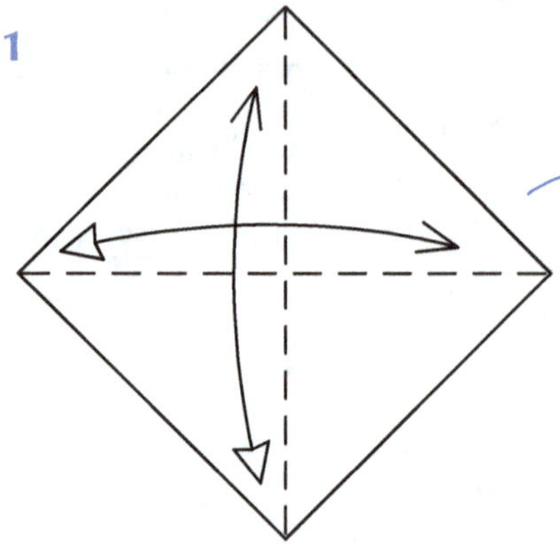

Fold and unfold.

2

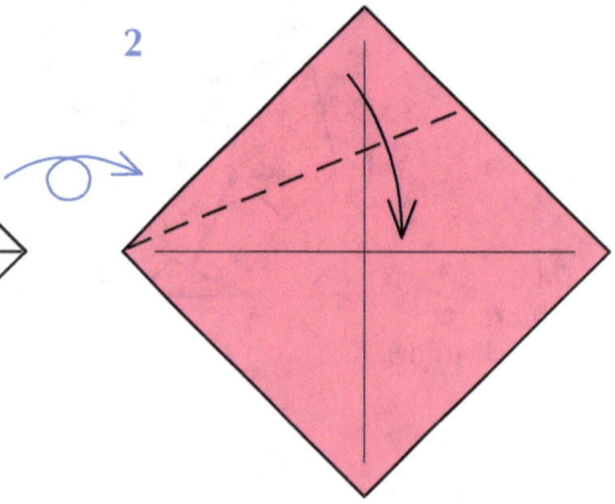

Fold to the center.

3

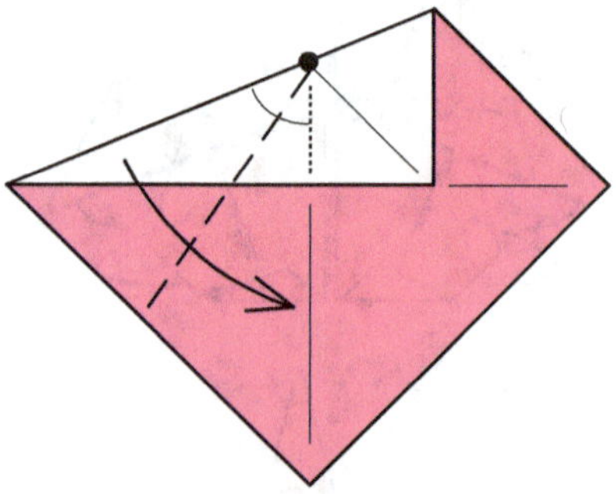

4

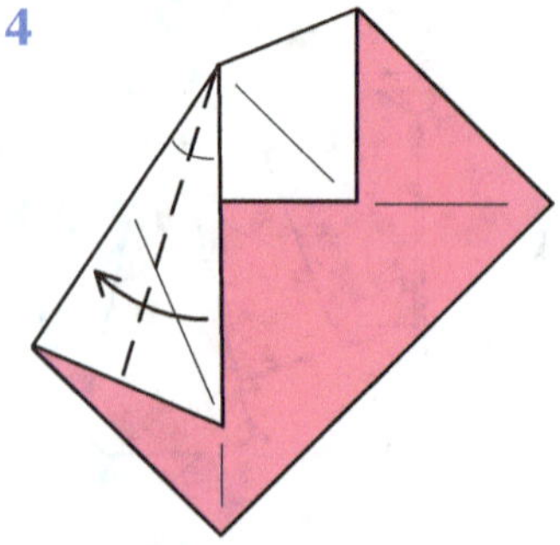

5

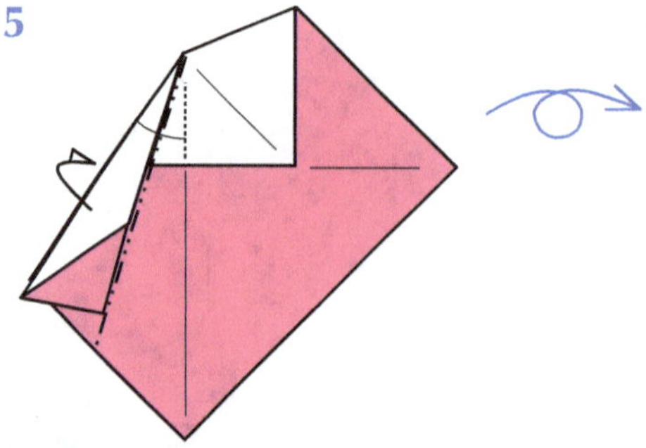

Fold to the center.

6

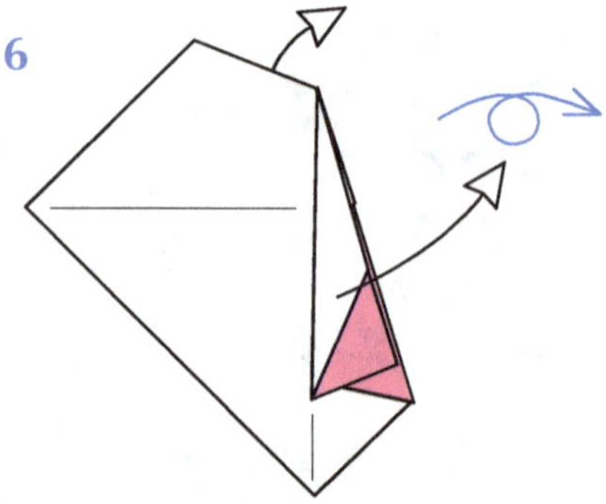

Unfold everything.

112 *Origami Gnomes of the Forest Wonderland*

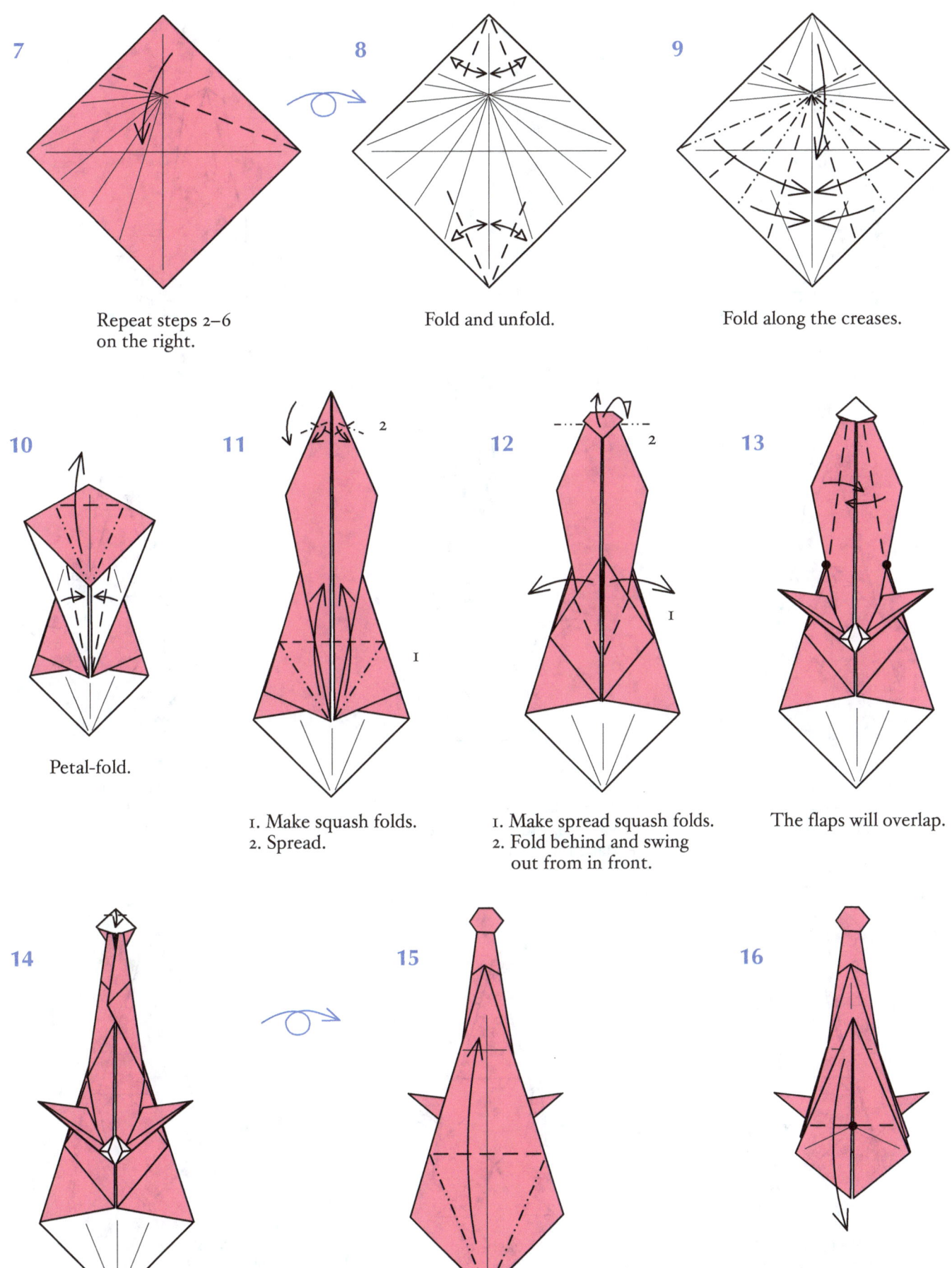

Bramblethorn Whistlewind 113

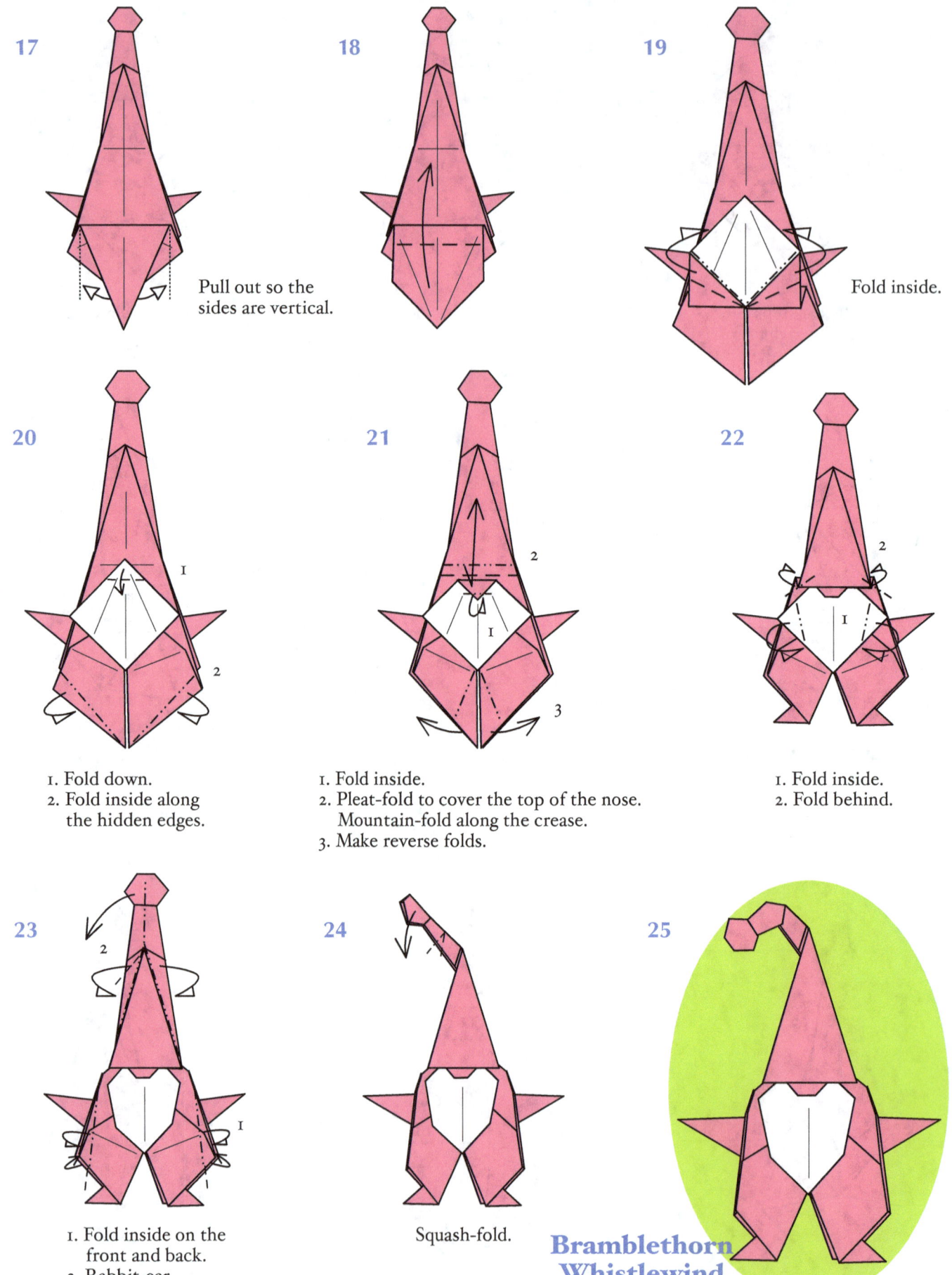

114 *Origami Gnomes of the Forest Wonderland*

Zindle Bramblewhip

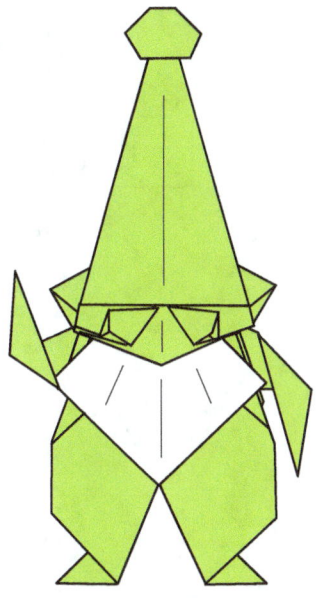

Zindle can make small sparks jump from fireflies into playful patterns. Birds chase them, squirrels leap toward them, and even snails pause to admire the tiny fireworks. These sparks keep the forest glowing all night long.

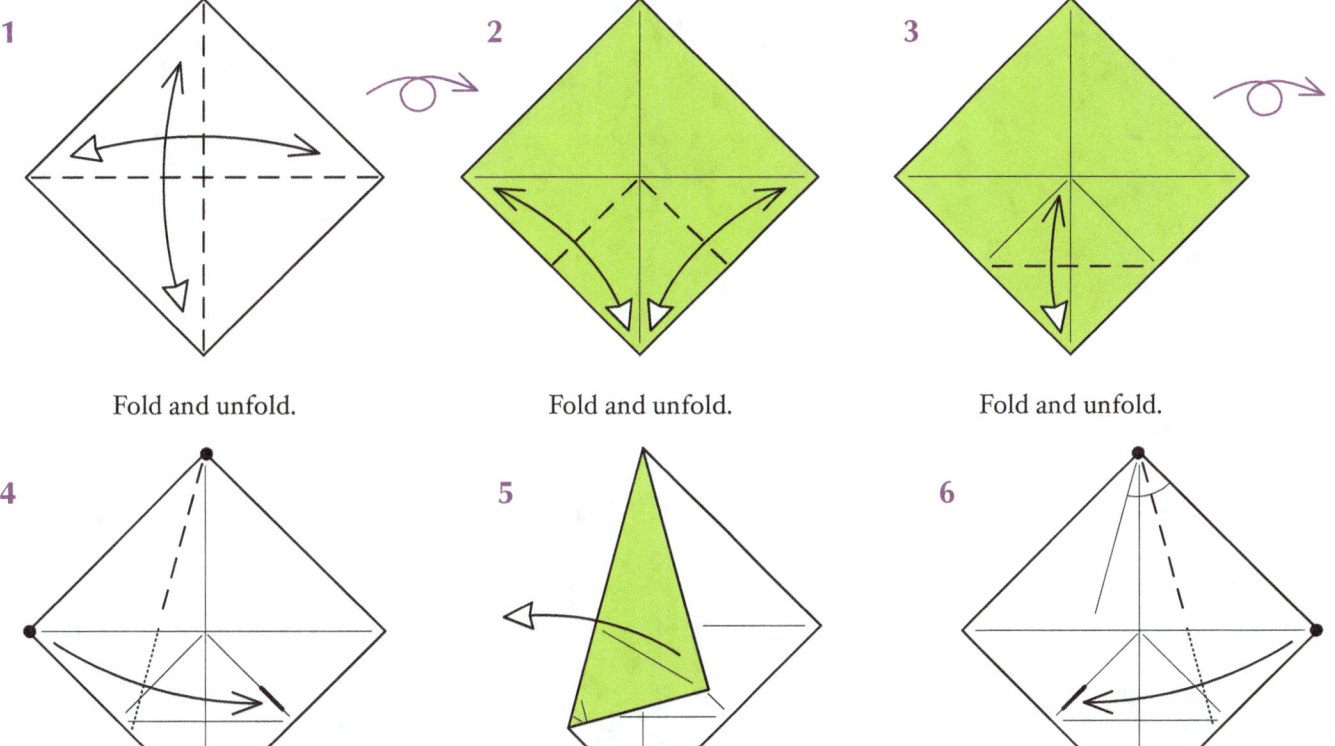

1. Fold and unfold.
2. Fold and unfold.
3. Fold and unfold.
4. Bring the dot on the left to the line.
5. Unfold.
6. Repeat steps 4–5 on the right.

Zindle Bramblewhip 115

7

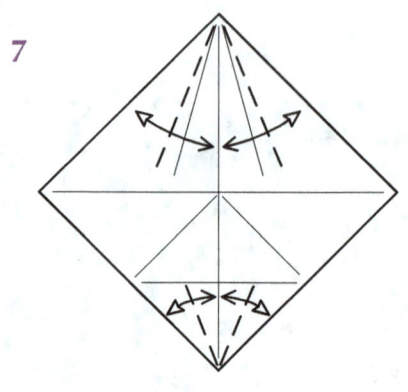

Fold and unfold.

8

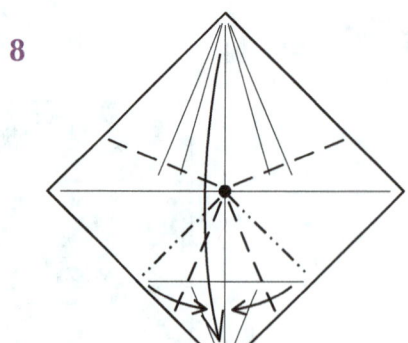

Push in at the dot, mountain-fold along the creases, and flatten.

9

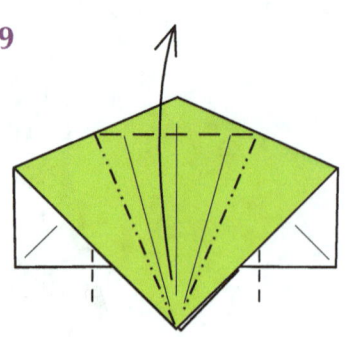

Petal-fold.

10

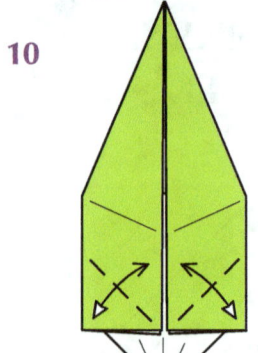

Fold and unfold.

11

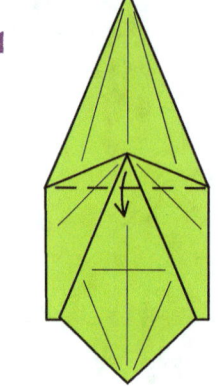

12

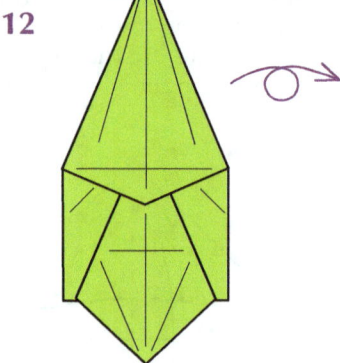

13

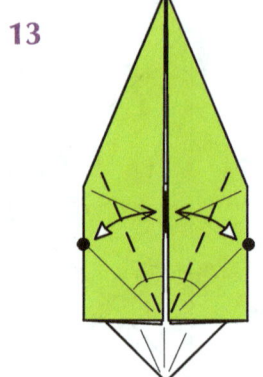

Fold and unfold.

14

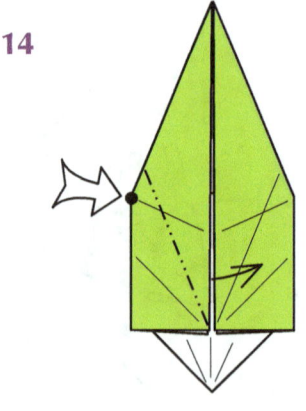

Push in at the dot for this reverse fold.

15

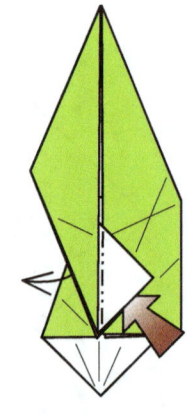

Reverse-fold.

116 *Origami Gnomes of the Forest Wonderland*

16

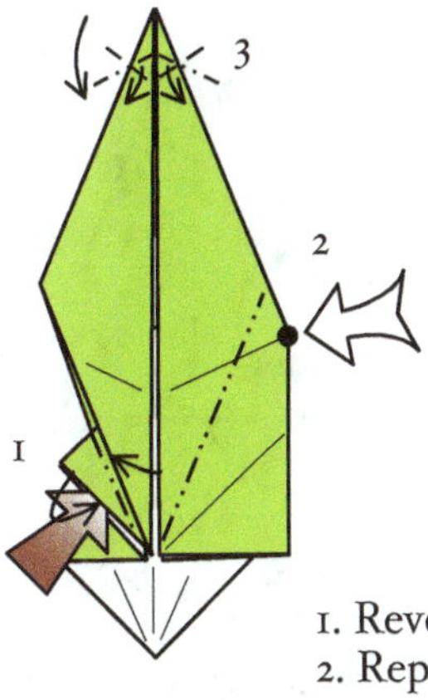

1. Reverse-fold.
2. Repeat steps 14–16 on the right.
3. Spread.

17

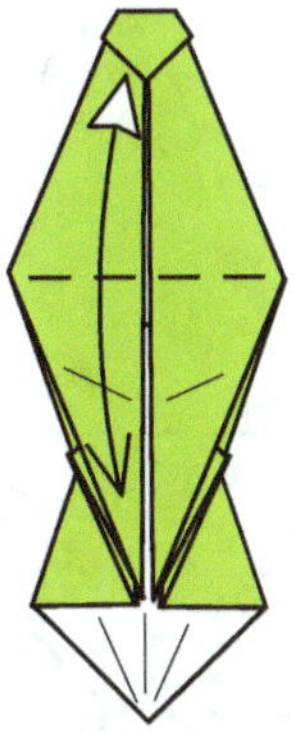

Fold and unfold.

18

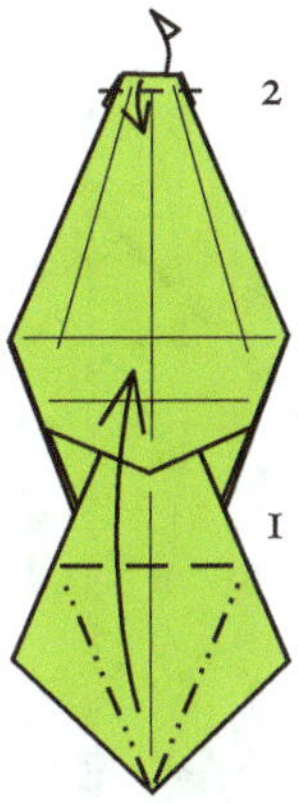

1. Petal-fold.
2. Fold down and swing out from behind.

19

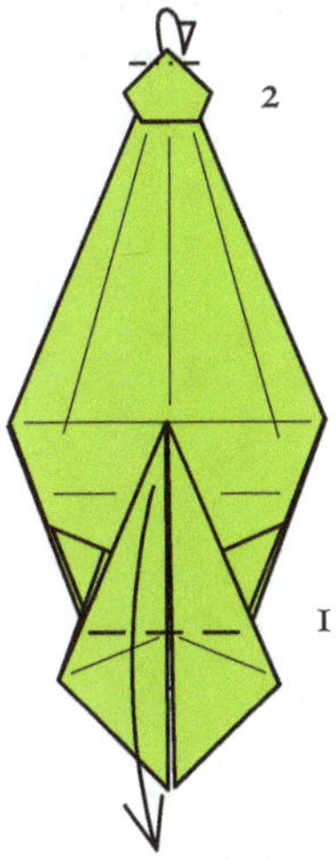

1. Fold down.
2. Fold behind.

20

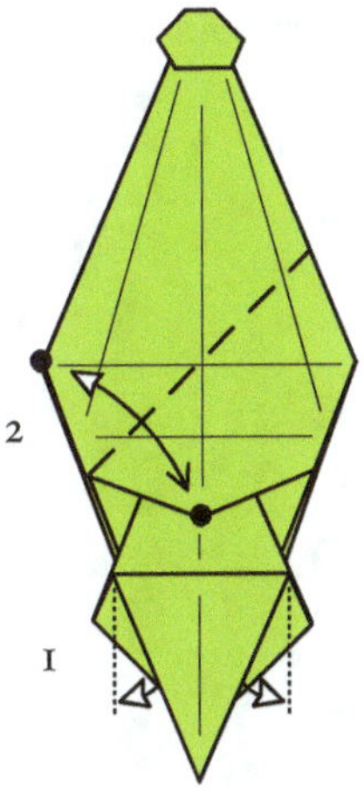

1. Pull out to the vertical dotted lines.
2. Fold and unfold.

21

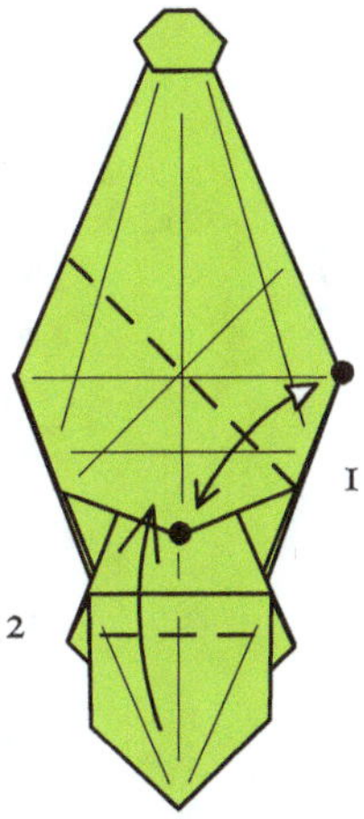

1. Fold and unfold.
2. Fold up.

22

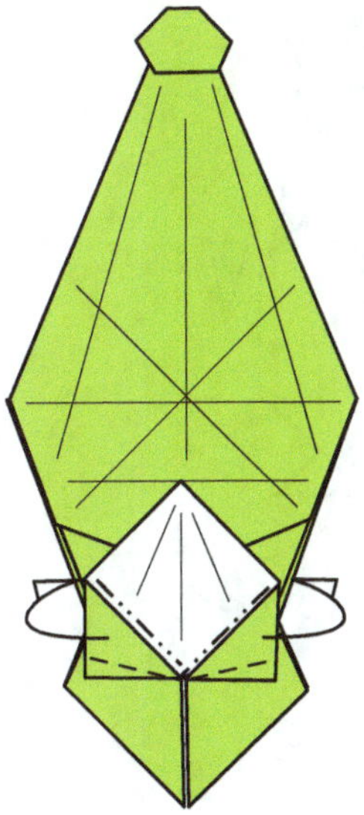

Fold inside.

23

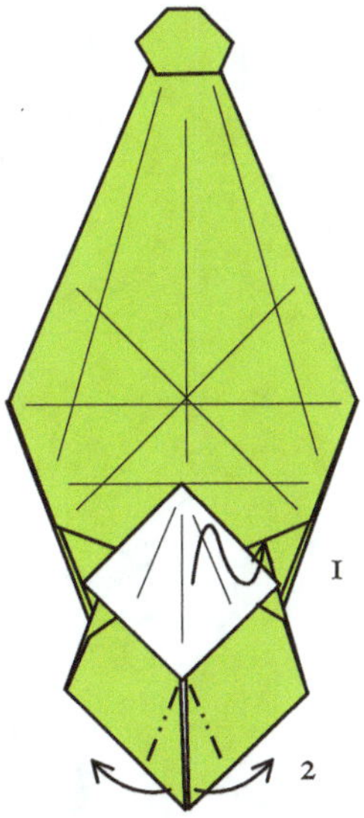

1. Tuck inside.
2. Make reverse folds.

24

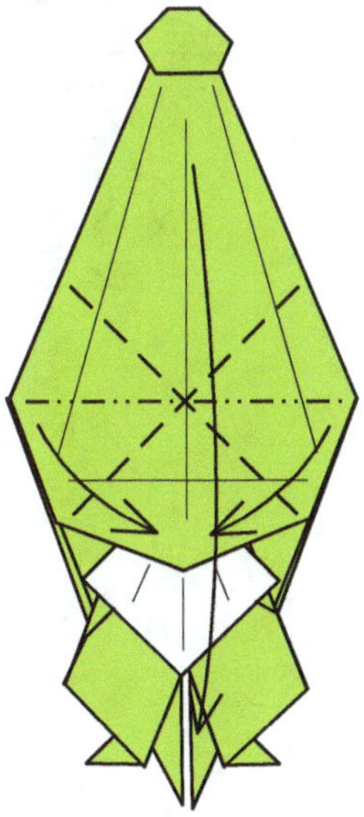

Fold along the creases.

Zindle Bramblewhip 117

25

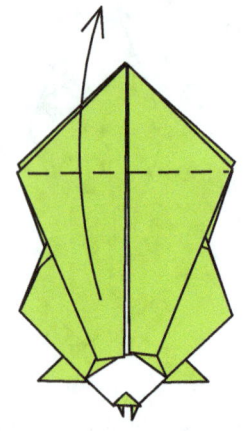

26

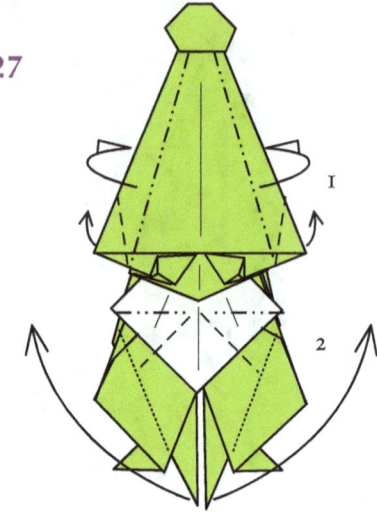

1. Make squash folds to form the eyes.
2. Make reverse folds.

27

1. Mountain-fold along the creases for these pleat folds.
2. Fold the arms with crimp folds.

28

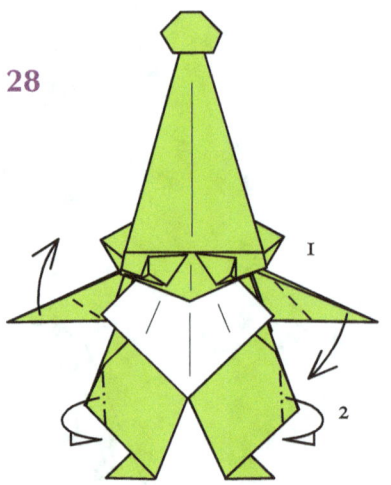

1. Fold the arms.
2. Fold behind.

29

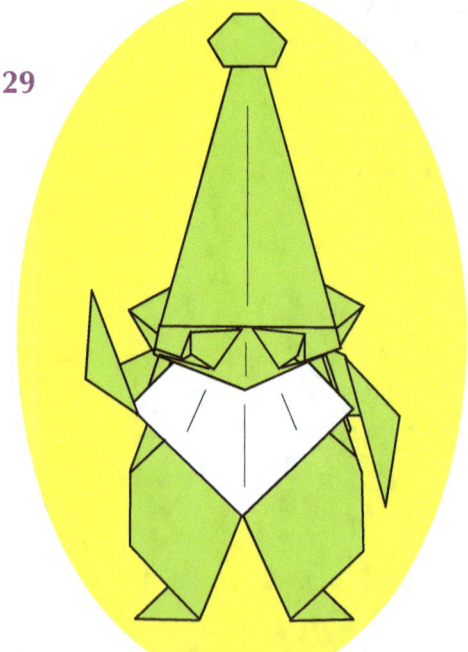

Zindle Bramblewhip

118   *Origami Gnomes of the Forest Wonderland*

Fizzlenip Puddlehopper

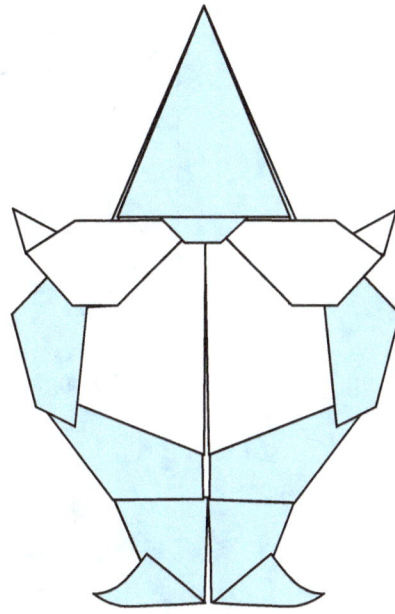

Fizzlenip magically moves puddles. Just when a gnome or rabbit thinks the path is dry, *SCHLOOP*, the puddle slides two feet to the left and splashes their toes. Fizzlenip claims puddles "enjoy socializing."

1

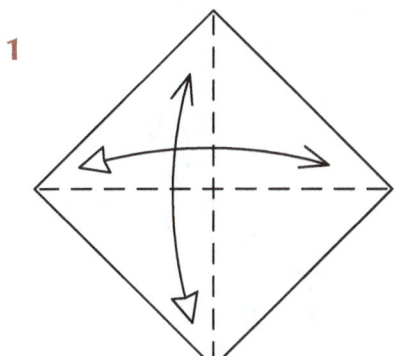

Fold and unfold.

2

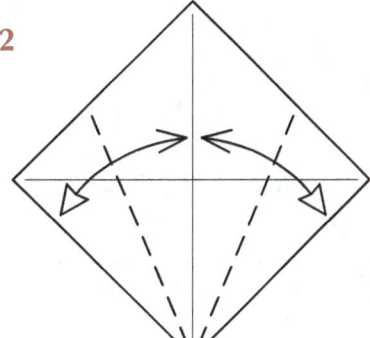

Fold to the center and unfold.

3

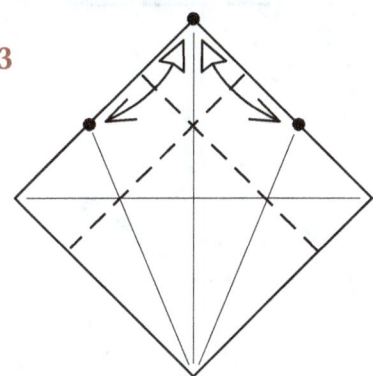

Fold and unfold on the upper half.

4

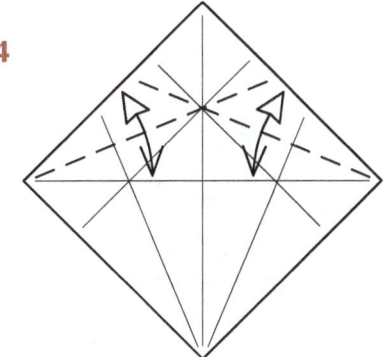

Fold and unfold.

5

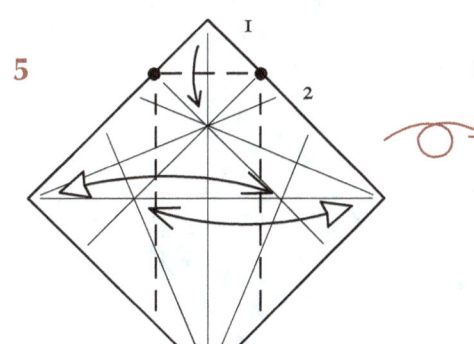

1. Fold down.
2. Fold and unfold.

6

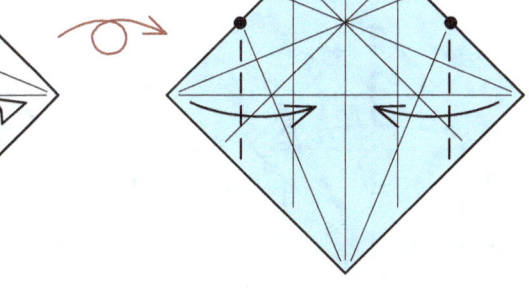

Fizzlenip Puddlehopper 119

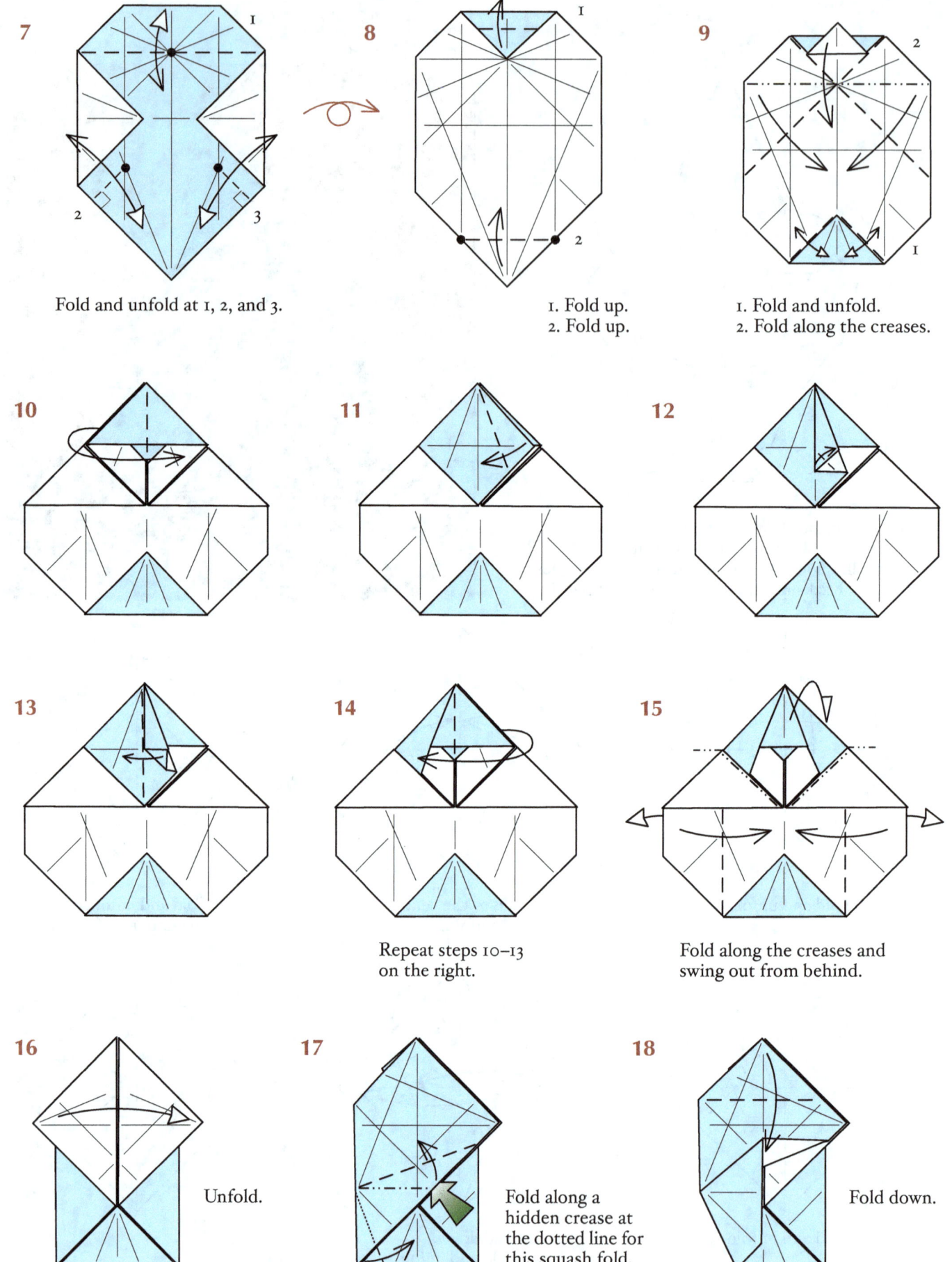

120   *Origami Gnomes of the Forest Wonderland*

19

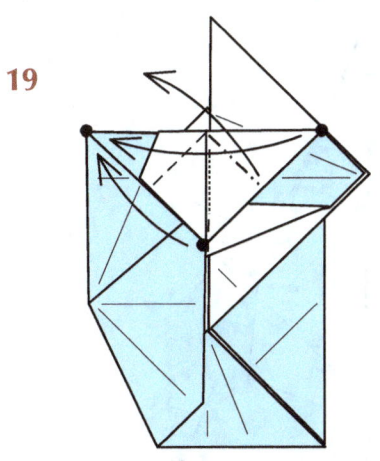

Squash-fold so the three dots will meet. Valley-fold on a hidden layer, at the dotted line.

20

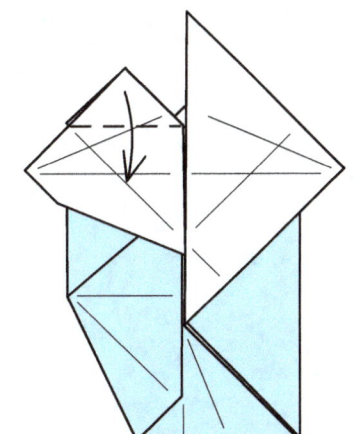

21

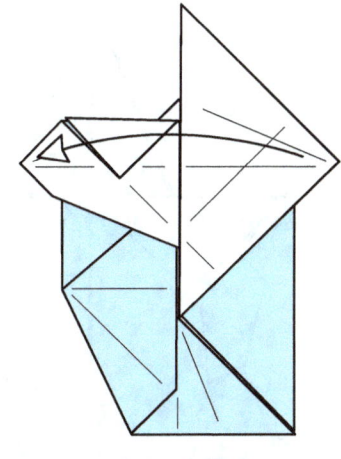

Repeat steps 16–20 on the right.

22

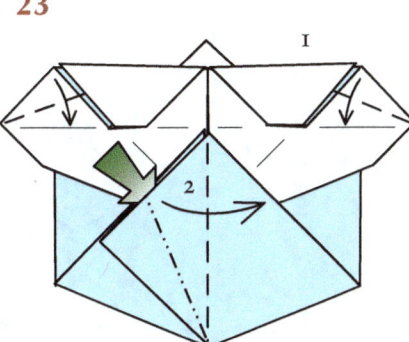

1. Make small reverse folds.
2. Lift up and make a squash fold.

23

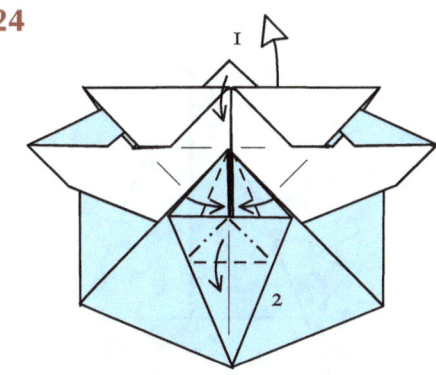

1. Valley-fold along the creases.
2. Squash-fold.

24

1. Unfold, or lift up from behind.
2. Petal-fold.

25

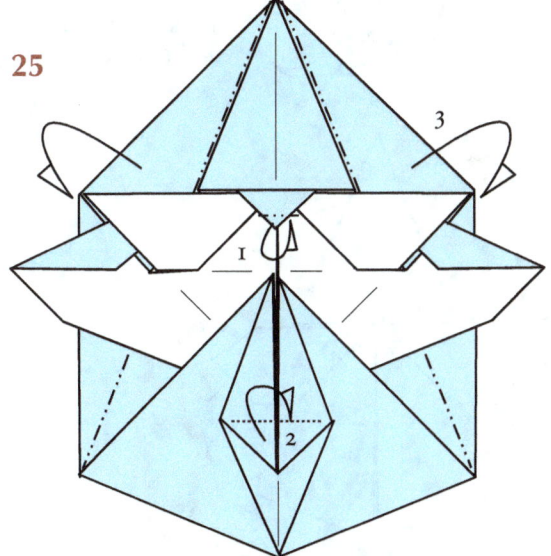

1. Fold inside.
2. Wrap around and tuck inside.
3. Fold behind on the left and right.

26

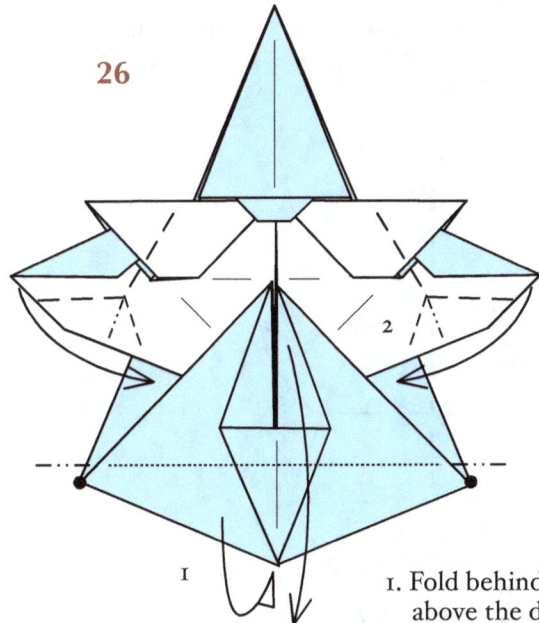

1. Fold behind slightly above the dots and swing out from in front.
2. Make rabbit ears.

Fizzlenip Puddlehopper 121

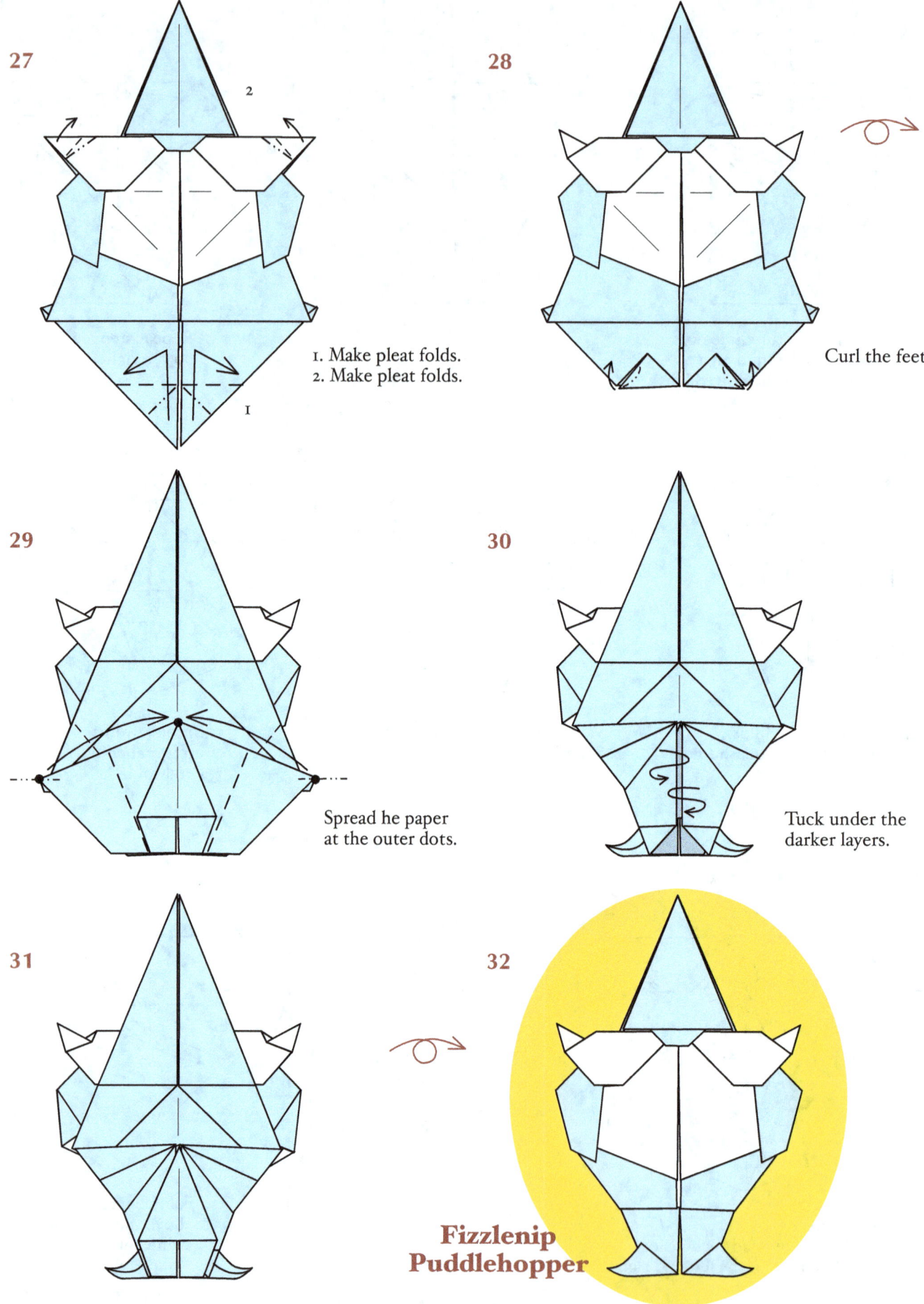

122 *Origami Gnomes of the Forest Wonderland*

Tinkerflip Fizzlegear

Tinkerflip created an amusement park where gnomes and forest animals could whirl, bounce, zoom, and whoosh through the trees. He did all of this with a toolbox full of acorn bolts, mossy gears, and glowing powered lights. Tinkerflip turned three giant hollow stumps into spinning teacups powered by cheerful chipmunks racing in tiny wheels beneath the platforms. He built a Mossy Merry-Go-Round. A favorite is the Pinecone Drop Ride, where passengers are carried up a towering pine trunk and then dropped holding tightly to a falling pinecone. The Glowbug Ferris Wheel lifts gnomes high above the treetops to see the whole night sparkling beneath them. A Gnome-Launch Trampoline used a giant mushroom cap capable of launching a gnome high enough to ring a bell tied to the top of a tall cedar tree. Soon, Tinkerflip's amusement park became the most wondrous spot in the entire woodland. Every evening, with sawdust in his beard, he would grin and say: "Just wait till they see what I'm building next."

1

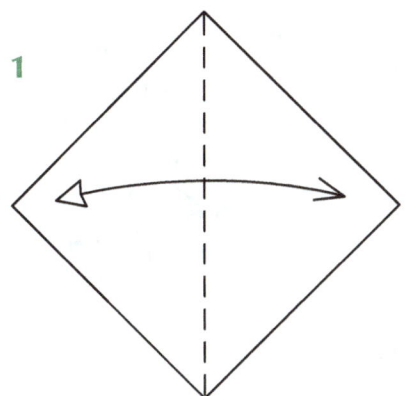

Fold and unfold.

2

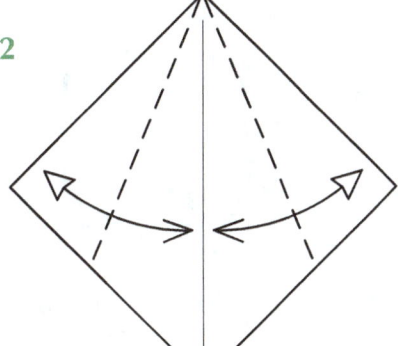

Fold to the center and unfold.

3

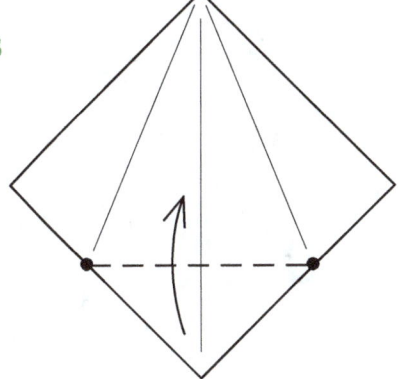

4

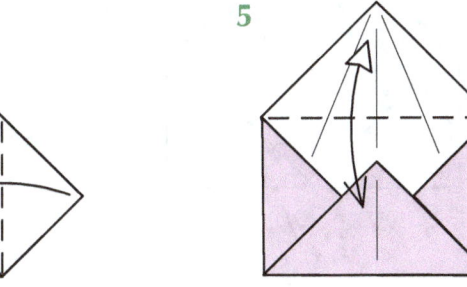

5

Fold and unfold.

6

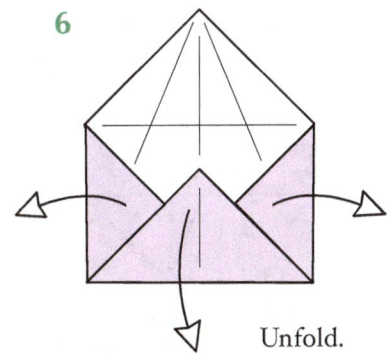

Unfold.

Tinkerflip Fizzlegear 123

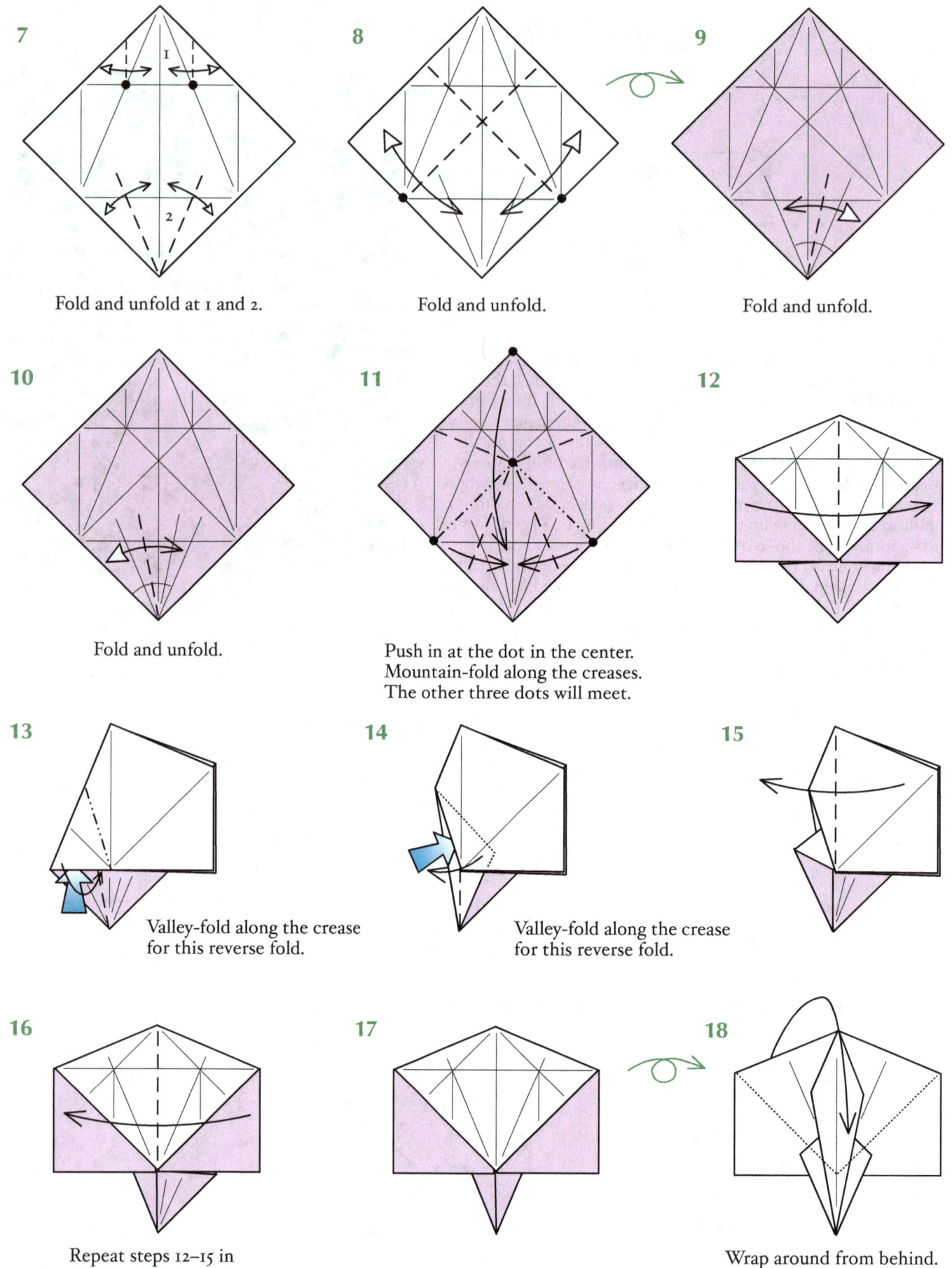

124 *Origami Gnomes of the Forest Wonderland*

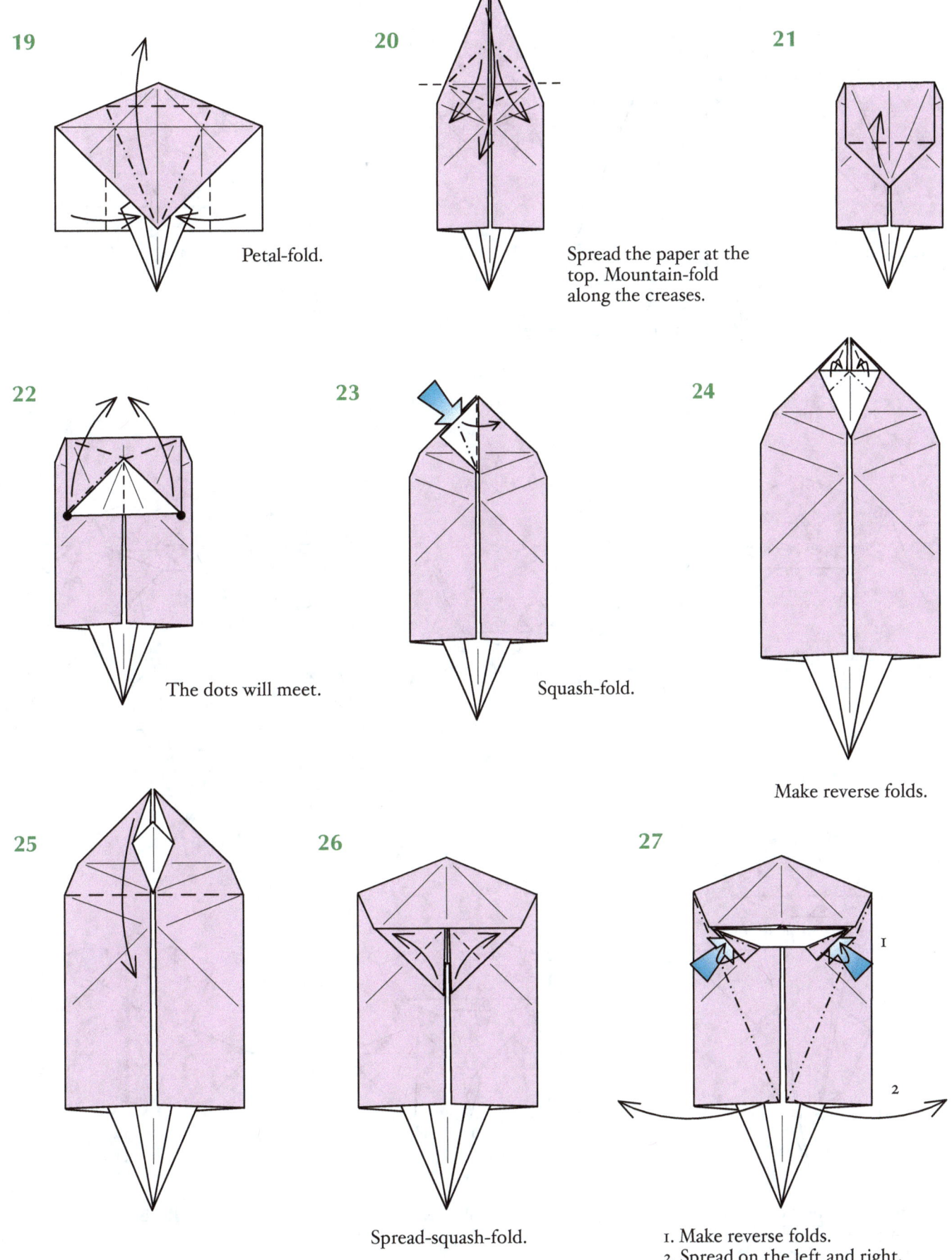

Tinkerflip Fizzlegear 125

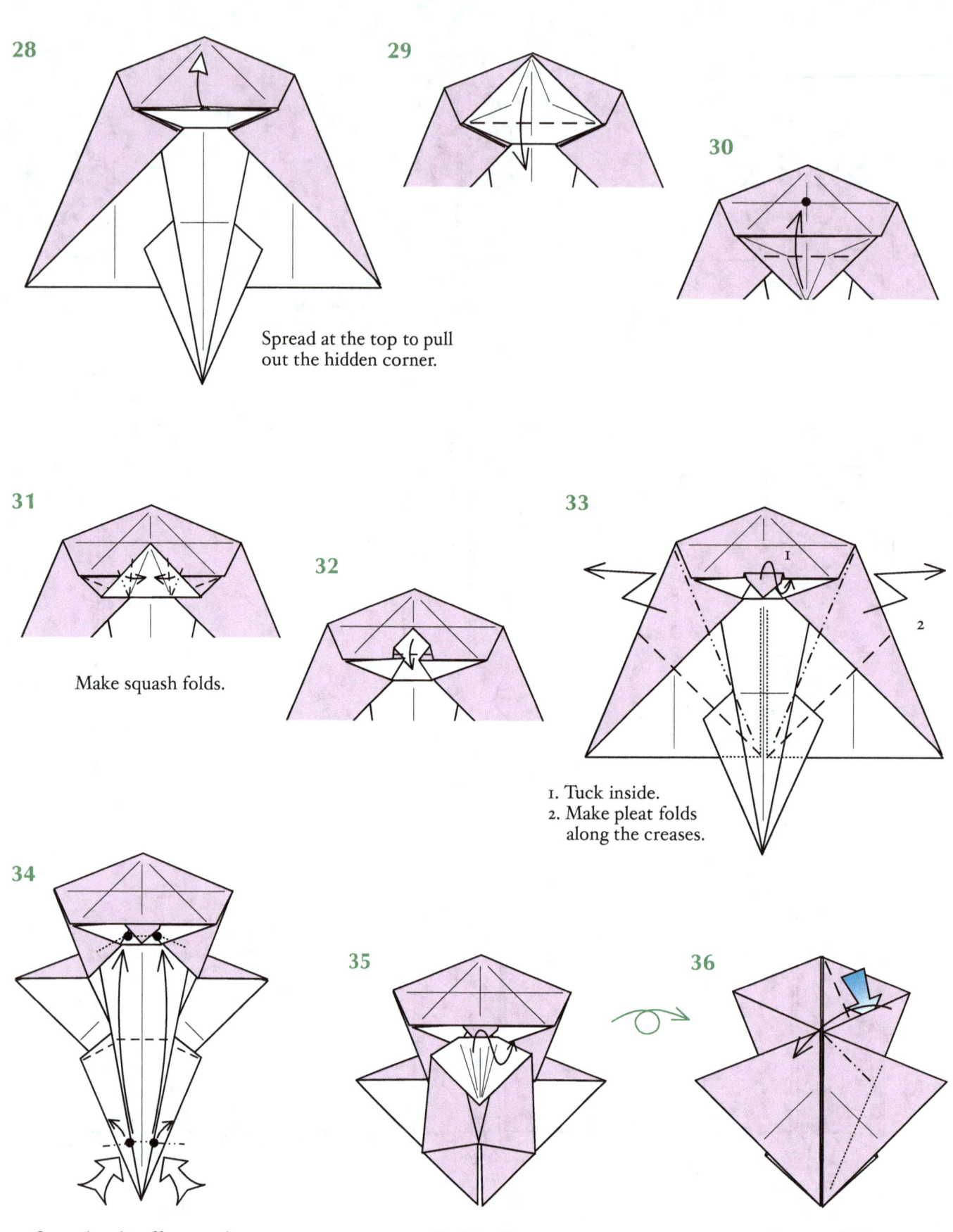

126 *Origami Gnomes of the Forest Wonderland*

37

Wrap around and tuck inside.

38

Repeat steps 36–37 on the left.

39

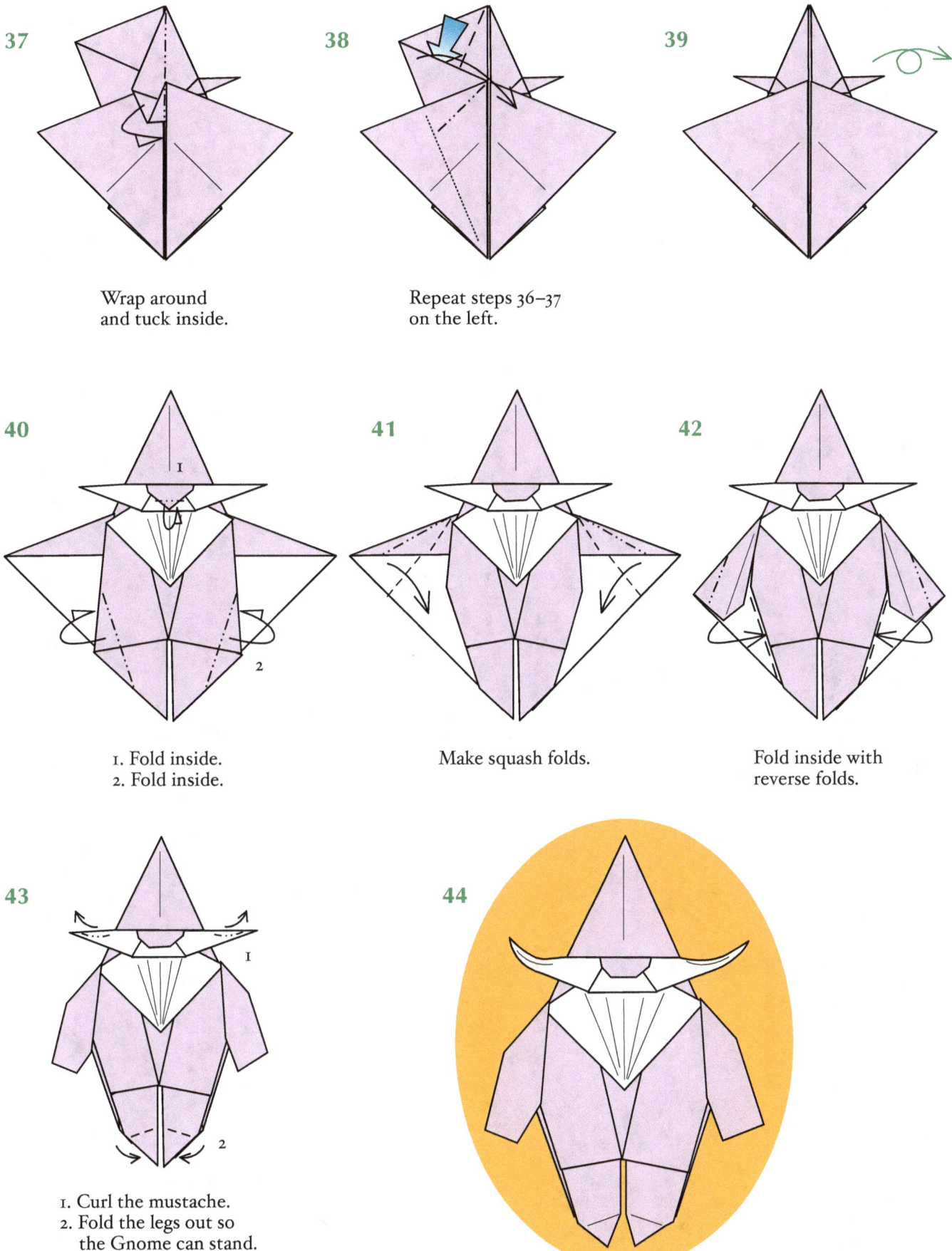

40

1. Fold inside.
2. Fold inside.

41

Make squash folds.

42

Fold inside with reverse folds.

43

1. Curl the mustache.
2. Fold the legs out so the Gnome can stand.

44

Tinkerflip Fizzlegear

Tinkerflip Fizzlegear 127

www.ingramcontent.com/pod-product-compliance
Lightning Source LLC
Chambersburg PA
CBHW051417070526
44584CB00023B/3469